DOG BREEDING

The Theory and the Practice

DOG BREEDING

The Theory & the Practice

Frank Jackson

The Crowood Press

First published in 1994 by
The Crowood Press Ltd
Ramsbury, Marlborough
Wiltshire SN8 2HR

This impression 1996

British Library Cataloguing-in-Publication Data

A catalogue record for this book is available from the British Library.

ISBN 1 85223 794 5

Throughout this book, 'he', 'him' and 'his' have been used as neutral
pronouns and refer to both males and females, be they human or
canine.

Line-drawings by Annette Findlay, except those on pages 69–70, 80,
88, 91–2, 125 (top), and 148, which are by Aileen Hanson.

Photo credits: as indicated in text.
Frontispiece: Border Terrier bitch and puppies. (Photo: Jackson)

Acknowledgements
The author would like to thank all those who kindly supplied some of
the photographs for use in this book: Lyn Anderson, Alan Carey and
Jennifer Lloyd Carey, Iris Combe, Joyce Ixer, Elspeth and Jean
Jackson, Chris Kernick, Karina Le Mare, Shirley Rawlings, Mrs. E. J.
Walker and Dr. L. Roberts, Ivor Ward-Davies and Roger Wright.
Thanks are also due to all those who assisted in the research and
provided valuable information.

Typeset by Avonset, Midsomer Norton, Bath
Printed and bound in Great Britain by Redwood Books, Trowbridge

Contents

	Preface	6
1	Responsible Breeding	9
2	Genetics and Selection	22
3	Breeding Systems	39
4	Hereditary Abnormalities	56
5	The Brood-Bitch	64
6	The Stud-Dog	82
7	Mating	95
8	Care of the Pregnant Brood-Bitch	108
9	Whelping	117
10	Post-Natal Care	134
11	Kennel Management	167
12	Finally	173
	Appendices	
I	Schedule of Hereditary Abnormalities	174
II	Whelping Calendar	191
III	Postnatal Development	192
IV	Position and Frequency of Progenitor within Pedigree	193
V	Registration Totals, Litter Size and Weight	194
VI	Canine Calorie Intake	203
	Bibliography	204
	Index	206

Preface

The main purpose of this book is threefold: to discuss the way in which attitudes to breeding have changed and are changing, to examine the methods that are currently regarded as best practice and, perhaps for the first time in a book of this kind, to consider some of the new techniques that have recently become available or may become available to dog breeders in the next few years. It also looks briefly at some of the attitudes of and methods employed by dog breeders of the past, and at the beliefs on which their methods were based.

The book is written after a period in which the techniques available to dog breeders expanded at a hitherto undreamt of rate, but dog breeders did not always take full advantage of these new techniques. Occasionally they were prevented from doing so by the restrictive policies of kennel clubs, which sometimes seemed to resist even the changes that were necessary in order to support the efforts of breeders to produce top-quality, healthy pedigree dogs. Breeders themselves were also sometimes at fault for their apparent reluctance to give health and temperament at least the same importance accorded to breed type and appearance.

Now, the transmission and control of disease, whether induced by infection, a want of care, or as a result of faulty genes, is better understood than ever before. As the threat of infectious disease recedes in the face of improved veterinary knowledge, hitherto unrecognized genetic problems come to the fore. As knowledge of these increases, the means to exercise effective control over them become available. Strict control over the quality of breeding stock, coupled with the wise use of genetic principles already provide the means by which the incidence of many genetically transmitted abnormalities could be dramatically reduced. Growing knowledge of the canine genome already enables the carriers of a few hereditary diseases to be identified and to be avoided by breeders.

It is probable that the majority of dog breeders intend to produce dogs that will live their lives as companions, though some of these will also take part in shows and other competitive events from which millions of dog owners all over the world derive so much enjoyment. Even so, it would be quite wrong to give the impression that breeding dogs is something which has little or no relevance outside the home or canine competitions. Dogs are still needed for traditional tasks, for herding, search and rescue, and for sport. They are also in demand for a growing range of new tasks, for guiding the blind, as ears for the deaf, to provide therapy for people who live their lives outside society, and even to give warning of the onset of illness. The practices described in this

Health and temperament must be afforded the same importance as breed type and appearance. (Photo: Ixer)

book are of great importance when applied to the breeding of dogs intended for all these tasks. Indeed, some of the techniques described were originally developed for one or other of these purposes and only later achieved a more general application.

In Britain, Guide Dogs for the Blind is a principal supporter of investigation into many of the problems which beset dog breeders. Elsewhere in the world, other organizations are at the forefront of investigation. For example, in 1977, research carried out at the Yarraview Veterinary Hospital, Victoria, Australia, resulted in the establishment of a systém for freezing canine semen. In the years that followed,

the services were extended to include artificial breeding, the diagnosis and treatment of infertility, DNA analysis, genetic investigation, and controlled breeding techniques. Experience of human in-vitro fertilization was later combined with Yarraview's existing techniques to launch a research programme aimed at further expansion of services available to dog breeders.

The May 1992 issue of the Victorian Canine Association Inc. Gazette said:

> The objectives of this project are to improve the quality and working performance of the rural farm working sheep, cattle and goat dogs; thereby

increasing the efficiency of these working dogs to aid farmers in effective stock husbandry and management.

To identify and select proven performance elite sires which will offer breeders the potential for rapid genetic improvement of working dogs throughout rural Australia and exported to expanding markets in similar agricultural countries overseas.

New diagnostic and breeding techniques, new insights into canine behaviour and development, the availability of scientifically formulated, balanced diets, and of the means to eradicate parasites and to protect against many diseases, are all available to assist breeders' efforts. The combination means that breeders are now far better equipped to produce good dogs than ever before. If breeders, their breed clubs, and the kennel clubs which exercise overall control over the breeding of pedigree dogs, do not take full and enthusiastic advantage of what the newly available knowledge has to offer, any claim that they exist to promote the improvement of dogs can only be regarded as unconvincing.

It is beyond the scope of this book, and certainly of its author, to offer a definitive text on genetics, anatomy, canine nutrition, behaviour, the process of reproduction, inherited disease, and veterinary medicine related to breeding. Nor has it been possible to examine each of the 500 or so breeds that exist throughout the world in the sort of detail with which their breeders must become familiar.

However, the book does offer an introduction to a complex, rapidly changing and enormously fascinating subject and contains, it is hoped, something of interest and value to both novices and experts, whether they be breeders or those who make themselves available to provide breeders with professional advice.

The research that has gone into this book has confirmed what was already suspected. There is very little reliable information available about many of the differences between the various breeds. Information about conception rates, actual litter size, survival rates, actual birth and adult weight, growth rates, rates of behavioural development, expected life span, causes of death, and much more, is usually available only as it relates to dogs as a whole, without any regard for the certainty that there are significant differences between breeds and then between countries. Here is a virtually untouched and totally unfunded field for research.

In spite of the obvious need for guidance from a higher plane than either science or the school of hard knocks are able to offer, dog breeders do not appear to have adopted or to have been adopted by a patron saint. Yet there appears to be an obvious candidate. This book is therefore dedicated, with understanding born of more than thirty years of trying to breed good dogs, to the man who appears to have the very best credentials for being regarded as the patron saint of dog breeders: Sisyphus.

Frank Jackson, 1994

CHAPTER 1

Responsible Breeding

Man's conceit encourages the belief that the first contact with wolves – the precursors of domestic dogs – began when wolves scavenged on kills made by man. If further thought were to be modified by a little humility it might seem more likely that man was the scavenger on kills made by wolves, the more efficient hunters.

Whatever may have instigated the first contact, man's early association with wolves began about 20,000 years ago. Initially the association was probably a very loose one, which did little more than exploit different skills and needs. Man's upright stance enabled him to see down-wind quarry which wolves could neither see nor scent. Wolves, however, were better able to chase and harass large animals, though after the animals had been brought to bay, man, with a variety of tools and weapons at his disposal, might have been better able to dispatch them. Once a kill had been made, wolves would be obliged to wait until man had satisfied his own appetite; but more powerful lupine jaws and teeth enabled wolves to make use of parts of the animal which man could not readily use.

Domestic dogs were developed during the next 12–15,000 years, and by 12,000 years ago man was an accomplished breeder of a number of varieties of domestic dog, not all of which – even at this early stage in the history of civilization – appear to have been solely

Confidence and mutual respect are important in any human–dog relationship. (Photo: Jackson)

intended for hunting or herding. There were already small dogs which, perhaps, served as playthings and companions, as watchdogs, as domestic scavengers, and as a source of food in hard times.

The popularity of dogs, in all their varied uses, has tended to increase throughout history and to do so in spite of occasional, and usually short-lived, bouts of anti-dog hysteria. It is, however, probably true that the dog population in several countries is now lower than it was fifty years ago when the human population was considerably smaller. In 1982, 42 per cent of all USA households contained at least one dog. In Australia the figure was 39 per cent, in France 35 per cent, in Canada 33 per cent, in Belgium 30 per cent, in Denmark and the Netherlands 26 per cent, and in the UK 23 per cent. In just these eight countries, over 410 million people were sharing their homes with a dog. To suggest, as some misguided people are inclined to do, that there is something reprehensible about owning a dog would be extreme arrogance.

Economic Importance of Dog Ownership

Dog ownership is important for several reasons, and ownership depends on breeding. Dog breeding is most often a hobby or a cottage industry, but it supports a series of massive, international industries whose economic importance cannot reasonably be ignored.

In 1988, the Royal Society for the Prevention of Cruelty to Animals (RSPCA) commissioned a report from the London School of Economics (LSE), which argued that dog ownership in Britain imposed a cost – derived from accidents allegedly caused by dogs, losses incurred by farmers, treating people injured by dogs and dealing with stray and abandoned dogs – to the public purse of about £70 million a year, roughly £1.25 for each person and about £11 for each dog in the country. The report totally ignored all the considerable economic, health and social benefits which, directly or indirectly, derive from dog breeding and ownership.

The first source of trade and employment to be derived from dogs stems from the sale of dogs themselves. The Kennel Club registers about 200,000 dogs each year, possibly not much more than one third of the total production, though many of the rest are the product of unwanted and unexpected misalliances, or of callous attempts to cash in on the popular interest in dogs, the major source of many of the problems for which dogs themselves are unjustly blamed. Even so, the minority share of the trade which is represented by Kennel Club registered dogs produces an annual turnover of well over £20 million and, if the increased value of dogs exported or retained in the UK for show or other competitive purposes is taken into account, turnover probably exceeds £40 million a year.

An excellent RSPCA publication, *Dogs and Puppies*, which sought to promote a more responsible attitude towards dog ownership by education and encouragement, claimed that the cost of feeding a dog might vary from '25p a day to feed a small dog and from £1.20 a day to feed a very large dog.' On this basis, the turnover generated by feeding 7.25 million dogs lies somewhere between about £662 million and £3,175 million. There are a number of international petfood companies whose products admirably fulfil this need.

In addition, dog ownership requires a service from the veterinary profession. Figures produced from Anval Limited, the profession's UK advisory service on practice management and finance, showed that about 63 per cent of the profession's total turnover was derived from the treatment of dogs. This represents an annual turnover of over £300 million in the UK alone.

To these factors must be added the publishing industry maintained by interest in dogs, canine insurance – a small but rapidly growing part of the insurance industry – and the revenue generated by advertising dog foods and other canine products.

There is also the economic benefit to dog owners, as well as to the community, which derives from the established fact that households that contain dogs are less likely to be burgled than those that lack both the deterrent and the alarm system which dogs provide. Surely, too, there is economic benefit to be found in the way in which dogs provide guides for the blind, ears for the deaf, are used to search for illegal substances, and to find and rescue people lost in hostile country. Considerable benefit is derived from the use of dogs to herd sheep and cattle, to protect industrial and domestic property and, in hospitals, special schools and prisons, to help some of the confused and unhappy members of our society.

It would be possible to further extend the list of economic benefits, but the point is already overwhelmingly made: far from representing a drain on the public purse, in the UK alone dog ownership supports a series of interrelated industries which, at a very conservative estimate, produce an annual turnover of well over £1,000 million a year. These industries are a major source of employment throughout the country, often in areas where alternative employment is not plentiful. This employment produces economic benefit for individuals, corporations and for both local and central government. There is no

The straight, strong timber that is the hallmark of good breeding and rearing. Here, a beautifully matched couple await their turn at the Royal Hound Show. (Photo: Jackson)

need for dog breeders to feel guilty about the economic effect of their activities.

There is, however, every reason for guilt if the dogs produced by breeders are not the very best it is possible to produce. Dog breeding is not and should not be merely an exercise in producing dogs in large numbers to satisfy an apparently insatiable and unselective market.

During the last 12,000 years the uses to which dogs are put have changed. Originally, dogs would have been used as hunters, as guards and herders, and, as now, as companions. Man, however, is a competitive animal as remarkable for his ability to create games which satisfy his need for competition as for anything else. It would have been surprising if, from a very early stage in their association with man, dogs had not been enrolled to support some competitive activity. It may well be that the need to test the abilities of dogs used for hunting or for pastoral duties led to the first competitions in which dogs were involved. The puppies of those which performed best would be in greatest demand. It is a moot point as to whether the existence of competitions – sheepdog trials, working trials, gundog tests, agility, and even dog shows – derives from a desire, if not an actual need, for breeders to demonstrate their success, or whether the main purpose of these activities is to provide breeders with the information on which success is built.

But why use the defensive phrase 'even dog shows'? Dog shows are a very popular source of competition and recreation throughout the world. The commonly accepted, but totally erroneous view is that competitive events involving dogs are of recent origin, arising out of an event for setter and retriever bitches, held in Newcastle in 1859. John Warde, one of the eighteenth century's peripatetic huntsmen, was certainly running hound shows at least from the mid-1770s. Even before that, in 1603, the Duke of Bavaria's seventeen-year-old daughter had embarrassed her father by declining to marry Rudolf II, the fifty-one-year-old bachelor King of Austria, Emperor of the Holy Roman Empire and son of Maximilian II, and in order to expiate the Emperor's understandable disappointment, the Duke sent Rudolf a gift of twelve hunting dogs. The Emperor quickly became so captivated by the dogs that he decided to test them against his friends' dogs. A field trial was organized. It took place, over an eight-day period, in the extensive grounds of the Hradcany Castle in the city of Prague. Taking part were 480 dogs, some coming from as far away as Spain. Following the trial the Emperor established the Society of Experienced Hunters, which remained active until the Emperor was deposed by his younger brother in 1611.

Competitive canine activities, and organizations to control them, have a history at least 400 years long, but it was not until a little over one hundred years ago, when the development of industry obliged man to accept an urbanized life style that forced him to live without close, daily contact with species other than his own, that attitudes towards companion animals began to change. Man's daily contact with animals over tens of thousands of years, during which he developed from a hunter to a farmer, from a farmer to a trader and then to an industrialist, cannot have failed to have reached into the very core of man's being. Urbanization resulted in many people losing contact with species other than their own, although the instinctive need for that contact remained and continued to exert its influence. Not only did popular attitudes towards animals change as society became more industrialized but pet keeping and the breeding of pet animals prized for their appearance and the companionship they provided became far more widespread.

Even while the nineteenth century was still young, clubs had been formed which enabled dog breeders to gather together to share their experiences and compare the results of their efforts. It was from these clubs that urban dog shows have grown. Charles Darwin took a close interest in this rapidly growing fancy and this, coupled with his experience of breeding exotic domestic pigeons, helped him to develop and enlarge the theories which had begun to germinate during his voyage on *The Beagle*.

Early British dog shows probably attracted no more than a handful of entries. A painting belonging to the Kennel Club depicts a show which took place a few years prior to 1855, when the painting was completed. It shows just seventeen dogs. The 1859 Newcastle show attracted sixty entries. The Kennel Club's first show, in 1873, attracted 975 entries. The Crufts Centenary Show, which took place in 1991, attracted over 25,000 entries to become the biggest dog show the world had ever seen, and this in spite of the fact that the Crufts entry is limited to dogs which have qualified by winning at previous championship shows. Crufts is just one of well over 500 championship shows and over 5,000 events licensed each year by the Kennel Club. The popularity of dog shows in Britain is repeated all over the world.

The Kennel Club in Britain registers about 200,000 dogs each year. These form about one third of the total (7 million plus), canine population of Britain. The American Kennel Club which, unlike the Kennel Club in Britain does not have a monopoly of USA registrations, registers

Showing dogs is an activity that can be enjoyed by all ages. (Photo: Jackson)

nearly 1.5 million dogs each year. There are almost 50 million dogs in the USA. In Japan over a quarter of a million are registered and the total population approaches 5 million. There are very few countries anywhere in the world which do not now have a kennel club to regulate the growing interest in breeding dogs and in the activities which involve dogs.

Science or Art?

Breeding dogs remains much less of a science than breeding farm stock. The qualities required in farm animals, the ability to thrive in certain conditions, to grow quickly and produce maximum profit, can be easily and precisely defined. Breeding can be planned on an entirely scientific basis. Companion animals are valued for reasons that are far less open to scientific analysis. That is why periodic attempts to feed the qualities of the ideal companion dog into a computer in the hope that the components of the perfect dog will emerge are doomed to inevitable failure. Even the 500 or so recognized breeds of dogs, in all their variety, with their varied histories and associations, are insufficient to satisfy every dog owner. Attempts are continually being made to create new breeds or to adapt old ones to meet fresh demands. The needs of dog owners are not susceptible to computer analysis and neither can dog breeding be entirely based on scientific breeding techniques. Breeding dogs remains an art, but it is an art in which science cannot be denied an important influence.

Individual and even official attitudes towards breeding, and particularly to some of the processes and techniques involved – inbreeding and line-breeding, the use of artificial insemination, storage of semen and embryos, embryo transfer, induced fertility, genetic manipulation, plotting the canine genome and the like, which more recent scientific advances have made available – seem often to stem from Luddite prejudices rather than from reasoned thought. Part of the purpose of this book is to examine the new tools which are or could be available to breeders in the hope that such attitudes may be eroded.

Breeders may no longer believe that pre-natal influences and mental impressions can affect the appearance of puppies. Jacob believed that planting particoloured sticks in a field would induce the birth of particoloured lambs, hence, it is alleged, the particoloured appearance of Jacob's sheep. Nor is there likely to be any remaining belief in saturation, the process of repeatedly mating a bitch to the same dog in the belief that her blood will progressively become saturated with his blood and successive litters more and more like their sire. The theory of telegony – that a pedigree bitch mated to a mongrel dog will henceforth never be able to produce pedigree puppies – is probably also thoroughly discredited, as must surely be the belief that acquired characteristics can be inherited. (Darwin himself believed that the huge biceps developed by blacksmiths would be inherited by their children, though he appears not to have considered how this might affect the blacksmith's daughters!) Breeds that have been docked for hundreds of years still do not produce naturally short-tailed puppies any more than man's habit of shaving has produced a beardless race.

Any residual belief that the male is the

dominant partner and as such is largely responsible for the transmission of virtues, has no basis in fact, and terms such as tail-male and tail-female descent have no biological validity. Elementary school biology is more than enough to demonstrate that the male does not exercise total control over the number of offspring conceived by the female. Although these and other beliefs are no longer common currency among dog breeders, attitudes towards some aspects of breeding – particularly those aspects which are frowned upon in our own species – probably still owe more to superstition, folklore and religious taboo than to reasoned judgement.

Popular attitudes towards inbreeding and line-breeding, matings between more or less closely related individuals, provide a telling example of the way in which moral attitudes may override scientifically valid precepts. Leviticus, Chapter 20, sets out a scale of punishments for various unions between people who may have been, but may not have been, related by blood. The effect of these edicts would be to maintain genetic variation within the population in which they were practised. As such they were, in small and relatively static populations, entirely sensible. Unions between a man and his father's wife, a man and his daughter, and a man and his mother-in-law were prohibited on pain of death. Unions between a man and his sister or his father's or mother's daughter were punished by banishment. Unions between a man and his father's or mother's sister appear to attract no more than condemnation while union between a man and his uncle's wife foreshadows a childless marriage. The prevention of incestuous relationships in small communities preserves genetic variability and so inhibits the spread of deleterious genes.

On the other hand, the Old Testament also provides an example of extremely close inbreeding. It is alleged that man is descended from Adam and from a female, Eve, created out of Adam's rib. This early example of genetic engineering would have created an individual genetically identical to Adam. Their offspring, Cain, Abel and Seth, were very closely inbred indeed and would have been genetically identical to both their parents. Since it apparently was God's purpose to establish a distinctive human breed it was entirely sensible to begin the process with closely inbred stock homozygous for the desired human characteristics. Undesirable characteristics unfortunately found their way into the foundation stock and because the stock was very closely inbred these have not yet been eliminated from the human species. Herein lies the principal danger of inbreeding.

In practice, it is impossible for dog breeders to avoid some degree of inbreeding or line-breeding, no matter how slight. If the pedigree of any dog is traced back through twenty generations, to perhaps no more than forty years ago, the twentieth generation in the pedigree would contain 1,048,576 individuals. Yet forty years ago, no breed would contain more than a few hundred individuals and most may have had less than a hundred from which the next generation was derived. Indeed, twenty-eight of the breeds then recognized by the Kennel Club had fewer than a hundred annual registrations. The next generation of these breeds probably derived from no more than ten or a dozen individuals whose names appear time and time again in the twentieth and subsequent generations of the pedigrees of modern dogs. Every breed has gone through at least one, and usually more, bottlenecks which have created a degree of background inbreeding which, in some breeds, is far higher than is desirable.

This high level of background inbreeding has, in part, been created by successive bottlenecks during which the population of various breeds sank to dangerously low levels. Even the most popular breeds would be regarded as rare by zoologists. Captive breeding stocks should be carefully managed to protect genetic diversity.

The original kennel club registries allowed, and might even be said to have encouraged, some degree of cross-breeding. Nowadays they maintain hermetically sealed registries for individual breeds irrespective of whether the breed exists in sufficient numbers to be capable of maintaining a healthy population. Far from actively promoting the improvement of breeds they have unintentionally created the conditions in which hereditary defects can flourish and in which their control becomes increasingly difficult.

Why Breed Dogs at All?

Apart from the perfectly valid economic arguments already put forward in support of dog breeding, there are a number of other valid reasons for doing so. Even in this mechanized, computerized, industrialized age, dogs are still needed for herding farm livestock, as guards and

Numerically weak breeds present breeders with particular problems. (Photo: Jackson)

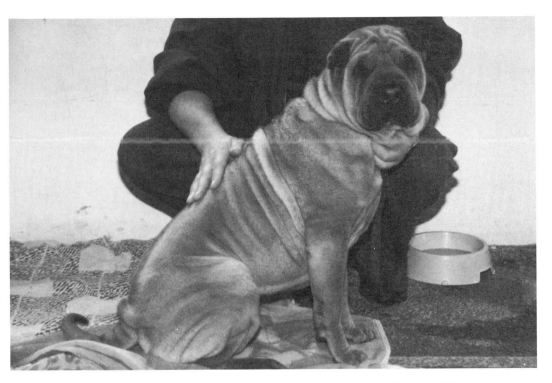

Reduced emphasis on exaggerated features is improving the Sharpei's health. (Photo: Jackson)

deterrents to malefactors, for search and rescue, to assist handicapped people, for sport and recreation, and to provide companionship, comfort, security and interest.

Our ingrained needs are slowly being charted as the medical profession recognizes that contact with animals helps to relieve stress, that animals can offer much needed companionship to the lonely, stimulate habitually sedentary people to take exercise, give security to the weak, provide interest for those whose lives lack motivation, pride to those who feel neglected, and help to relieve many of the stresses which modern living imposes.

It has been shown that people who own pets not only live longer than those who do not but are also more likely to recover from illnesses – and recover more quickly – than people who have no pets. Tests have shown that contact with a dog or a cat has the effect of lowering blood pressure, slowing the heart beat and modifying respiration, all indications of relief from the effects of stress. People who are obliged to spend their lives locked away from society can have some meaning restored to their existence by the presence of animals. Ronald Stroud, the famous bird man of Alcatraz, is not an isolated example of the way in which an interest in animals has helped someone to survive in very difficult circumstances. These factors are now being increasingly used to help people survive in prisons, in

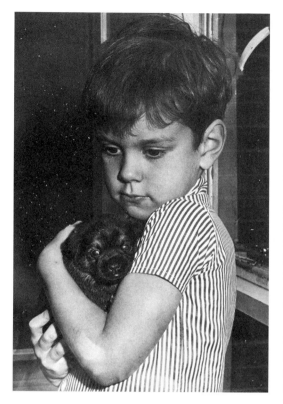

Mutual companionship, one of the many benefits that arise from the close association between man and dog. (Photo: Jackson)

mental institutions, in homes for the aged, and in hospitals. Doctors know that the benefits which accrue from contact with animals far outweigh any disadvantages which may arise. Far from being a threat to health, dogs in our society are the source of positive benefits which not only promote good health but, by doing so, appreciably reduce the overall cost of providing health services.

These benefits have not yet been fully investigated. In 1993, Dr Andrew Edney reported the results of a trial which showed that some dogs were capable of recognizing and warning of the onset of epileptic fits in their owners. Previously Dr Edney had suggested that, 'it may also be possible to identify animals which can anticipate other acute episodes in human illness, such as hypoglycaemic coma, coronary heart disease, syncope or even migraine attacks.' He went on to suggest, 'there is an opportunity to encourage the trait present in some dogs.' Clearly dog breeding has hitherto unexplored areas to investigate.

Just as they have been for hundreds of years, dogs continue to be used for experimental and testing purposes. Breeding dogs for such purposes is a highly specialized business with a number of requirements which fundamentally differ from the demands made by breeding sporting, utilitarian, companion or assistance dogs.

Carefully bred dogs of various types are required for many purposes. Some dogs – guide dogs and police dogs for example – are increasingly being bred in carefully controlled breeding colonies but the majority of dogs are still bred by individuals whose skills, abilities and motives are subject to wide variation. To most of these people breeding dogs is simply a means by which the enjoyment and interest derived from dog ownership can be extended. Some breed with the intention of making a profit or, at the least, of recouping the cost of their own dog and its upkeep. Some do so simply to perpetuate the characteristics of a favourite companion; some to provide a young family with a practical lesson in sex and the care of young things. Others do so in order to provide themselves with the means of continued involvement in some canine activity. Quite often breeders are motivated by a combination of several of these factors. Perpetuating the characteristics of a favourite and competitively

Foxhounds arguably represent the zenith of the breeder's art. (Photo: Jackson)

successful bitch may produce the profit which will support competition with one of her offspring. There is no need to cavil about any of these motives providing that each and every one is allied to the only good reason for breeding dogs: the desire and intention to breed and raise good dogs.

What is a Good Dog?

A good dog exhibits the characteristics of its type, is capable of fulfilling the tasks for which it was intended; he can move, eat, and breathe without distress, can see and hear, can reproduce naturally, is resistant to disease, does not suffer from unreasonable fear or nervousness, and can reasonably be expected to preserve all these qualities throughout most of a normal span of life. No good breeder would even begin to be satisfied with his efforts until he was confident that his puppies had all these qualities, but the best breeders would also aim at something more. They would be continually striving to reach a quality of excellence which, except rarely, is probably unattainable.

The problem breeders face is that the need to conform with a particular Breed Standard which, since it was written down many years ago, has probably been refined and its meaning narrowed, directs them towards uniformity, whereas health and vitality are best protected by variation. It is not a coincidence that the

Brachycephalic breeds present problems for breeders. (Photo: Jackson)

breeds whose standards are most specific are often also the ones that suffer most from hereditary defects. What may have happened is that in pursuit of exotic breed points, breeders may have been unaware of or have chosen to ignore the existence of hereditary disease. As a consequence breed type may sometimes have been achieved at the expense of breed health.

Breeders, however, must not be allowed to carry all the blame. Kennel clubs have been and continue to be far more anxious to preserve and develop breed type by maintaining separate breed registers than protecting breeds from the proliferation of inherited defects. It may not be coincidental that as kennel club registration became increasingly selective, exercising total discrimination against dogs which could not prove descent from a narrow gene pool, the incidence of inherited defects has increased dramatically.

Nor should the veterinary profession be absolved from responsibility. Improved veterinary skills now enable animals to breed which previously would either have died or been incapable of breeding. Furthermore, the proper exercise of veterinary skills in order to relieve the pain or discomfort produced by some inherited conditions often obliterates evidence of the condition's existence. Unknowing or unscrupulous breeders may then breed from dogs carrying hereditary defects. In the UK during 1991, the Royal College of Veterinary Surgeons and the Kennel Club came to an agreement by which Kennel Club services would only be made available to those who agreed to allow their veterinarian to report any instance of surgery which had the effect of hiding an inherited condition. Precisely the same condition was included in the Kennel Club's Code of Ethics, with which all breeders are expected to comply.

Released from a code of confidentiality, vets would be able to play a major part in the control of some serious hereditary defects. In spite of its obvious flaws, the scheme might have made a valuable contribution to canine health had vets chosen to play their part. Sadly, after almost two years, only a handful of vets have made reports to the Kennel Club.

The Responsible Breeder

Canine well-being is the responsibility of the veterinary profession, of kennel clubs and of breed clubs, but there can be no avoiding the fact that the major share of responsibility must remain with the breeder. The activities of puppy farms and mills and of their callous owners and the equally callous owners of puppy supermarkets have, in recent years, focused attention on some of the unacceptable aspects of dog breeding. Attempts to expose and subsequently control those whose standards leave much to be desired have achieved only limited success but during the next few years the spotlight that shines on the practices of unscrupulous dog breeders is likely to become far more intense. Bad breeders may well find themselves isolated and exposed as kennel clubs progressively tighten their procedures, and the worst breeders are likely to be called upon to answer to the courts.

National and local legislation intended to impose minimum standards, some of which are specific to breeders and some more generally applicable, is already in place. Many breed and kennel clubs already have codes of ethics with which members and those who make use of services are expected to comply. Co-operation between veterinarians and kennel clubs, the growth and analysis of computerized records and a growing public concern are all likely to impose new obligations on breeders. Some of these, as in the past, will be troublesome and even unworkable; others will achieve their effect only at the expense of breeders whose standards require no such control. It will be necessary for breeders to be aware of all the control measures with which they must comply if they are not to fall from grace.

The qualities required of a judge are easily defined: it has been said, perhaps unkindly, but not without a grain of truth, that he must be clever enough to be capable of accomplishing the task in a competent manner and stupid enough to believe that what he is doing is important. The qualities required of a good breeder are less easily defined. Charles Darwin made a brave attempt to do so in his *Origin of Species*.

> Not one man in a thousand has accuracy of eye and judgement sufficient to become an eminent breeder. If gifted with these qualities, and he studies his subject for years, and devotes his lifetime to it with indomitable perseverance, he will succeed, and may make great improvements; if he wants any of these qualities he will assuredly fail.

He returned to the subject in *The Variation of Animals and Plants Under Domestication*.

> Indomitable patience, the finest powers of discrimination and sound judgement must be exercised during many years. A clearly predetermined object must be kept steadily in view. Few men are endowed with all these qualities, especially that of discriminating very slight differences; judgement can be acquired only by long experience; but if any of these qualities be wanting, the labour of a life may be thrown away.

It is little wonder there are so few really good dog breeders.

CHAPTER 2

Basic Genetics

When, in the early 1870s, Thomas Hardy wrote *Moments of Vision* he could not have known the principles of genetics, yet in just two verses he managed to encapsulate all that genetics is about:

I am the family face;
Flesh perishes, I live on,
Projecting trait and trace
Through time to times anon
And leaping from place to place
Over oblivion.

The year-heired feature that can
In curve and voice and eye
Despise the human span
Of Durance – that is I;
The eternal thing in man
That heeds no call to die.

Genetics is the study of the way in which 'the family face' survives from generation to generation and becomes 'The eternal thing in man/That heeds no call to die.'

The word genetics derives from a Greek word meaning 'to produce', itself a derivation of a word meaning 'a race or family'. It is the study of the means by which characteristics are inherited, and owes its existence as a science to the efforts of an Austrian monk, Gregor Johann Mendel, from the Augustinian monastery at Brünn who, in 1860, discovered the basic laws of inheritance. Mendel's findings were published in 1866 and were then neglected until 1900 when their importance was confirmed by the independent findings of three biologists, de Vries, Correns, and von Tschermak.

In the ensuing years, scientists have unravelled many more of the laws that govern the way in which physical and mental attributes are inherited. Research has tended to concentrate its principal interest on those economically important animals and plants which can be made more profitable by the principal application of genetics. The study of canine genetics has been relatively ignored. Nevertheless, the published work of canine geneticists now enables breeders to exert far more control than was once the case over the quality of the puppies they produce. If this ability may sometimes have been ignored or mis-used, that is not the fault of the science but of breeders and of their advisers.

During a symposium on 'Heredity and Disease in Dogs and Cats', which took place in London in 1988, Dr Donald Patterson recognized that research and the availability of new diagnostic techniques, possibly rather than an actual increase in the incidence of hereditary defects, had led to the identification of a large number of diseases of genetic origin. Dr Patterson also warned breeders that inbreeding was the route by which genetic disorders were spread most quickly through a group of breeding animals, whether within a kennel or a breed.

Breeders must, of course, have access to the best possible advice. A paper written by Professor B. Denis of the Nantes Veterinary School faced the question of vets as advisers:

> Nowadays, genetics proper is given a place in symposiums on hereditary pathology and in publications with a view to continued education. Actually veterinary surgeons are above all clinicians and very few really master this discipline.

Even so, Professor Denis recognized that the fact that clinicians are 'readily interested in genetics is an indirect way of showing, if necessary, the growing importance of hereditary pathology'.

Like veterinarians, very few breeders master the increasingly complex science of genetics. Many more, deterred by the complexities, do not even make the attempt. Yet, since it is impossible for a breeder to avoid the effects which genetics exerts, it is surely essential to have at least a rudimentary grasp of the subject.

The basic unit of all life is the cell. Bacteria, yeasts and amoebae may consist of single cell; more complex creatures contain many millions of cells, some of which have specialized effects, but all, nevertheless, consist of a nucleus and surrounding cytoplasm. The nucleus contains the chromosomes which themselves contain the genes on which are recorded all the information necessary to replicate the individual. Because chromosomes are paired, the total number (the diploid number) is of less importance than the number of pairs (the haploid number). Our own species has twenty-three pairs of chromosomes, sheep have twenty-seven,

cows thirty, donkeys thirty-one, and dogs (both wild and domestic), have thirty-nine. It could, therefore, be said that dogs are, in genetic terms, more complex than man, sheep, cows and donkeys.

Cell Division

During the process of sexual reproduction the cells which contain the chromosomes divide in the testes and ovaries, by a process called meiosis, to produce cells which each carry the diploid number of chromosomes. When fertilization takes place the sperm, carrying genetic information derived from the male parent, and the ova, carrying the female parent's genetic information, unite following sexual union to produce cells which again carry the normal haploid number of chromosomes, half of which have been derived from the male and half from the female parent.

Dominant/Recessive Relationship

In order to resolve any possibility of conflict between genes carrying opposing messages, nature devised the dominant/recessive relationship, which Mendel was the first to recognize.

The place that individual genes occupy on the chromosome is known as the locus. Genes occupying the same locus are called alleles or allelomorphs. A gene that is capable of masking the effect of its allelomorphic partner is referred to as dominant; genes whose effect is masked by their allelic partners are known as recessive. This simple relationship becomes complicated because some genes

A harlequin Great Dane bitch has produced two black puppies in a litter of harlequins. (Photo: Le Mare)

may be incompletely dominant or incompletely recessive, because the information which produces some characteristics may be carried by more than one gene (such characteristics are referred to as polygenic), and because some characteristics are genetically linked to others, so that all are inherited as a sort of package.

When each allelic pair carries the same genetic message, the animal is said to be homozygous for that characteristic (in such animals, the characteristic will be apparent, rather than merely carried); if the allelic pair are dissimilar the animal is said to be heterozygous for that particular characteristic, and in these animals the characteristic may either be apparent or merely carried.

Thus, to take a simple example, a black-spotted and a liver-spotted Dalmatian would both carry genes that gave rise to Dalmatians with spotted coats; if the pair were mated their offspring would all be spotted Dalmatians. However, since black is dominant to liver, it might be expected that all the offspring would be black-spotted. Liver is recessive to black and so the liver-spotted parent must be homozygous for liver-spotting, because if he had inherited one gene for black-spotting, he would actually be black-spotted; the black parent, on the other hand, may be either homozygous or heterozygous for black-spotting. If the black-spotted parent is homozygous, all the offspring would be black-spotted, since black would mask the liver inherited from the liver-spotted parent; however, such offspring would be heterozygous for black-spotting because they will have inherited one gene for liver-spotting. If the black-spotted parent

24

were heterozygous, the offspring would carry genes for both black- and liver-spotting, in which case some, about one quarter, of the offspring would be black-spotted but heterozygous, and the rest would be homozygous for liver-spotting.

Suppose then that two heterozygous black-spotted Dalmatians were mated. The offspring would, on average, consist of one quarter homozygous black-spotted Dalmatians, one quarter homozygous (as they must be) liver-spotted Dalmatians, and one half heterozygous black-spotted Dalmatians.

In selecting for the recessive characteristic, in this case liver-spotting, it would be easy to eliminate the dominant characteristic, in this case black-spotting. Selec-

The unusual coat pattern of Weimeraner puppies fades with age. (Photo: Edminson)

tion for black-spotting, the dominant characteristic, would, however, do no more than progressively reduce the incidence of liver-spotting, but would never entirely eliminate it. Even so, simply by selecting against phenotypically affected animals the incidence could be reduced from 20 per cent to under 3 per cent in a matter of thirty generations. If entire litters in which the character appeared were removed from the breeding programme the incidence would be reduced to less than 2 per cent.

Unfortunately, the majority of undesirable characteristics and hereditary defects in dogs are carried on recessive genes. Their total elimination is a practical impossibility but simple means exist to reduce their incidence quite dramatically if breeders choose to do so.

Gender

Sex Determination

One pair of chromosomes carries the information which will decide whether the offspring is to be male or female as well as information which is linked to gender (sex-linked). The male's sex chromosome carries an X and a Y chromosome, the female two X chromosomes.

When these chromosomes divide, they produce four chromatids, X, X, X and Y. When mating takes place these unite to produce XX, females, or XY, males. Genetically, therefore, the male parent is entirely responsible for the sex of the offspring but the environment during pregnancy has a considerable effect on which survive. It is entirely possible that some bitches may, whether consistently or from time to time, provide an environment which is more or less hostile to one or other sex and so produce a predominance of dogs or bitches.

Sex-Linked and Sex-Limited

Any characteristic carried on the X or Y sex chromosomes can only appear in the relevant sex and is said to be sex-linked. Haemophilia, as in the human species, is linked to the X chromosome and so can appear only in the male, which carries two X chromosomes, though females, which carry only one X chromosome, may be carriers of the disease.

Sex-limited characteristics are somewhat different in that they are not carried by the sex chromosomes and so are inherited by both sexes, although, because of the nature of these characteristics, only one or other sex can exhibit them. The most obvious are those characteristics such as maternal fertility, maternal drive and lactation, male fertility, including the effects of monorchidism and cryptorchidism and masculine sexual drive.

Epistasis

Some genes, epistasic genes, can affect others which are not their alleles. Albinism is carried on these epistasic genes so that no matter what colour other genes may indicate, their effect is masked by the epistasic albino genes.

Mutation

Further complications arise because, from time to time, the effect of a gene may be modified by mutation. In the wild, mutation is the means by which new species evolve, but because mutation is a random element it does not indicate the direction evolution takes; evolutionary direction is controlled by natural selection.

It is likely that a significant number of the characteristics which now differentiate one breed from another may have arisen because of mutation. In the wild, mutants survive to breed only if their mutation confers some advantage over the normal population. Natural selection keeps undesirable mutants ruthlessly in their place. Selection employed by dog breeders is far less ruthless and may well favour a long-coated or hairless mutant, one with unusually short legs, or one that differs in size or in some other way from its normal siblings. The mutant may then be used as the basis for a breed.

It also seems probable that a number of undesirable inherited abnormalities appeared as a result of mutant genes and that these have survived simply because the process of artificial selection practised by breeders is not nearly as stringent or effective as natural selection.

Threshold Traits

A number of inherited abnormalities owe their existence to a more complex effect of several genes, all or some of which affect a particular characteristic. When the effect of all is exerted, the characteristic will be seen in its most extreme form; when a few exert their effect that effect will be milder; and the effect of very few may be so mild as to be scarcely discernible.

Cryptorchidism is probably a threshold trait which varies in expression between, perhaps, unnoticed late descent into the scrotum of one of the testes, to the obstinate refusal of both to take up their normal positions.

The majority of kennel clubs bar cryptorchids from the ring and several refuse to register them or their offspring, whether male or female. The Kennel Club in Britain currently takes a totally different view: cryptorchids may be both bred from and shown, though judges are instructed to regard the condition as a fault. However, since castrated dogs may be freely shown, how is a judge in Britain to differentiate between a cryptorchid, which should be faulted, and a previously normal castrated dog, which should not be faulted? Even worse, how are breeders to collect the information needed in order to avoid this serious condition if its existence can be hidden by surgery and if the Kennel Club does not take steps to record its incidence?

Population Genetics

Although the science of genetics is directly concerned with the way in which parents transmit their characteristics to their offspring, the wider effect – on a kennel, a particular breed and even on pedigree dogs as a whole – is perhaps of even greater importance and significance. Unfortunately only in recent years have a few breed clubs begun to show that they are aware of this wider significance.

Hellmuth Wachtel is one of the growing number of visionary experts who are expressing fears about the degree of uncontrolled inbreeding which is taking place in dogs:

Regarding an 'acceptable' inbreeding coefficient, in literature I have read six per cent is suggested as a desirable limit. Up to now it is impossible to know a dog's true coefficient as mostly just the pedigree coefficient is calculable but not the background homozygosity derived from former inbreeding, bottlenecks, etc., in the breed's history. So we have to wait for DNA-figures from different breeds, a thing that now is under way for six breeds in Sweden. . . . Lots of work is going on in this field (homozygosity studies in wild and domestic animals) and people are very concerned about genetic soundness of both wild and domestic (farm) animals. I think it is a shame that almost nobody cares (with the few exceptions I mentioned to you) about the domestic dog. Some time ago, a most prominent Canadian veterinarian, Dr Mac Keown, told me he thinks the domestic dog is an 'endangered species'. He meant genetic defects. I think there are three calamities to fight: a rising hysterical antidog wave and the two capital sins of breeding – inbreeding and type exaggeration. I don't know which of the three is worst, just that two of them depend on the dog fancy community itself that seems to obstinately ignore modern scientific tools like population genetics and molecular biology.

Kennel clubs throughout the world claim, in slightly different ways, to exist in order to promote the improvement of dogs. The aim is a noble one, and yet it appears that kennel clubs have been powerless to curb the obscene practices of puppy farms and mills, or to prevent hereditary disease from spreading through breed after breed. It must be hoped that in the future they will find both the means and the will to take effective action on both fronts and that in the future they will be enabled to supply the services and support which breeders need and have sought in order to

Grooming is important but can it become too important? (Photo: Jackson)

protect the breeds in which they have a particular interest.

During the early 1990s it was becoming increasingly apparent that the failure by kennel clubs to assess and exert effective control over the genetic health of individual breeds, and especially of those which for many years had existed on the basis of a dangerously small breeding population, was reaching crisis point. The eminent Canadian veterinarian who described pedigree dogs as 'an endangered species' probably exaggerated the situation, perhaps deliberately, but he did draw attention to a real problem.

Some breeds have existed for many years on the basis of breeding populations which, had they been wild species, would certainly have placed them in the notorious zoological red book of endangered species. Once listed as endangered species their pedigrees would have been analysed and their breeding carefully managed in order to preserve genetic health and breed type, indeed to protect them from the imminent danger of extinction. No breed of dog, no matter how numerically small the breeding population may be, has yet enjoyed the benefit of such carefully managed breeding programmes.

Within a population of infinite size, in which matings take place on a random basis, there would be no significant genetic variation from generation to generation. With small populations, especially when these are isolated, or in sub-populations – such as exist within kennels – in which breeding is selective, gene frequency is subject to considerable variation.

For example, in a large population, in generation after generation roughly half the offspring are male and half female. But supposing the population were to be reduced to a single pair and the pair produced only female offspring. This would leave the sire as the only male who would have to produce male children out of his own daughters if the population were to survive. This would mean that any deleterious genes he happened to carry would be spread through the entire population and these might easily result in the population's demise.

Suppose that the sire was a cryptorchid. Obviously his daughters would not exhibit the defect but they would all carry the gene, even if the female parent did not. When these were mated to their father, all the male offspring would be cryptorchids. The breed would have lost the ability to produce normal male offspring. It would not be long before it became extinct.

The science of population genetics has enabled breeding programmes to be devised which will maintain the genetic health of small breeding populations of animals threatened with extinction, such as Whooping Cranes and Mauritius Kestrels. There are certainly some breeds of dog that would benefit from the application of similar management techniques.

Population genetics is the science which is concerned with the means to counteract such effects. The science is only now beginning to be applied to dog breeding and the fear must exist that, for some rare breeds, kennel clubs may have left it too late to take effective action.

Change

Change in the appearance of livestock, wild or domesticated, is inevitable without a positive and determined effort to prevent it. Different breeds adopt different attitudes towards change: some strive to prevent it, some allow it to happen, and some actively encourage it. In the wild, change is the product of what the available gene pool has to offer and of adaptation to the demands exerted by the need to survive. Among domesticated animals change is also a product of the contents of the available gene pool and of the process of artificial selection employed by breeders.

Changed appearance as a result of superficial cosmetic fashions, particularly to grooming techniques can, to a large extent, be disregarded. Exquisitely groomed terriers, hounds or gundogs would not be prevented from working, though their coiffures may not survive the attentions of brambles and brackens. The tendency to scoff at superficial fashions in the dog show world is invariably based on prejudice and ignorance. None of these critics nowadays dress in the fashions that were current when Queen Victoria was on the throne. However, changes tend to be progressive and should be carefully managed.

Fashion apart, the appearance of all animals is partly a product of environmental factors, the way they have been reared, the exercise they get, and their age. All these combine to produce what is known as a phenotype. As environmental conditions change so the animal will change.

The Bulldog is one of the many breeds that have opted for change.
(Photo: Ward-Davies)

Mice living in cold stores tend to have smaller ears and longer coats in order to conserve body heat than do their brethren living in less hostile conditions.

Children in Western countries are now roughly ¾in (2cm) taller than their counterparts at the same age thirty years ago. They are several centimetres taller than their Victorian counterparts who, in their turn, were taller than sixteenth-century children. The change has been brought about by improved nutrition and medical care. Precisely the same tendency is to be seen in dogs. Improved nutritional standards, and more effective control over internal parasites, result in bigger, stronger and healthier dogs. If dogs from the past were to be born now and reared by the methods now available they would not, as adults, look as they did having been reared by the methods available even in the 1950s. Some breeders, however, tend to resist this particular change. They do not want Chihuahuas as big as Cocker Spaniels, or working terriers too big to follow a fox to ground. So they tend to select against an increase in size and, in practice, this may mean selecting the least robust individuals.

On the other hand, although the significance of a greater modern emphasis on grooming has been dismissed, it may go alongside selection for a longer or more profuse coat which will enable exhibitors to demonstrate their grooming skills. This profusion of hair causes no problems when the dogs are regularly groomed but is a threat to the welfare of neglected dogs. Surely breeders should examine all the consequences of any changes that they would like to make. Several breeds nowadays grow far more hair than they did even thirty years ago, and the change has been brought about by deliberate selection.

In a large population, changes resulting from inherited factors are unlikely to be dramatic, and may be imperceptible except to the keenest observer. The effect that an individual may have, however, can be seen to be quite dramatic when that effect is confined to a small area, and especially to certain kennels. In a small population, overall changes might be rapid and dramatic. Thus even a prolific dog who is different in some way and whom breeders find attractive, will have little effect on the appearance of a numerically strong breed, whereas he might totally change the appearance of a numerically small breed within a single generation.

Various breeds have adopted different attitudes towards change. Bulldogs, Sealyhams and Scottish Terriers are among those breeds that have, deliberately or fortuitously, opted for change which, while it makes them unsuitable for their original purpose in life, makes them more attractive to their modern supporters. Breeds such as Deerhounds, Manchester Terriers and Border Collies have opted for what might be seen as the conservationist approach. Breeders have resisted change to the extent that in some breeds dogs born during the last century are identical to those born recently. Between the two extremes are a multitude of positions. It is for breeders to decide whether they want to try to resist

change and preserve their breed in the form it had at a particular time in history, to allow change to happen and only to exert slight influence over the direction it takes, or actively to encourage change. No course has a monopoly of right or wrong.

The Gene Pool

The gene pool is the sum of the genes available to a population. If the gene pool is small then variation, other than by mutation, will also be limited. If the ingredients of a gene pool that has been allowed to shrink produce non-typical or abnormal animals, there will be no opportunity to restore typicality or normality.

If the pool is large then variation can also be large. It is then possible to select in favour of typical and normal animals. Random breeding (outcrossing) tends to maintain the size of the existing gene pool but cannot increase it. Selection, inbreeding and line-breeding all have a tendency to decrease the size of the available gene pool. A small gene pool restricts the ability to select and to make breeding progress. Only by importing unrelated breeding stock can the gene pool in a particular population be increased.

Dog breeders maintain the gene pool available to their kennels by making careful use of stock from other kennels. The gene pool available to a breed in a certain country may be increased by importing breeding stock from other countries. If the gene pool internationally available to a breed becomes dangerously small, the danger may be averted only by means of crosses with other breeds, a strategy which is anathema to modern kennel clubs and so largely unavailable to breeders. The strategy was one which old breeders used wisely and without compunction, and may well have been one of the factors that kept dogs of former years relatively free from hereditary defects.

Variation

Richard Jeffries may have been the first naturalist to draw attention to the way in which indiscriminate breeding among street dogs, between them exhibiting almost every feature to be found in domestic dogs, would eventually produce a dog of consistent type and appearance. Jeffries referred to this universal, ubiquitous dog as 'The Little Red Dog'.

He is a common type, widely distributed on the earth; I doubt if there are many countries where you will not meet him – a degenerate or dwarf variety of the universal cur, smaller than a fox-terrier and shorter-legged; the low stature, long body, small ears, and blunt nose giving him a somewhat stoaty or even reptilian appearance among the canines. His colour is, indeed, the commonest hue of the common dog, or cur, wherever found. It is rarely a bright red, like that of the

The ubiquitous 'little red dog' identified by Jeffries is alive and well on many a hearth-rug. (Photo: Parkinson)

Irish Setter, or any pleasing shade of red, as in the dingo, the fox, and the South American Maned Wolf; it is dull, often inclining to yellow, sometimes mixed with grey as in the jackal, sometimes with a dash of ginger in it.

An indiscriminate and varied mix of genes gives rise to a common type of feral dog, rather in the same way as indiscriminate and varied mixes of paints will invariably produce the same colour. On the other hand differences between breeds are maintained by restricting gene variety in order to eliminate undesirable characteristics and encourage desirable ones.

Thus a uniform appearance may be the result of genetic variety, while the varied appearance to be found among pedigree breeds is the product of deliberately restricting genetic variation. There may be a basic contradiction between the maintenance of breed type and what is required to maintain genetic health. Every genetic defect found in pedigree dogs would be found, if anyone cared to look, among mongrels but, because mongrels are the product of random matings, these defects are unlikely to spread through the entire population or even through a significant part of it. The maintenance and enhancement of breeds and of breed type tend to restrict genetic variety; in order to sustain health and vitality within breeds breeders must seek to reduce phenotype variation while maintaining genotype variety.

No other species shows as much phenotype variation as does the domestic dog. Even if we ignore the variation which exists in such things as physical shape, coat colour, texture, and length of leg, and instead consider weight alone, the range,

defined by breed standards, extends from the 2lb (1kg) Chihuahua to the 154lb (70kg) Neapolitan Mastiff. The norm for dogs is about 25lb (11kg); for our own species it is about 140lb (64kg). If the same range existed in our own species we would not be surprised to encounter normal, healthy adults who weighed little more than 11lb (5kg) and others who weighed nearly 62 stone (400kg).

If the concept of breeds is to retain any meaning, a recognizable breed type must exist within a fairly closely defined degree of variance. Kennel type, which exists between even narrower limits of variance, is to be found within old established kennels.

Variation is reduced and a changed appearance created by close breeding. In time all animals within a closely bred population would be genetically and physically identical. Before that stage had been reached, however, it is probable that nature would have taken a hand and, for one reason or another, the population would have become extinct. It is generally accepted by zoologists that when a population reaches a point at which somewhere between a third and a half of the individuals in that population are descended from a particular individual, that population is in dangerous territory. Several breeds of dog have been in this territory for many years, and some may have reached the point at which it is impossible to avoid some particular ancestor.

It is this tendency to reduced variation which gives rise to the changed appearance of breeds in different countries. The same phenomenon is also responsible for what breeders refer to as kennel type, the family likeness which exists among dogs from closely bred kennels.

Although the science of population genetics is still in its infancy, it might be argued that the regulations which appear in Leviticus 20, to which we have already referred, represent an early text on the subject. Only recently have a few breed clubs and kennel clubs begun to regulate in order to protect the genetic health of complete breeds.

Bottlenecks

Some breeds of dog have existed for many years on the basis of a breeding population which is far too small to maintain their genetic health and may even threaten their existence unless steps are taken to control breeding within the population as a whole.

Most breeds go through periodic bottlenecks which restrict their numbers and, in the absence of appropriate control, could lead to closely bred populations in which the effects of deleterious genes are impossible to avoid. The first bottleneck might occur when a breed is being developed: Count Hamilton, Louis Dobermann and the rest, all probably evolved closely bred strains consisting of relatively few individuals which formed the basis for the breeds that now carry their names. The next bottleneck may occur when the breed receives official recognition, a process which, at one sweep, usually takes unregistered dogs out of the breeding population and so exacerbates an already potentially dangerous situation.

Prior to official recognition it is possible to maintain genetic health by the use of judicious outcrossing with other breeds. In breeds where breeding populations have been depressed for some time, and in

Recently imported breeds may suffer from rapid popularity, exploitation and a restricted gene pool. (Photo: Jackson)

which there is no opportunity to improve matters by means of imported breeding material, the only way to sustain genetic health might be by the use of outcrosses to other breeds.

Other bottlenecks occur during wartime when breeding is restricted. In Britain this has occurred twice during the course of this century and on both occasions the effect on Kennel Club registrations was dramatic.

Bottlenecks are also created when a breed is first introduced to a country. A few individuals then tend to form the basis for the breed in its new home and even though these have been selected with care they are unlikely to provide all the genetic variation that exists within the breed's major populations. Further carefully selected imports, and the use of imported and stored semen will help to reduce the risks but in the absence of carefully designed control systems, which breed clubs and kennel clubs appear reluctant even to contemplate let alone provide, the genetic health of the new population is at risk.

Survival

Even in fairly recent years a number of breeds have become extinct. In Britain the list includes Blue Pauls, Drovers Dogs, Old English White Terriers, Clydesdale Terriers and Welsh Greys. Other breeds which struggle to find public favour seem destined to follow them. The same tendency is doubtless repeated in other parts of the world, but in the United States there is a strong interest in reviving old breeds or developing new ones which, perhaps, acts as some sort of counterbalance. Determined efforts are being made to promote new or revived breeds such as Alapaha Blue Blood Bulldogs, American Bulldogs, American Pit Bull Terriers, American Staffordshire Terriers, Australian Shepherds, English Sheepdogs, Louisiana Catahoula Leopard Dogs, Miniature Shar Peis, Rat Terriers and Toy Fox Terriers.

Recent political events in the Eastern bloc countries seem likely to lead to several breeds hitherto unknown in the West making their debut at shows. Closer co-operation between the American

Wire-haired Fox Terriers have fallen from popularity to the verge of becoming a rare breed. (Photo: Jackson)

Kennel Club, the Kennel Club (UK) and the Federation Cynologique Internationale (FCI) may well mean that breeds familiar in mainland Europe will find their way to British and American shows.

Breeds cannot survive unless breeders take an interest in them, and it is surely right that the breeds that have been so much a part of human existence for so many years should be given the opportunity to survive.

Testing for Genetic Abnormalities

Although genetic defects may seem to appear spontaneously, and occasionally as a result of mutant genes they do, they will usually have been lurking among recessive genes which close inbreeding has brought together to reveal and spread the defect. At this stage breeders need to know how prevalent the problem is in order to plan a strategy for its control.

The Federation Cynologique Internationale (FCI) has recently announced that 'the number of breeds recognized by the FCI is already too large, and difficult to survey; numerous countries keep applying to the FCI for the recognition of new breeds, most of which are only of regional importance. At the moment (September 1993), for example, three new breeds are being dealt with: the Bulgarian Hunting Dog, the Korean Gindo Dog, and the Brazilian Terrier. Another three breeds have already been registered; the Fila di San Miguel (Portugal), and two Italian breeds, the Lagotto and the Cane Corso.

Establishing the prevalence of a problem involves the collection and examination of information, which may be acquired from club members, from kennel club registration systems and from systems such as the Canine Genetic Disease Information System. The availability of programmes, and the increase in the use of personal micro-computers, makes it possible for any breed club, with the appropriate guidance, to make valuable use of this information in order to protect and improve the health of the breed. Indeed it could be said that checking on the hereditary health of the breed has become the prime responsibility of all breed clubs.

Every control scheme must be based on carefully collected, carefully analysed information. The more information that is available and the more detailed its analysis the more effective control is likely to be. Unfortunately, the hysteria and 'witch-hunting' which too often surrounds efforts by breed clubs to collect information severely impedes the exercise. Veterinary surgeons may also inadvertently obscure the existence of some hereditary defects when they carry out surgery to relieve their effect. If this means that information is withheld or is inaccurate, efforts to control hereditary disease may be frustrated.

An empirical method of calculating the incidence of a particular inherited defect, but one that produces results that are sufficiently accurate to form a firm basis for control, requires examination of the offspring of particular dogs. In order to identify a 2 per cent incidence of some particular inherited defect it would be necessary to examine nearly 600 offspring. To identify a 10 per cent incidence, fifty-nine puppies would need to be examined and to reveal a 20 per cent incidence it would be necessary to examine only twenty-nine offspring. It may well be that a 2 per cent incidence could be regarded as insignificant but a 20 per cent incidence is certainly very serious indeed.

If just one dog out of each sample was found to be carrying the defect it could be assumed that the brood as a whole is affected. There are certainly breeds, generally supposed to be free from hereditary defects, in which the same inherited defect can be found in one in sixty and possibly one in thirty.

Genetic Screening

Many diseases of genetic origin produce a recognizable biochemical anomaly which makes it possible to identify clinically normal heterozygotes. This is important in creating effective control systems for diseases which are inherited as recessives. The use of test matings is wasteful and the result can be distressing, since the puppies produced by these matings have to be slaughtered, neutered or in other ways prevented from breeding. Biochemical screening offers a means to exercise control without the waste and much of the distress.

Commenting on the need for teamwork in assessing tests, R.D. Jolly and P.J. Healy insisted that:

Genetic screening will usually be carried out by a partnership involving at least the breeder, a veterinarian and a laboratory. The responsibility for the diagnosis should not be abrogated to the biochemist performing the laboratory tests unless he or she is familiar with the inherent problems and has access to all the information that might influence the decision. Similarly a veterinary surgeon may not have sufficient information to assess an individual's genetic status merely on the basis of the laboratory data and an involvement with the client. A specialist diagnostician is usually required to interpret all the information pertinent to the test and to make uniform diagnoses within predetermined probability limits.

Control procedures are best based on a mass screening programme if only because this enables more effective control to be exercised over the entire population. The absence of effective control has already led to overseas registration being conditional on the results of compulsory screening in some breeds which are known to be at particular risk. The need for the existence of such procedures can do nothing to enhance the international reputation of the breed, of breeders or of the national control body.

In the absence of a national screening programme it is possible for an individual kennel to undertake its own testing programme, although unless the kennel is largely self-contained, or is able to rely on the co-operation of others, the value of testing may be much reduced.

Gene Register

A relatively new technique, molecular genetic linkage, is now available which makes it possible to use blood samples to identify defective genes which may give rise to some hereditary diseases, including progressive retinal atrophy, hip dysplasia, retinal dysplasia, Von Willebrand's disease, hereditary cataract and fucosidosis.

Use of these techniques would enable kennel clubs and others who run registration systems, as well as individual breeders, to discover the genetic health of breeding stock. A genetic register could provide the means by which the results of these tests can be recorded and made available to breeders; it should then be possible to make a large and rapid reduction in the incidence of many hereditary diseases.

If kennel clubs were also to make proven genetic health a condition of the confirmation of major awards, such as championship status, or even make genetic health a condition for the acceptance of puppies for registration, then eventual elimination of some hereditary diseases would be a real possibility.

Environment

Characteristics which are inherited are referred to as the genotype. Those that are the product of environmental influence are called the phenotype. The com-pounded effect of the two offer problems which all breeders must face.

Suppose that a dog is admired for some particular quality. How is a breeder to know whether this quality is inherited, and so is likely to be transmitted to his offspring, or whether it is the product of environmental factors, and so cannot be transmitted to another generation? In the past it was believed that environmental conditions could influence such things as coat colour and that acquired characteristics could be inherited. Such ideas have long been discredited but the way in which a puppy is reared and subsequently cared for undoubtedly has a profound effect on its temperamental and physical characteristics.

To complicate things even further, litter size, birth weight, growth weight, mature weight, temperament, coat and skin condition, musculature, skeleton construction, life span and many more qualities are affected by both inherited and environmental conditions.

CHAPTER 3

Breeding Systems and Methods

Even the worst puppy farmer or commercial breeder must make use of some sort of system in order to ensure that puppies are of the desired breed. Bulldog puppies can only be produced by bulldog parents. But the majority of breeders aim at something more than merely producing puppies of a particular breed. Every good breeder has in his mind's eye a picture, no matter how ill-defined the picture might be, of what he is aiming towards. The picture will become clearer and more refined as knowledge and experience grow; it may even change quite dramatically, but it is always there to guide the breeder's efforts.

Parson Jack Russell was an example of this. He was not only a very talented breeder but he enjoyed an unusually long career. Among several stud-dogs from outside Devon that he made use of was a well-known show and working fox terrier dog called Old Jock. He did so because Jock, more than any other terrier, fitted the Parson's picture of the ideal.

> I never saw a sweeter animal than Jock, so perfect in shape, so much quality. He is as near perfection as we poor mortals are ever allowed to feast our eyes on. His temper is so beautiful and his pluck undeniable.

The Parson, a breeder of terriers intended for work, listed appearance, temperament and courage in that order, and though it would be quite wrong to suggest that he regarded courage as of less importance than appearance it is undeniable that he regarded appearance as being very important. He certainly did not subscribe to the 'handsome is as handsome does' philosophy which has done so much harm to several sporting and working breeds. It was his mind's picture, combined with the Parson's considerable talent as a breeder, which enabled him to produce a distinctive type of fox terrier recognized and acclaimed by his peers.

The picture must, of course, be a realistic one. To a breeder intent on producing greyhounds for the track or for coursing, appearance will be of less importance (though seldom totally ignored) than the readiness to chase and the ability to run. If, however, the intention is to produce greyhounds for the show ring or as companions, appearance and temperament will rightly have priority, though it is hoped that readiness to chase and ability to run will not be totally ignored.

Unfortunately, few breeders begin their careers with a clearly defined picture of what they want to achieve. More often they buy a bitch and then become increasingly captivated by the breed; an ambition develops and they embark on a career as a breeder. Only later do they discover that their original bitch provides an unsuitable foundation for their growing ambitions.

In his novel *The Life of a Sportsman* Nimrod, C.J. Apperley, that most arrogant but most readable of nineteenth-century sporting journalists, offered advice to his hero, Frank Raby, who was about to set up his own kennel. Now, 150 years later, the advice remains relevant.

I must start with your start. Do you purchase, or get together a pack of your own? I should recommend the former at a liberal price. It will save you much trouble, and be the cheapest plan in the end. If you collect a pack – like Harlequin's snuff, a pinch out of every man's box – have nothing to do but with kennels of the highest character, for the better the hounds are, the less bad, of course, will be the drafts, and *vice versa*. For example, who would accept of a hound drafted from C——'s pack? At all events, if you determine on forming a pack by drafts from different kennels, don't fail purchasing twice as many as you may require for, depend on it, one half of them will be useless. Ask yourself the question, 'Who would draft *good* hounds?' You are then purchasing faults, which you never again get rid of. And do not trust to your eye; I have had hundreds of beautiful hounds in my time not worth one day's meal.

... If you attempt to form a pack of fox-hounds yourself, you must not, clever fellow as you are, expect *perfection* under ten years, and that makes a hole even in a young man's life. I can only say it cost me that time to form what I considered a steady and stout pack. Some sorts prove vicious, however highly bred; some unsound, some delicate; and, forasmuch as it requires

three years to find out the results of any cross, how favourable soever may the expectation from it, the breeder of hounds is too often, if not working in the dark, involved in uncertainties and perplexities to no small amount. As is the case with breeding horses, faults of generations back, on one side or the other, will appear; and with hounds, even should the cross suit the first time, there is perplexity again; the produce must be three years old before their real goodness can be verified; and their sire must be at least five or six, as no man would breed from a hound much under three year's standing at his work. Should the cross nick, however, spare no pains to continue it, if circumstances will enable you to do so – that is to say, if the dog and the bitch are within 500 miles of each other.

Nimrod's message is clear: kennel owners must define their needs and ambitions as precisely as possible, they must acquire stock from the best available source, aim only at perfection, discard any which subsequently fail to reach the required standard, choose the very best available mates for them, and be prepared to persevere. All of which can be expressed in one word, that word is selection.

Selection

Selection is inevitable. Only about 10 per cent of all registered dogs ever produce registered offspring; 90 per cent are effectively discarded by breeders. At the outset of their careers, when they may be ill-equipped to make such decisions, breeders select the foundation stock for their kennels. Eventually a mate will be chosen for the bitch; once more selection has been exercised. A litter will be produced and, in all probability, one or more puppies will be selected to extend the kennel's breeding potential. Already the new breeder has made decisions which could have a profound effect for many years to come.

Selection, therefore, is a matter of the greatest importance to breeders. It is imperative that the principles on which it is based are well defined. The principles must be closely related to the kennel's objective. There is no point in selecting dogs with a particular quality unless that quality is important to the kennel's objectives.

The principles on which selection is based must also be easily, quickly, accurately and cheaply measured. It would, for example, be difficult – though not impossible – to use longevity as a basis for selection simply because by the time the principle could be exercised the dogs would no longer be available for breeding. If selection principles can be exercised while dogs are young, not only can the economic loss entailed in keeping dogs which will not contribute to the breeding programme be avoided, but progress towards the objective can be that much more rapid. In most breeds the colour of a puppy at birth will not have changed by the time the puppy is an adult. It is, therefore, usually easy to select for colour at birth. It is not possible to select for regular dentition at this age and even when milk teeth erupt these may not offer a reliable guide to the placement of adult teeth. Thus, selection for regular dentition can be made only when adult teeth are in place. If the breeder is able to rely on every puppy having regular dentition, a troublesome and expensive area of selection will have been avoided.

Selection, then, is the process by which the parents of the next generation are chosen. It is this process which has given rise to the different breeds, which maintains their differences, and which enables breeders to exercise their own preferences.

Originally, selection would have been based on little more than toleration of man's company, though whether man or wolf was responsible for the selection is debatable. As domesticated wolves began to take part in hunting expeditions, those which would co-operate most readily, and especially those which would respond to commands or were fastest or had the best noses or the keenest eyesight, would have been selected. As time passed and the business of keeping body and soul together did not entirely preoccupy man – though functional requirements would still have been uppermost in his mind – he began to allow himself the luxury of selecting dogs whose appearance pleased him.

At this stage, if man had wanted to breed dogs with enormous heads or with very short, crooked legs or some other unnatural feature he could probably have done so but the extent of these unnatural attributes would have been kept in firm check by nature itself. Dogs had to be naturally conceived and born. They then had to survive to maturity in order to reproduce their kind. If the characteristics that breeders produced prevented any of these things, they could not be sustained. Nature still had the upper hand. Even when the standards of some breeds asked for exaggerated features these were kept in check by being practically unattainable.

The advance of veterinary skills since about 1900 has made it possible for dogs to be conceived, born and to live to reproduce their kind, when previously they would have died. A Pandora's Box containing a plethora of exaggerated features has been thrown open and its contents have escaped. Breeds began to run into trouble when veterinary science enabled breeders to reach and, in some cases, even go beyond exaggerations described in breed standards.

The Conference of World Kennel Clubs' response to this unacceptable level of exaggeration was to ask kennel clubs to re-examine all breed standards and wherever necessary rewrite them so that exaggerated features were no longer required. Only the Kennel Club (UK) responded to the challenge. The exercise was a long and difficult one, and although it was finally completed in 1988 all the anticipated benefits have yet to materialize.

Bowman offers, as a telling example of the effect of selection, a breeding programme involving White Plymouth Rock poultry. The foundation stock were divided into two groups selected only by weight. The heaviest were placed in one group, the lightest in the other. Random breeding, avoiding only close inbreeding, was allowed, and selection by weight from the two groups was continued for four generations. When the experiment was concluded the flock selected for heavy weight were 33 per cent heavier than the foundation stock, while the flock selected for lightness were 9 per cent lighter. Dog breeders could expect to make similar progress by means of careful selection. Breeders, however, are often in favour of using the sharper and more powerful tools provided by inbreeding and line-breeding.

Breed

It is selection that originally gave rise to breeds. The concept of 'breed' is one which has become progressively narrower during the course of this century and especially so during the last twenty-five years. Few breeders deliberately set out to produce crossbred dogs, the production of which, in any case, relies on the existence of pure bred animals as a basis for crossbreeding. None deliberately set out to produce mongrels, whose existence is almost entirely the product of irresponsible, careless and, to an extent, callous ownership.

Breeders are interested in breeds and, most often, in one particular breed. But what is a breed? The term has no biological significance. Biologically, physiologically and genetically there is no significant difference between domestic dogs and wolves, or between any two breeds of domestic dog. All will readily mate with any other and produce fertile young. The only thing that prevents Chihuahuas from mating with Great Danes is size. The only thing that prevents the Australian Dingo from mating with the Arctic Wolf is distance.

Breed originally meant no more than a group of dogs which had a common purpose and, within quite broad limits, a common appearance. The occasional indulgence in crossbreeding did not destroy the concept of breed but was used to strengthen some particular aspect of it. Even as late as the 1970s, it was possible for dogs of unknown breeding to be incorporated into a Kennel Club breed register, providing only that an independent championship show judge of that breed was prepared to verify their resemblance to it. The weakness of the system was that it placed total emphasis

In some breeds the dichotomy between show and working types poses unnecessary problems. (Photo: Jackson)

on appearance and none at all on performance. Previously, as is seen in Parson Jack Russell's attitude to Old Jock, appearance was just one of the criteria to be considered.

Eventually, appearance rather than function came to be the principal criteria. Such relatively insignificant minor qualities as colour, coat texture and slight differences in size were enough to differentiate one breed from another. Dachshunds were divided into six separate breeds differentiated only by size and coat texture. Fox Terriers were divided into smooth- and wire-coated, Norfolk and Norwich Terriers were separated on the basis of ear carriage.

The consequence was that the range of genetic material available to some breeds fell below that which was necessary to maintain a healthy population. This might not have mattered had not kennel clubs chosen to prevent crossbreeding, sometimes even to the breed's colour, coat or size variant, and so deny access to a larger and potentially healthier gene pool. Once crossbreeding was prohibited, small populations were forced to rely on their own, often inadequate, resources.

There seems little point in the concept of breeds unless this is allied to a strong concept of type, that indefinable quality which separates one breed from another and the dogs of one kennel from those bred elsewhere, but when health and soundness are sacrificed on the altar of type the priorities of breeders, of breed clubs and of kennel clubs must be questioned.

It cannot be too much to expect that

Should coat type and colour be enough to differentiate one breed from another? (Photo: Jackson)

type and health must be regarded as equally important, neither ever being sacrificed to the other.

Breed Fertility

There have been no large-scale investigations of fertility levels in different breeds, which take account of stillborn puppies and early postnatal deaths. Investigations that have been carried out suggest that puppy mortality at this stage is between 12 and 33 per cent, far too high to be acceptable. In 1988 and 1990, however, information was published by the Kennel Club and by Dr Herm David, which allowed comparison to be made of breed fertility levels in Britain and the United States (*see* Appendix V). The published figures relied on the number of puppies registered and so exclude stillborn and early postnatal deaths.

The figures seem to show that fertility levels in the United States are appreciably higher than in Britain. Ninety-three breeds had bigger litters in the USA than in Britain, while only twenty-one had bigger litters in Britain than in the USA. Over all breeds, the British figure is 4.8 puppies per litter; the USA figure 5.2 puppies per litter, an 8.3 per cent difference in favour of the USA, but in some individual breeds the difference is even more marked.

In an effort to explain the difference one breeder, who it is hoped is untypical, suggested that, 'In America they have the

Small, short-backed breeds are not among the most fecund. (Photo: Jackson)

vitamins to build up the genetics.' The global influence of international petfood firms makes it unlikely that different nutritional levels do, in fact, provide an explanation. It is possible that fewer puppies succumb in unheated houses and kennels in America. It is also possible that the ready availability of antibiotics, vaccines, wormers, and so on in the USA encourages their use and results in appreciably higher survival rates among puppies. There is also another possible explanation: it is simply that the smaller British breeding population, especially noticeable in some breeds, results in an unavoidably high level of inbreeding which reduces fertility and gives rise to higher puppy mortality.

Whatever may be the explanation for differences between British and US breed fertility levels, it is noticeable that three factors recur in breeds which have low

Exaggerated physical conformation is a sure route to breeding problems. (Photo: Jackson)

levels of fertility: they tend to have low body weight; they have exaggerated physical characteristics; and they have small populations. Small breeds, such as Chihuahuas, Italian Greyhounds and Papillons, cannot be expected to produce as many puppies as larger ones. Exaggerated breeds, such as the Pekingese, Dandie Dinmont Terriers and Boston Terriers, are likely to lose more puppies at birth than breeds with less exaggerated features. In breeds that exist only in very small numbers, such as Affenpinschers, English Toy Terriers and Chinese Crested Dogs, inbreeding depression may contribute to reduced fertility.

Random Matings

Selection and the maintenance of breed type both require that matings should be planned. The nearest approach to random matings among dogs are those that take place on street corners between two wandering dogs of unknown parentage and pedigree. Nevertheless, although it has to be accepted that the very act of choosing to mate a bitch to a dog of the same breed reduces the random element of the process, some breeders undoubtedly do come close to planning matings on what is little more than a random choice.

People who mate a bitch to a particular dog for no reason other than it happens to live conveniently close by, is available at a discounted stud fee, or just happens to be the current fashionable sire are, within their breed, doing little more than mating at random.

That is not to say they have no chance of producing an outstanding puppy but if they do so it will be more by good luck than by good judgement. They have as

When two breeds combine, the result can be very attractive. (Photo: Jackson)

much chance of breeding a quality puppy as of picking a winner by blindly sticking a pin in a list of race runners.

Breeders are far more likely to make use of methods from which the random element is absent and which have more right to be regarded as systems even though they may discount the effect of genetic influences.

Like to Like

Breeders may totally ignore genetics as well as the undoubted fact that, in terms of breeding, beauty is far more than skin deep. They may simply plan matings on the basis of appearance, assuming that like begets like. Nor are they entirely wrong; if two dogs are mated the progeny will be dogs; if two Greyhounds are mated the progeny will be Greyhounds. However, if two unrelated animals of identical appearance are mated it is probable that, unless that appearance stems from genetic rather than environmental influence, their offspring will resemble neither.

There is, however, some probability that like individuals have a closer genetic relationship than do unlike ones, in which case like to like matings may be successful, but what they cannot do is fix the ability to reproduce the desired type. Like to like may produce the desired phenotype but without recourse to inbreeding cannot fix this as a genotype.

Compensatory Matings

Compensatory matings, a system sometimes referred to as unlike to unlike, involves the choice of mates in the hope that the exaggerated qualities of one will counter-balance the faults of another. And so they might, but it is no more likely that the offspring will inherit the virtues of both parents than it is that they will inherit the faults of both.

Breeders who use this method often choose mates that vary about a desirable norm. A short-headed bitch will be mated to a long-headed dog in the hope that the offspring will have heads of intermediate length. A bitch that is straight in stifle may be mated to an over-angulated dog in the hope of producing puppies with sound hindquarters. This is unlikely to happen: the offspring are more likely to consist of a mixture of long- and short-headed, and of straight-stifled and over-angulated puppies.

Crossbreeding

Crossbred dogs are the product of matings between two animals of different breeds. They should not be confused with mongrels, which are the product of matings between dogs of unknown breeding.

When, in 1814, Princess Charlotte invited Charlie Aistrop to mate his terrier, Billy (famous for having killed 100 rats in five and a half minutes), to one of her tricolour Toy Spaniels she probably did so not because her home was overrun with rats or because she intended to compete in the rat pits, but simply because she realized that her dogs required an infusion of vigorous blood. Eskimos indulge in precisely the same practice when they contrive to get their sledge-dog bitches mated by wolves.

The breeders of some unrecognized breeds make regular use of crossbreeding in order to improve the qualities of their breed. There is no doubt that, in Britain, white working Lakeland Terriers were used to overcome the hereditary problems which beset stumpy-legged Jack Russell Terriers, to impart quality and smartness and to bring them up on the leg. Breeders of unrecognized Jack Russell Terriers retain the freedom to indulge in crossbreeding. Breeders of recognized Parson Jack Russell Terriers can no longer avail themselves of the advantages it might have to offer. The vigour of recently recognized breeds provides evidence of the value of the wise use of crossbreeding. These crosses will make it easier for the breeds to retain genetic health after recognition, which places a severe restriction on the size of the available breeding population and will call for a very different system of breeding management if the breeds are henceforth to survive in a healthy state.

Official recognition as a breed need not end the ability to indulge in judicious crossbreeding. In the UK, the Kennel Club has allowed it between Bull Terriers and the miniature version; between the Long- and Short-Coated Chihuahuas and, more recently, has gone to the extent of amalgamating the four Belgian Shepherd Dog breeds in order to facilitate cross-breeding between Malinois, Tervueren, Groenendael and Laekenois, to which the majority of breeders are vehemently opposed. However, it must be accepted that these are rare exceptions to the general rule. Official recognition usually ends or at best makes it more difficult to make use of crossbreeding.

The Lurcher is probably unique in that it is a breed that exists, and has existed, for hundreds of years on the basis of crossbreeding. Breeders make use of Greyhounds, Whippets and Salukis as the source of speed and chasing ability; they use various collies and other working breeds to impart intelligence; and ter-riers, of various sorts, to give a dash of fire to the mixture. The result is a sound, intelligent and uniquely resourceful dog which comes in a variety of sizes and shapes, all of which are undoubtedly Lurchers.

The value of crossbreeding is utilized by farmers who often cross two pedigree animals: Cheviot ewes to Suffolk rams, Charolais bulls to Friesian cows, in order to produce crossbred offspring (known as F1 cross) which, as a result of the hybrid vigour or heterosis which frequently occurs in the first (F1) generation of such crosses, will thrive better than either of their parents. Hybrid vigour seldom persists into the second (F2) generation (produced by mating two F1 hybrids), and is absent from the product of subsequent gen-erations. Hybrid vigour is entirely the prod-uct of matings between totally unrelated pure-bred animals, not mongrels. It is a quality which can be maintained by a care-fully controlled outbreeding programme.

Outcrossing

Outcrossing, or out-breeding, the mating of two unrelated animals from the same breed, must not be confused with cross-breeding, the mating of animals from different breeds.

In the human species, there is a very large number of individuals, approxi-mately equally divided between the sexes. Many have the means to travel long distances, which means that almost any individual may find a partner in almost any part of the world. This leads to regular outcrossing, which supports and encourages variety, based on a wide range of genetic types. It is this variety which tends to retain general, though not always individual, genetic vigour and health.

In the human species, outcrossing may give rise to a genius with a puny body or a superb athlete with a puny brain. Both can make valuable contributions to human society but if the aim was to produce a creature with the stamina and intelligence to herd sheep, to guide the blind or to work as a gundog, neither would be of the slightest value. That is why dog breeding must be based on something which, though it runs the risk of dangerously decreasing genetic vari-ation, can be relied upon to produce what is necessary for a given narrowly defined purpose.

Even so, outcrossing is a useful and at times a valuable tool which enables breeders to introduce characteristics not present in their stock. If a closely inbred kennel has lost the ability to produce puppies with, say, dark eyes the only way to regain that ability is to introduce blood from a strain which has dark eyes; and the way to ensure that the quality was not again lost in future generations would be to inbreed or line-breed to dark-eyed puppies.

Strains

As with the term 'breed', there is no scientifically precise definition of 'strain', though the word is much used by breeders in order to promote the exclusive quality of their kennel. It is a word which is in some ways synonymous with 'family', but perhaps 'tribe' or 'clan' would be nearer in meaning. A family may consist of no more than parents and their immediate offspring. A strain cannot be created in one generation but implies a relationship which extends over a number of generations. A strain, then, is a group of individuals who are more closely related to one another than to the breed as a whole.

Breeders who airily refer to their 'strain' after breeding for one or two generations are certainly deceiving themselves and are probably attempting to deceive others.

Selection alone will not produce a strain; what is also needed is a system that increases the degree of relationship between individuals, and breeders have devised a number of systems for doing just this.

Inbreeding and Line-Breeding

Inbreeding may be seen as a variant of like-to-like breeding, based not on appearance (phenotype), but on pedigree (genotype).

'Inbreeding' and 'line-breeding' are not scientific terms with accepted, well-defined meanings. Inbreeding is usually taken to refer to the process of breeding from closely related individuals, father to daughter, brother to sister, and so on. Line-breeding is generally taken to refer to matings between more distant relations, cousin to cousin, aunt to nephew, and so on.

Both terms are used, in an Alice in Wonderlandish sort of way, to mean all sorts of different things. They imply only that an individual dog appears more than once in a pedigree. It might be convenient to define inbreeding as the appearance of a parent in earlier generations and line-breeding simply as the repeated appearance of an individual in other than the first generation.

Veterinary prejudice sometimes gives the impression that inbreeding and line-breeding are practices that have only recently been used by dog breeders and that are largely employed by those who breed for the show ring. Two examples will show that this impression is false. The first can be found in Old Foiler: few modern dogs are as closely inbred as this Smooth Fox Terrier who was born, probably in the Grove Hunt kennels, in 1870, out of a bitch who had been bred in the Eggsford Hunt kennels. On studying his pedigree (*see* overleaf), it becomes apparent that Victorian breeders practised – for good or ill – far closer inbreeding than is customary today. His parents were full brother and sister, as

Old Foiler's Pedigree

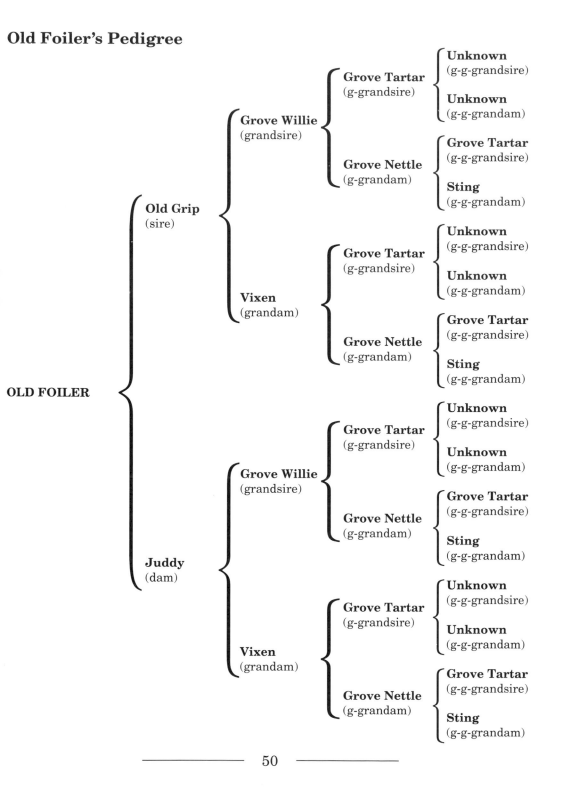

were his grandparents, while his great-grandsire was the father of his great-grandam.

The second example can be found in the working Border Collie: few domestic dogs require as much stamina, intelligence, or ability to learn as does this breed, and yet every working, trial-winning collie is a descendant of Old Hemp, whose grandam was Shotton's Pose, who was also the grandam of Turner's Cleg who, mated to a great-grandson of Old Hemp, produced Snowdon's Old Kep, one of very few dogs to have won the International Sheepdog trials in successive years. Old Kep was mated to his mother, Turner's Cleg, to produce Scott's Ancrom Jed, who sired Wallace's Moss, both winners of the International.

The old breeders, whose aim was to produce sound, tough and sensible working dogs, made good use of the advantages that close breeding can offer. They avoided its perils by their ability to identify outstanding stock, by a rigorous process of selection and, when necessary, by the judicious use of outcrosses, sometimes even to other breeds.

Nor should it be assumed that close breeding is practised only by the breeders of domestic animals. In fact a number of wild animals and insects that breed in colonies tend to become closely bred. A strong male will collect a harem and protect it from all other males. Next year his harem will include some of his own daughters and this will continue until he is deposed by a younger and stronger male, probably one of his own sons, who will then take over the harem to produce offspring from his mother, aunts and sisters. The ingredients which keep this closely bred stock healthy is rigorous natural selection and the regular introduction of unrelated new blood by opportunist males or by the harem being taken over by a male bred within another harem.

Even animals that do not live in colonies may become closely inbred. Research, using tests of mini-satellite DNA, carried out by Dr Alec Jeffreys at the Brackenhurst College of Agriculture, Nottingham, revealed a surprising degree of inbreeding among nesting House Sparrows, with some nestlings being the product of father to daughter matings.

It is probable that some of the most closely bred domestic dogs are to be found among populations of street mongrels in which a virile sire may mate all the bitches available to him and will subsequently mate his daughters until such time as his place is taken by a dog who may be one of his sons.

There are two reasons for close breeding. The first is quite simply that in a numerically small population it is impossible to avoid, and the second is that it offers the best means to perpetuate the desirable qualities of particular dogs.

Close breeding does not introduce characteristics which the breeding stock does not carry, though all the characteristics they do carry may not always be apparent until close breeding reveals them. For this reason, a thorough knowledge of pedigrees is essential to successful close breeding. Close breeding cannot itself discriminate between desirable and undesirable characteristics. That is the breeder's task. The breeder who is blind to faults in his own kennels or to qualities in other kennels is likely to find that inbreeding may offer nothing more than a rapid road to ruin.

The breeder who makes good and careful use of close breeding can produce related dogs which have a strong family likeness and which have the ability to reproduce that likeness. There is, however, a price to pay. Prolonged close breeding will lead to inbreeding depression, the first symptom of which will be reduced fertility: bitches will fail to conceive, will produce fewer puppies, and there will be an increase in postnatal deaths. The next symptom will be a reduction in size and this is likely to be coupled with reduced vigour, leading to reduced life spans and reduced ability to resist infection. Furthermore, if the original selection failed to give proper regard to the propensity to produce some hereditary defect, close breeding will spread that defect through the population more quickly than any other means. The wise breeder protects his stock against this by unremitting vigilance, rigorous control over the degree of inbreeding, and careful control over the selection of breeding stock.

Inbreeding is a sharp and powerful tool and it is important that its use should be both controlled and measured. Its effect, for good or ill, is achieved by increasing homozygosity within the breeding colony. Because a dog can produce far more litters than a bitch, and because his breeding life is likely to be far longer in practice, close breeding tends to rely on the repeated use of a certain sire. It follows, therefore, that any benefits to be achieved are limited by the dog's ability to transmit his qualities to his offspring and, since no dog is perfect, it must not be forgotten that undesirable qualities will be transmitted as well as desirable ones.

Sib Mating

As the name implies, sib mating is a system based on repeated matings between siblings, full brothers and sisters. Sib mating is, therefore, a restricted and unusually close form of inbreeding. It is not a system which dog breeders often use for more than a single generation.

In Old Foiler's pedigree (*see* page 50), Grove Willie and Vixen were full brother and sister; so too were Old Grip and Juddy. The advantage of sib mating is that it achieves its effect very rapidly. The disadvantage is that once this effect has been achieved no further improvement is possible and the likelihood is that the stock produced will begin to decline in vigour. Sib mating should, therefore, be regarded only as a means of achieving quickly a particular end product.

Background Inbreeding

Calculated on the basis of a four-generation pedigree, Old Foiler's coefficient of inbreeding (*see* Appendix IV) was 28.1 per cent to Grove Tartar. But suppose that Sting was also a daughter of Grove Tartar or, worse still, that Grove Tartar's unknown parents and Sting shared one or, yet worse, both parents. The actual level of inbreeding would then be far higher than is revealed by calculations based only on a four-generation pedigree. It is this background level of inbreeding which is becoming a matter of very serious concern in some numerically small, as well as in some not so small, breeds.

The background level of inbreeding provides a measure of the ability of breeders to control the transmission of inherited characteristics, both desirable and undesirable. Once the background level of inbreeding has risen to 6 per cent that ability may be restricted in a way

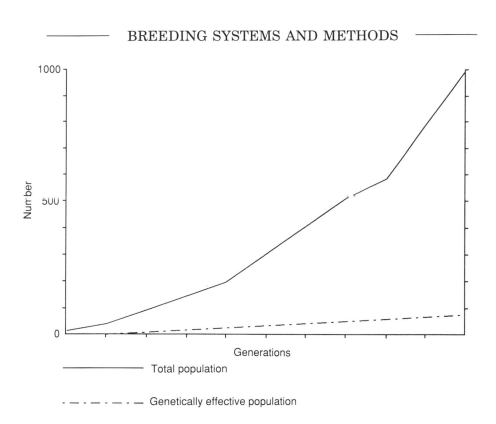

If a breed is reduced to, or begins with, ten breeding animals, and increases its number to 1,000 within ten generations, that population will consist of the equivalent of only about seventy individuals and the inbreeding coefficient will increase in each generation. (Copyright: Kyonics)

which exposes the breed to the uncontrollable spread of genetically transmitted defects.

It is becoming increasingly apparent that unless breed clubs and kennel clubs take steps to control the level of background inbreeding in some numerically small and isolated breed populations, these may face extinction or an increasingly unhealthy future.

Closed Stud System

Whether by accident or design many breeding kennels, rather like wild species in which breeding harems are main-tained, operate systems which are variants of the closed stud system. They make frequent use of a particular stud-dog mated to several, perhaps unrelated, bitches. The effect is that the next generation largely consists of half-brothers and sisters. Some of these may be mated to their own sire to increase dramatically the degree of close breeding, but more usually matings between half-brother and sister are used to increase the degree of close breeding somewhat less dramatically.

One advantage of a closed stud is that the degree of close breeding can be controlled by means of matings between

Breeders in numerically small breeds must co-operate if problems are to be avoided. (Photo: Jackson)

more or less closely related individuals. Another advantage is the flexibility which the system offers. Comparatively large kennels are able to keep all the animals they need to operate the system. The breeder is in total control. Smaller kennels may still operate the system, though they must accept some loss of control. They must rely on making use of dogs sired by their chosen dog and occasionally buying in puppies sired by him or his sons. It is even possible to base a closed stud on a dog in another kennel, and some breeders contrive to operate the system without keeping a stud-dog. What they must do is rely on the continued availability of their chosen dog and of his sons produced by suitable bitches. If circumstances conspire to make suitable sires unavailable the breeder has no option but to select another dog and begin the process again.

Close breeding within a kennel is unlikely to affect the breed as a whole and so, providing, of course, that it does not threaten the welfare of the puppies being bred, it may be regarded as a matter that is of concern only to the breeder. There are, however, circumstances in which a particular kennel's methods might have wide implications. If the kennel contains a numerically small breed the stock it produces may well have a considerable effect on the breed as a whole. A popular, closely inbred dog could be so widely used that, within a very few years, he might have mated virtually every bitch in the breed. When this stage is reached it becomes difficult for breeders to avoid his influence. Numerically small breeds, therefore, need to have regard to the overall effect of the efforts of individual breeders.

In Sweden and Switzerland the use of stud-dogs in some numerically small breeds is restricted in order to prevent the production of a population with a dangerously high level of background inbreeding. It seems likely that other kennel clubs must contemplate the imposition of similar restrictions if some breeds are to be protected from the effect of unco-ordinated breeding.

Repeat Matings

Among the aphorisms coined by Raymond Oppenheimer, that most talented of Bull Terrier breeders, was that the efforts of breeders are most often ruined by staying too long in their own stable than by any other cause.

The statement contains a general warning against the dangers of prolonged close breeding and of kennel blindness but it is also a warning against the dangers of repeat matings.

It is arguable that repeat matings are one of the most damaging practices in which breeders are inclined to indulge. They reduce the available gene pool in a way which could be dangerous to a numerically small breed and which in a small basically closed breeding unit inevitably leads up a blind alley in which further progress is impossible, and from which there may be no escape other than by returning to the beginning, if that is possible, and taking a different route.

Repeat matings are invariably carried out in an effort to reproduce the quality achieved by a previous exceptional litter. Matings that have proved to be dis-appointing are seldom repeated, except by the most confident and optimistic breeders. That which is exceptional, whether exceptionally good or excep-tionally bad, is, by definition, unlikely to be repeated. It would, therefore, make more sense to repeat soundly based matings which have produced dis-appointing results than to repeat those that proved to be exceptionally successful, but for no apparent reason.

From the point of view of a small breeding kennel, repeat matings tend to build a brick wall rather than a doorway to progress.

Kennel Blindness

The inability to see faults in one's own kennel and to see nothing but faults in every other kennel is one of the most damaging diseases from which a breeder can suffer. The disease totally erodes the ability to make the sort of objective decisions on which success as a breeder depends.

CHAPTER 4

Hereditary Abnormalities

Dog breeders are, quite rightly, deeply concerned about the incidence of inherited defects in a number of breeds and it has to be accepted that reducing their incidence must be given the highest priority by all good breeders, by kennel clubs and by the veterinary profession. Even so it is important that the matter should not be unduly exaggerated or sensationalized.

The terms in general use to describe these problems, themselves have a tendency to sensationalize the issue. Genetic disease, hereditary abnormality or inherited defect, create an alarming Dr Frankenstein sort of picture which is far from accurate. Many of the hereditary abnormalities found in dogs are trivial and are accepted in the human species without alarm or even comment. Many, indeed most, of the inherited diseases to be found in dogs are also found in the human species as well as other animals both wild and domesticated.

Farm animals and, to a lesser extent, sporting animals do not live in close association with man. Their purpose is fulfilled when they are slaughtered, often at an early age, or when advancing age ends their sporting careers. Defects which do not affect their purpose are of little interest to breeders. Companion animals on the other hand live in close association

with man. Their every breath and tremor is closely observed, they are expected to live long, disease-free lives, and failure to do so becomes a matter of the greatest concern for their owners. It is for these reasons that many inherited defects which might be and are, perhaps, ignored in other domestic species are of such importance. The disease itself may cause little or no trouble to the patient but may be the source of immense concern to the owner. Nevertheless, the importance of all inherited defects must not be underestimated. Breeders strive for perfection, and toleration of even the slightest inherited blemish is difficult since it must detract from perfection.

Some abnormalities, which have no deleterious effect on the individual, are regarded as highly undesirable in some breeds but may be perfectly acceptable – even desirable – in others. Other conditions, and again many exist both in dogs and in the human species, threaten the individual's well-being and some are lethal. It is against these that breeders and all those who profess a care for canine welfare must wage all-out warfare.

About 3,000 inherited abnormalities have been identified in man. Some of these are sufficiently common to give support to the suggestion that whenever most people look into a mirror they will probably see evidence of at least one inherited abnormality. Man also carries severe inherited defects, which are either lethal or which lead to a drastically shortened and painful life. Dog breeders are severely castigated because similar conditions are also to be found in dogs.

In 1928 only five inherited diseases had been identified in dogs; by 1958 the number had risen to fifty-five. The number doubled by 1968, and again by 1978, and it has since risen to over 300. The existence of a new disorder is revealed almost every month. Apart from the fact that increased awareness and interest in inherited characteristics has resulted in greater knowledge of inherited conditions, they have also become more apparent as veterinary science and improved husbandry led to a dramatic reduction in the overlying levels of disease of non-genetic origin. The effect of these diseases, which had previously produced a high level of puppy mortality that tended to be concentrated on the least strong individuals, was to mask the existence of hereditary defects. Prior to the widespread use of effective vaccines for distemper and similar diseases, the death rate among puppies was very high and many survivors incurred permanent damage. How many puppies suffering from genetic abnormalities died before the abnormality could be recognized? In how many damaged puppies was the damage ascribed to their illness rather than to some inherited defect? To what extent might an unrecognized abnormality, of heart, respiratory tract or nervous system, have contributed to an early death ascribed to some other unrelated cause?

During the last seventy years, muta-tions must also have increased the number of hereditary diseases just as mutation has increased the number of diseases of non-genetic origin. It is necessary only to look at the way in which parvovirus – having mutated from a disease whose effect was confined to cats swept through the canine world during the late 1970s and early 1980s to realize how mutant diseases can inflict a hitherto untroubled species.

The major part of the increase in the number of identified hereditary abnormalities is probably more apparent than real, and is probably owed to improved survival rates and to increased knowledge and interest in inherited conditions. This will inevitably mean that the number of abnormalities identified in dogs, as in our own species, will continue to grow. Knowledge is always preferable to ignorance though it may be far less comfortable. It is important that everyone concerned with pedigree dogs should do their utmost to reduce the incidence of these abnormalities.

The paper by Professor Denis, to which reference has already been made on page 23, ended with a stirring call to arms:

> The interest that breeders, veterinary practitioners and scientists take in hereditary diseases in dogs is always increasing. Breeders are beginning to be truly worried and they ask for more and more information and advice. Breed clubs as well as veterinary surgeons feel the need to make an exact assessment of the situation so as to define suitable preventive measures and to enhance the possibility of success. It is highly desirable that national and international canine authorities should work to the utmost of their ability to join this trend.

Although the nature versus nurture arguments that so intrigued Victorian biologists have now largely been resolved, there is still no clearly defined line to be drawn between the perceived effects of some inherited and some acquired characteristics. A dog's genotype (its physical appearance) is a product of its phenotype (what has been inherited) and the way in which it has been reared and is kept.

Hip dysplasia, for example, is an inherited defect which produces a shallower than normal socket in the pelvis. The result of mating two animals in which the degree or defect is known remains unpredictable, not only because the condition is the product of a complex mode of inheritance but also because the degree to which the abnormality is manifest is dependent on the way in which puppies are reared. Thus two puppies with precisely the same degree of inherited abnormality may, if reared in different conditions, exhibit quite different symptoms. Yet each may carry precisely the same genetic message to be passed on to the next generation.

Control of inherited abnormalities is further complicated by the fact that not all have yet been studied in sufficient depth to reveal their mode of inheritance with any degree of certainty. The list in Appendix I provides evidence that the way in which some abnormalities are inherited remains unclear or uncertain. Indeed it remains uncertain whether some are inherited directly or as a consequence of some predisposition. Furthermore, what appears to be the same abnormality may be inherited in a different way in different breeds or may appear in a slightly different form in different breeds.

Still further complications arise because some diseases that are undoubtedly not inherited may occur more frequently or with greater severity in some breeds because of some inherited characteristic of those breeds. For example, it has been found that both Dobermanns and Rottweilers have an appreciably higher risk of contracting parvovirus, a viral disease, than do other breeds. They do not inherit parvovirus, but they appear to be unusually susceptible, perhaps because of some inherited weakness in their immune systems. In Basset Hounds a sex-linked characteristic produces a resistance to the effects of vaccination against distemper, thus preventing affected puppies – always males – from acquiring immunity. Many of these breeds, Dobermanns, Rottweilers and Basset Hounds, die of a disease not because it is inherited but because of some inherited deficiency.

Nor are the complications ended here. Some problems may arise as a result of injury, may be inherited in their own right, or may be produced by a related defect. Lens luxation might be produced, as in pugilists, by a blow to the head. It can also be produced as a familial and probably inherited condition, or it may be a side-effect of glaucoma, itself either inherited or produced by disease or trauma. The condition might also be inherited.

The appearance of what might be an inherited abnormality need not signal a need for immediate control measures but should ring warning bells. If breeders were to err on the side of caution, albeit a simplistic caution which may ignore much of what the science of genetics can tell us, by avoiding breeding from affected animals and maintaining vigilance over related animals, the problem may not

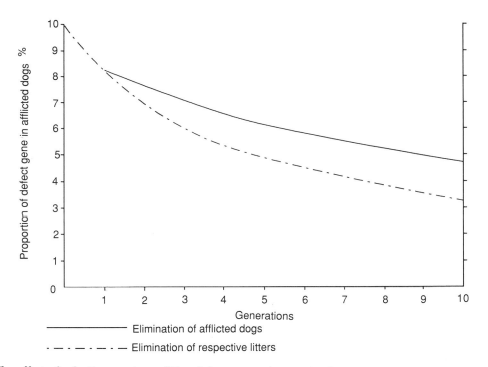

Elimination of afflicted dogs

Elimination of respective litters

The effect of selection against afflicted dogs or against entire litters containing afflicted dogs. Both this graph and the one below apply only to monogenic autosomal recessive defects. (Copyright: Kyonics)

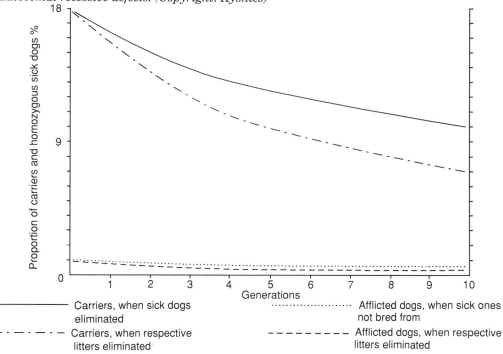

Carriers, when sick dogs eliminated

Afflicted dogs, when sick ones not bred from

Carriers, when respective litters eliminated

Afflicted dogs, when respective litters eliminated

The effect on the number of carriers and homozygous sick dogs in a population when afflicted individuals, or entire litters containing afflicted individuals, are removed from the breeding population. (Copyright: Kyonics)

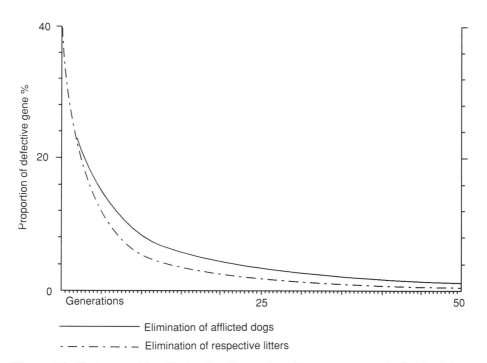

The rapid effect created by eliminating from a breeding programme individual dogs or litters carrying a recessive defect. (Copyright: Kyonics)

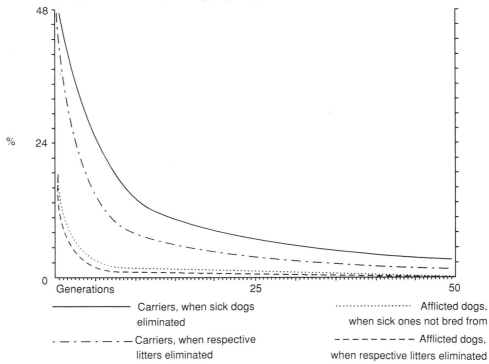

Reduction in the number of carriers and sick dogs when such dogs are eliminated from the breeding population. (Copyright: Kyonics)

recur. Such simplistic advice may not satisfy geneticists but it is, in practice, sound advice.

Breeders in some numerically small or seriously afflicted breeds may not be able to afford to accept such advice. The future of some numerically small breeds may be dependent on the readiness of breeders to breed from stock they suspect or even know carries inherited abnormalities. In breeds that have a high incidence of some particular hereditary abnormality, it may not be possible to find unaffected stock. In breeds that have a larger population or that do not have a high incidence of hereditary problems, surely the prudent course is to avoid breeding from suspect animals.

How then is a breeder to decide whether a previously unrecognized condition which appears in his kennel is of genetic origin? Unfortunately the rate at which knowledge of canine genetic disorders is progressing means that published information tends to be out of date even before it reaches the publisher, let alone the reader. In 1987, Professor Donald Patterson of the University of Pennsylvania, with support from the American Kennel Club, set up the Canine Genetic Disease Information System in order to provide up-to-date information about all the known canine disorders. Five years later it had become the foremost repository of information about canine genetic defects and was able to supply a service to all the world's kennel clubs and breed clubs, though many continued to ignore its existence.

Rather than make use of kennel clubs and breed clubs, breeders still tend to rely on their own efforts. They know that if a defect occurs more frequently in a group of related animals (whether within one kennel, a group of co-operative kennels or a breed), than in the population, the breed or pedigree dogs as a whole is likely to be genetically disposed. Studies (which are facilitated by the ready availability of home computers and of programmes that enable pedigrees to be analysed) of the relationship between affected animals may then reveal how the defect is inherited. The breeder can then take appropriate action.

In the past, the existence of hereditary disease many have become apparent only when the symptoms appeared in a number of animals. Sometimes the disease only appeared late in their lives when they had already been used for breeding. Unaffected carriers of the disease could be identified only by using wasteful test matings. Uncertainty about modes of inheritance made control problematical. Furthermore, some kennel clubs and even the veterinary profession, which had shown itself to be quite capable of taking decisive action on less important matters and was seldom slow to condemn breeders, often seemed reluctant to accept their own share of responsibility or to take action which might lead to effective control.

Research into genetic disease, increasingly accurate and sensitive veterinary diagnostic techniques, coupled with increased awareness and determination among breeders, supported by breed and kennel clubs, offer the means by which genetic disorders may be brought under control. Chromosome analysis, biochemical screening, computer analysis of pedigrees, assays of gene protein products and the availability of stored semen from tested animals all provide far better tools than have previously been available. Already understanding of basic protein

Mapping the canine genome is a new area of research which, it is hoped, will eventually enable breeders to predict with accuracy the long-term future health of their puppies.
(Photo: Anderson)

breeding systems which will avoid the procreation of diseased animals.

In some breeds responsibility for the unacceptably high incidence of hereditary defects can be laid directly at the door of breeders or of a kennel club that has failed to take appropriate action. There are still breeders who refuse to play their part in reducing the incidence of hereditary defects and a few who actively conspire to avoid the effect of control systems. There are also kennel clubs that have not yet taken the necessary action.

The unavoidable prerequisite of any control measures is a scheme for testing all breeding stock and for publishing the results of these tests. Tested animals must be positively identified and in the absence of widespread voluntary support by breeders, testing must be made a condition of registration if effective control over the incidence of hereditary defects is to be exercised.

Genome Analysis

One of the most exciting lines of research, as well as potentially one of the most rewarding in terms of preventative medicine, is concerned with mapping and analysing the canine genome, the complete set of hereditary factors contained on the haploid set of chromosomes.

Phil Spiby of the Animal Health Trust told a symposium which took place at the 1993 Birmingham Congress of the British Small Animals Veterinary Association that:

and DNA abnormalities enables carriers of some deleterious recessive genes to be identified. Eventually gene replacement therapy may provide another and even more effective tool by which improved genetic health can be sustained.

Techniques that enable carriers of some hereditary diseases to be identified are now becoming available. These involve the biochemical examination of blood or tissue samples and offer the means to formulate control measures and to plan

> Mapping the canine genome is likely to prove the ultimate in preventative medicine. Not only has it the potential to allow scientists to use something as

simple as a single strand of hair to predict in advance the diseases to which a dog will be susceptible, it will also allow many hereditary diseases to be eliminated through selective breeding when carriers of diseased genes are identified.

Carriers of diseases such as progressive retinal atrophy (PRA), which affects several breeds, and phosphofructokinase deficiency, which is of especial interest to the owners of Springer Spaniels, can already be identified from the analysis of a small piece of tissue. It should, therefore, be possible to breed stock that is free of both diseases.

It is difficult to predict how quickly this research will reveal the means to identify most of the hereditary canine diseases or, once they have been identified, what controls will be put in place to ensure that full advantage is taken of the new knowledge.

Initially it may be that they will be used to establish, with some degree of accuracy, how widespread certain diseases may be in particular breeds. The outcome would then indicate what sort of control measures may be appropriate, and these could range from banning the use of all untested and affected dogs to importing disease-free dogs or semen in order to establish disease-free lines.

While the new technique will not make genetic science obsolete it will offer breeders a simple alternative to grappling with the uncertainties of trying to breed disease-free stock on the basis of uncertain genetic knowledge. It will simply be a matter of identifying carriers and removing them from the breeding programme.

Breeders who refuse to make use of the technique and continue to breed diseased stock may well find that they have no satisfactory defence available if disappointed puppy buyers take legal action against them. Certainly too, breed clubs and, more particularly, kennel clubs which do not ensure that their members and all to whom their services are available make full use of the techniques will have no legitimate claim to exist in order to promote the improvement of pedigree dogs.

CHAPTER 5

The Brood-Bitch

The transition from dog owner to breeder often comes when it is realized that the qualities of a much-loved family pet might be perpetuated for longer than that pet's life span if she were given the opportunity to produce puppies. Sometimes less laudable motives are also evident. The desire to recoup the cost of the bitch, a desire to profit from the sale of puppies, a practical sex lesson for children, a belief (to which, even today, some vets subscribe), that every bitch deserves the supposed fulfilment of having a litter, and even that motherhood may cure temperamental problems, might all be advanced as reasons for breeding. It bears repeating that none of these is in itself adequate reason. The only good reason for breeding is a desire to produce top-quality dogs.

Acquisition

Perhaps the most important decision made by prospective breeders is when they acquire their first bitch. Almost certainly the acquisition will be made when they are least able to exercise judgement supported by detailed knowledge. With good fortune, it will result in a wise choice. In such circumstances the watchword must be 'Care'. Buying a puppy has a very different meaning to being sold one!

Vets and others who should know better are much inclined to suggest that selection of a breed is an entirely objective process, related to the prospective owner's established life style, analysis of the qualities required in the ideal companion dog, and much more pseudo-scientific assessment. It may, of course, make perfectly good sense if an habitually sedentary person avoids breeds that require considerable exercise, that physically weak people avoid large, strong breeds, and those who dislike grooming avoid dogs with a profusion of hair, but it has to be accepted that people are often prepared to change in order to accommodate the needs of the breed that captivates them. Choosing a breed is no more an objective process than choosing a marriage partner. It is certainly not a process that can be constrained by pseudo-scientific criteria.

What is important is that the potential breeder learns as much as possible about the chosen breed before acquiring it. Most breeds are well served by books written by acknowledged experts. Breed clubs exist to support interest in the breed; dog magazines often have a regular column devoted to each breed; and, of course, no opportunity to visit shows, or wherever the breed may be seen actively engaged, should be lost. By these means a prospective buyer will be able to confirm that the chosen breed is the right one and to

Three champion bitches showing distinct breed and kennel type. (Photo: Jackson)

learn where a suitable female may be acquired.

A prospective buyer should only accept a proud breeder's estimation of the quality and virtues of a particular puppy with appropriate reservations. Some breeders regard all their ugly ducklings as potential swans, not with the intention of deceiving but simply out of an excess of uncritical and misplaced pride. James Boswell refers to a visit made in 1777 by Dr Samuel Johnson to his good friend Dr John Taylor, a kennel-blind breeder of Bulldogs, 'who praised everything of his own to excess, in short, whose geese were all swans'. The propensity to be led astray by misplaced pride is not a new one among dog breeders.

It is not uncommon for dogs with serious and obvious faults to be sold as potential show dogs. It is not even uncommon for breeders whose success in the ring has been less than meteoric to sell every puppy out of a litter as a potential show dog. It has even been known for puppies to be sold with a guarantee that they will become champions, by breeders who themselves have never owned, let alone bred, a champion.

The story of the man who was persuaded that a mediocre puppy would mature into a good show dog comes to mind. The hopes and expectations he had for the dog were quickly dashed as, with predictable persistence, it remained a very ugly duckling. He decided to let the breeder know of his disappointment:

'You know that dog I bought from you? Well, it's for sale.'

'Yes, it was when I had it.'

Fit to Breed

If the decision to breed has been anticipated, care will have been taken not only to acquire a female – a basic requirement that is ignored surprisingly often – but to choose one that is likely to grow to be fit to breed from. This means buying a well-bred, well-reared, sound and healthy bitch that is the product of parents with similar qualities. Such bitches are usually available only direct from breeders, and the best breeders, without any need to advertise, often have a waiting list for their stock. The axiom that 'Good wine needs no bush' is entirely appropriate.

No one who genuinely intends to breed good dogs would ever think of breeding from stock that was not out of the very top drawer although, of course, each might define 'top drawer' slightly differently.

A well-known breeder and exhibitor was once severely castigated by an enthusiastic newcomer to the breed, whose strong opinions, based on little knowledge, were loudly broadcast with almost evangelical zeal.

Newcomer: 'You should not breed from bitches you don't think are good enough to show.'

Breeder: 'But you show bitches I don't think are good enough to breed from!'

Puppy or Adult?

In most cases, a breeding kennel will be founded on a bitch acquired as a puppy. No matter how well chosen the puppy may have been, the possibility that she may grow into an adult that cannot or should not be bred from cannot be ignored. Furthermore, if she lives a solitary life she may be reluctant to mate as an adult and will be embarking on motherhood in the hands of a breeder whose experience is also non-existent.

Buying an adult, especially one that has already been successfully bred from, will avoid these problems. Unfortunately such bitches are not readily available. Wise breeders seldom sell their seed corn, and the price asked for such bitches tends to reflect their scarcity value.

Buying

Only in the most exceptional circumstances should prospective breeders consider doing anything other than buying outright. Breeders often find it advantageous to offer bitches for sale on terms, known as breeding terms, which purport to reduce the initial price in return for a claim on one or more puppies from the first and sometimes subsequent litters.

Such arrangements are seldom brought to a conclusion without acrimony or disappointment. They are best avoided. If they cannot be avoided, the agreement should be explicit, put in writing and be legally binding. It should set out who is responsible for deciding when the bitch should be bred from, who selects the dog to which she will be mated, and who pays the stud fee. It should define how many puppies of what sex are to be given up, whether the bitch's original owner is to have a free choice from the entire litter, and at what age the choice must be made. The agreement must also face the possibility that the bitch may prove to be infertile or might die before giving birth; it must define precisely how these events will affect the agreement.

Outright purchase is a far better option. In either case, the buyer must make sure that the breeder gives him all the relevant paperwork, and that any certificates proving testing of the parents for certain defects are produced (for example, in the case of breeds that are routinely tested for hip dysplasia or progressive retinal atrophy). Since the breeder is the only person who can register a dog with the Kennel Club, registration papers should also be produced.

Care of the Potential Brood-Bitch

A prospective brood-bitch should be treated with due care. In order that her natural canine instincts are preserved she should be allowed and encouraged to mix freely with other dogs. She should be kept in the peak of physical condition. Few things cause more problems during whelping than poor physical condition, especially obesity.

A programme of injections which will protect her from the common infectious diseases must be scrupulously maintained as must a programme to keep her free from the debilitating effect of parasites.

If the breed is known to suffer from hereditary problems, diagnostic checks must be carried out at the appropriate time. The breed or kennel club will be able to supply details of what tests are appropriate and when and where they should be carried out. Failure to submit to routine testing may well mean that the best stud-dogs will not be made available for use on the bitch.

Bitches that are to be used for breeding usually enjoy a career as competitors before they depart for the nursery; and there is no better advertisement or way of enhancing the value of a bitch's puppies than a successful career.

There is no evidence to show that the

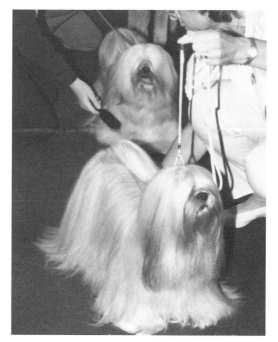

Coat quality and coiffeur may not survive raising a litter. (Photo: Jackson)

physiological welfare of a well-cared-for bitch is necessarily at risk if she is bred from at a young age, frequently, or into old age. Provided that she is well grown and mature, fit and healthy, and receives the sort of care that any breeding bitch deserves, a bitch may be bred from quite frequently from early maturity to relative old age. There are, however, many ill-cared-for bitches that are subjected to a callous regime by unscrupulous commercial breeders. The majority of these bitches are of poor quality. No breeder with a conscience would wish to add to the unhappy population of poorly kept, mediocre dogs. They want only to breed good and, it is hoped, outstandingly good dogs and to place them in homes where their welfare will be well protected.

Out of concern for the welfare of dogs, a number of kennel clubs throughout the world have imposed limits on the lower and upper ages of breeding bitches and on the number of registered puppies or litters they may have. These limits are also often reinforced by the codes of ethics which breed clubs impose on their members. The imposition of these limits is a response to concern about the large number of ill-bred, badly reared puppies, which are being produced by breeders who make use of registration to give their products an often spurious stamp of quality. The limits are primarily concerned with population control and general welfare considerations. As such they are welcomed by all caring breeders.

Even the best breeders will not always succeed in producing outstandingly good dogs, of course. Indeed they may seldom succeed, but the production of top-quality dogs remains their primary objective. They are most likely to succeed by breeding only from healthy, vigorous, top-quality bitches. In order to come close to success, they will need knowledge and a large slice of good fortune. These must be allied to a resilient spirit of optimism supported by unremitting attention to detail. Breeding good dogs is not easy. It is indeed quite probable that the difficulties and challenges entailed provide an important part of the attraction to the best breeders.

Diet and Accommodation

Potential brood-bitches require no special dietary treatment, the same balanced diet given to other dogs is perfectly adequate, though this, as is mentioned elsewhere, will need to be adjusted during pregnancy.

Accommodation, like that for all other dogs, needs to be dry, clean, warm, light, spacious and secure, whether it is in the owner's home or in an outside kennel. Damp and dirt are perhaps the main sources of ill health. Supplementary warmth is essential for some breeds though more hardy ones will be quite content in unheated kennels, providing that these are draught-free. The interior of some kennels is stygian, a condition conducive to misery and ill health. A source of natural light is essential and if windows can be placed so that they admit sunlight in which dogs can luxuriate then so much the better, but remember that summer sun may make a kennel interior oppressively and even dangerously hot, so proper ventilation is essential. Site kennels with care. Kennels, especially if the inmates are to be confined for long periods, should be big enough to allow room for play and it is as well to remember that daily cleaning in a low-roofed, small-doored, dark cell is not an easy task.

Whether the bitch is housed indoors or out security, especially when she is in season, is essential. There should be no possibility of her escaping and none of her being visited by unwanted suitors. It is also as well to remember that a good bitch and her puppies have monetary value which may attract the attention of thieves.

Female Reproductive System

The female reproductive system consists of a pair of ovaries, each surrounded by its protective bursa, in which the unfertilized eggs are produced to begin their

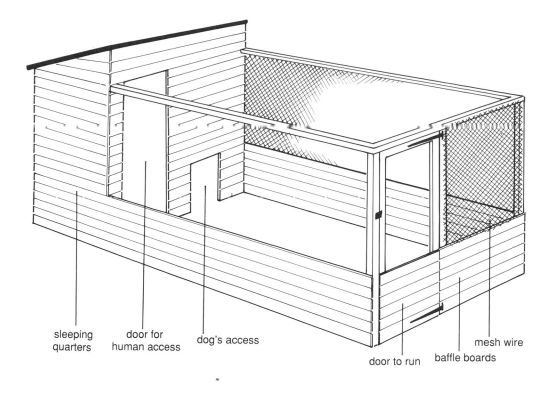

sleeping quarters · door for human access · dog's access · door to run · baffle boards · mesh wire

The design of this kennel and integral run is suitable for most breeders' purposes, although the dimensions will vary according to the size of the breed.

miraculous journey. The ovaries are connected to the twin horns of the uterus by the fallopian tubes. Following a successful mating, fertilized eggs grow into puppies both within the horns and main body of the uterus. At what (for an unborn puppy) is the exit from the uterus, is the cervix, beyond which is the vagina, to the floor of which is connected the urethra which carries urine from the bladder. The vagina connects with the outside world through the vulva. The entire reproductive system consists of soft tissue which changes in shape and size in response to the reproductive cycle and to the demands made on it by a developing pregnancy.

Many of the physical problems associated with parturition derive from the fact that this series of interconnected soft tissues passes through the cavity formed by three fused bones, the ilium, the ischium and the pubis, which together form the pelvic girdle. The shape of the pelvic cavity varies from breed to breed. In short-legged breeds it tends to be roughly equal in height and width; in longer-legged breeds its height tends to be greater than its width; in some breeds the pelvis is abnormally vertical thus creat-

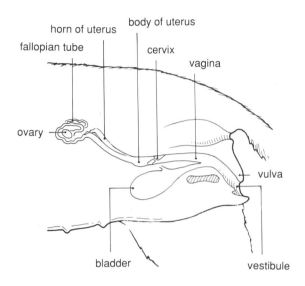

Reproductive system of the bitch.

ing a hurdle of the pubis over which puppies must be pushed before they can be born.

Once a bitch is fully mature the three bones are inflexibly fused together but prior to this the junction at the pelvic floor may be relatively flexible. It is sometimes suggested that by breeding from very young bitches advantage can be taken of this juvenile flexibility to reduce the possibility of some whelping problems. Certainly, if breeding from bitches that have an abnormal pelvic construction and alignment is delayed until the bitches are well into maturity, the likelihood of whelping difficulties will be increased.

Female Reproductive Cycle

Bitches will have had one and usually two or more seasons before they are mated. Their owners will have had the opportunity to observe the signals that precede a season. It is obvious that the reproductive cycle is of great importance to any owner with an ambition to breed from his bitch, but it is no less important to owners who wish to ensure that the bitch does not produce an unexpected and unwanted litter of puppies.

The female reproductive cycle follows a regular pattern which varies both in the timing of its initial onset and in length. Bitches of small breeds may reach

Breeds with exaggerated conformation and low popularity are prone to breeding problems. (Photo: Jackson)

puberty when they are little more than four months old. Bitches of larger, slower-maturing breeds may not have their first season until they are eighteen or more months old. Once the cycle has begun, its length may vary from as little as four months, in some small and exotic domestic breeds, to as much as twelve, in wild dogs and those domestic breeds that might be described as primitive. In some giant breeds the cycle may be even longer. Generally, however, breeders regard a six-monthly cycle as normal, though surveys carried out over several breeds suggest that normality is probably nearer seven than six months.

After a bitch has had two or three seasons the regularity of the reproductive cycle makes it possible for the owner of a bitch to predict, with a fair degree of accuracy, when she is likely to be in season. The interval between seasons may, however, be varied after the bitch has produced a litter, by the previous use of hormones to suppress seasons, by the weather, by ill health or trauma, and by the oestrus (or season) of other bitches with whom she is in contact. A mild winter and warm spring may bring bitches into season early, while cold weather may delay them. The presence of other bitches in season may provoke what some breeders refer to as the 'me too syndrome', whereby bitches in a kennel tend to coincide their seasons. A bitch's season may also be delayed if she has been or is in ill health, or has been subjected to any trauma, a change of home or loss of companions. If hormonal injections have been used to delay or

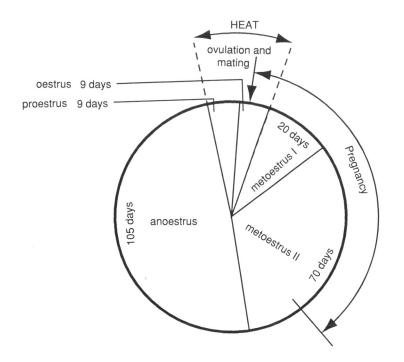

HEAT

ovulation and
mating

oestrus 9 days

proestrus 9 days

20 days

metoestrus I

Pregnancy

105 days

anoestrus

metoestrus II

70 days

The oestrous cycle, which may be as short as four months or as long as twelve.

suppress seasons her regular cycle may also be changed. These injections are sometimes routinely used to prevent a bitch's competitive career from being interrupted by seasons, to enable female sporting dogs to continue their activities throughout the season or even just to postpone a season which occurs at an inconvenient time. The makers of such products, and some vets, do not recommend their use on breeding bitches but, in practice, apart from making the timing of the next season less predictable, their use appears to have no untoward effects providing that use is not prolonged.

The season, or oestrus, is just one of the four parts – anoestrus, pro-oestrus, oestrus and metoestrus – of the reproductive cycle.

Anoestrus

Anoestrus is a sexually quiescent phase which, within a six-month cycle, usually lasts for about 120 days, but which may last for anything from sixty up to 240 days. During this phase the bitch's external genitalia retain their normal appearance and the bitch is not attractive to males.

Pro-Oestrus

Towards the end of anoestrus, an increase in oestrogen levels begins to prepare the bitch for the next stage and may result in some behavioural changes. The bitch may become quiet or restless, she may take an increased interest in her genital regions, which may become slightly swollen; and she may, especially when out at exercise, urinate frequently although she will usually pass no more than a drop or two of urine. It may well be that this is a means by which she advertises her approaching condition to likely suitors and so it is something to which the vigilant owner should respond with increased security.

Some owners may attempt to disguise their bitch's approaching condition from wandering attendants or at shows by the use of chlorophyll tablets or scented sprays. The use of such measures underestimates both the sensitivity of a dog's nose and the ability of experienced stud-dogs to recognize such diversionary tactics for what they are.

As pro-oestrus progresses, the bitch's vulva will become more swollen and will, normally, emit a blood-suffused discharge. In some bitches, perhaps less clean than others, the discharge may be

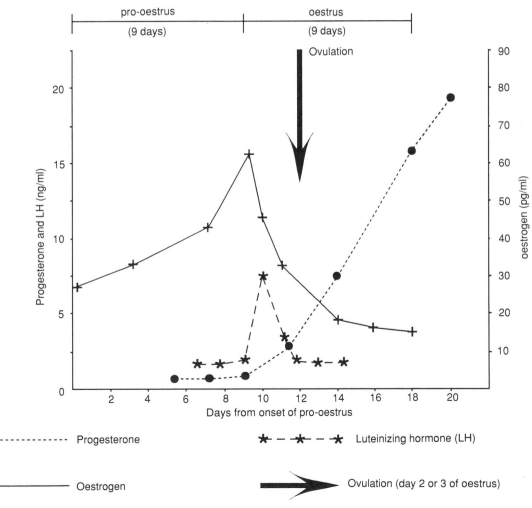

Oestrogen, progesterone and LH blood levels during pro-oestrus and oestrus.

sufficiently copious to stain furniture and clothing. It may be convenient, as well as more secure, to consign the bitch to a kennel for the duration. Some bitches, however, perhaps cleaner than others or, for some as yet not fully understood physiological reasons, may have what breeders refer to as a 'silent season' in which the discharge is colourless. Since the only visible sign may be a very slight swelling of the vulva it then requires a very observant breeder or a knowing dog to realize that the bitch is coming into season. During pro-oestrus the bitch will be especially attractive to dogs and to other bitches and may go through the motions of mating with both. She will not, however, be fertile.

Oestrus

The bitch cannot conceive until pro-oestrus gives way to oestrus, a short period which may last no more than two or three days, or for as long as twenty-one, although nine days is the average duration. During this time the vulva may be greatly enlarged and the discharge pale yellow. The vulva will also feel warm to the touch, hence the popular reference to bitches being 'in heat'. About two days after the start of oestrus, in practical terms two days after the discharge has become clear and between ten or twelve days after the early signs of pro-oestrus became evident, the bitch should be fertile and ready to be mated.

Most bitches will signal their readiness by 'standing'. They may respond to the presence of dogs, other bitches, even the household cat, by lowering their heads, arching their backs, curling their tails and elevating their vulvas in an unmistakable and characteristic manner. They may also indulge in simulated sexual activity with other bitches and household pets.

It is possible for the pro-oestrus and oestrus to be more precisely defined by taking swabs from the bitch, and these will assist the owners of bitches that have silent seasons, but for most practical purposes observation of outward signs remains sufficient to indicate to the breeder when the bitch is ready to be mated.

Once the bitch is standing or tests have shown that she has ovulated, she should be mated within a few hours. Some bitches may stand for the dog for as much as two days. Others may only be receptive for a couple of hours. Delaying or anticipating the mating in order to fit in with a time more convenient for the owner, or the owner of the dog, is to ignore the entire biological process and will reduce the chances of conception taking place.

Metoestrus

If the bitch has been mated – and has conceived – the next stage of the cycle will be interrupted by a developing pregnancy. If the bitch has not been mated, or rather if she has failed to conceive, metoestrus will follow; it is at this stage that hormonal changes may produce all the signs of pregnancy, and this is the so-called false pregnancy, a bane of the lives of many breeders and exhibitors. After about ninety days, metoestrus gives way to pro-oestrus and the cycle will have come full circle.

Induced Oestrus

Although oestrus occurs naturally as part of a regular cycle, some variation may be brought about by changes in the weather,

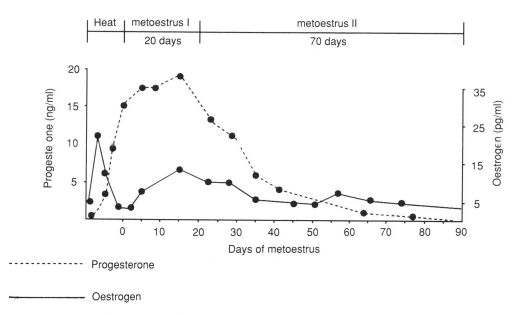

Oestrogen and progesterone blood levels during metoestrus in the bitch.

or more probably in the quality of daylight, by the presence of other bitches in season (what breeders refer to as the 'me too syndrome'), as well as by the bitch's state of health.

For some years experiments with drugs to induce seasons artificially have resulted in very low levels of fertility. However, new techniques, using hormone implants, now offer the means to induce fertile seasons. It thus becomes possible for breeders to arrange for puppies to be born at the most convenient times, when weather conditions offer the opportunity for them to be exercised out of doors, so that they are at an age which enables them to catch the flush of competitions or to have them available when sales interest is at its height.

It also becomes possible to synchronize seasons in different bitches and this removes one of the obstacles that has prevented embryo transplants from being used by dog breeders. (*See* pages 105–6.)

Gonadotrophin Releasing Hormone (GnRH) is a naturally occurring hormone, produced by a small gland in the brain, which controls the oestrus cycle through the release of Follicle Stimulating Hormone (FSH) and Lutenizing Hormone (LH). These three hormones act together to stimulate ovary activity.

Implanting a small GnRH tablet will induce the first signs of oestrus within seven days and will create the conditions for a fertile mating within twelve to fourteen days. It is possible, though perhaps undesirable, to induce another fertile season after a three-month interval.

There are no kennel club regulations which specifically prohibit the use of GnRH implants, but computer checks on dates of birth may produce queries which might result in a reluctance to register puppies born outside the naturally occurring cycle.

Irregular Oestrus

The delayed onset of puberty, unusually long or short, or irregular intervals between oestrus are not necessarily symptoms of underlying disease. Even so they, like anything that cannot be regarded as normal, should be treated with caution by breeders. The reasons behind these abnormalities are not yet fully understood but they do appear to be familial if not inherited traits. In which case it is wise to err on the side of caution and, whenever possible, avoid breeding from bitches that show an irregular cycle. If avoidance is not possible, such bitches should only be mated to dogs whose dams did not show similar irregularities.

False Pregnancy

False, phantom or pseudo pregnancies are one and the same condition, in which a non-pregnant bitch shows some or all of the signs of being in whelp.

The condition is a nuisance to anyone who owns a bitch that is prone to it, and is sometimes regarded as yet another example of the degeneracy of domestic, and especially pedigree, dogs. In fact it is simply yet another ancestral hangover from the days when dogs were wild.

Among wild canids, it is customary for puppies only to be born to a dominant pair, their dominance having been established because of their superior abilities. Obviously it is inconvenient and could be damaging to the group to lose the services of a superior bitch while she rears a litter of puppies but, on the other hand, it would be nonsense to delegate breeding to an inferior bitch. In order to overcome this problem, all the bitches in a wild pack tend to come into season together; the dominant one is mated and gives birth to puppies while the unmated bitches go through a false pregnancy so that together they can rear the puppies while the superior bitch returns to her hunting duties. Apart from freeing a superior bitch from maternal duties, the system also has the advantage that puppies are being reared by several females so that the loss of one bitch need not result in the puppies' death.

False pregnancies are a perfectly normal occurrence though they are undoubtedly often a nuisance. The symptoms of a false pregnancy vary from nothing more than a slight and barely perceptible tendency to put on weight to mimicry of all the symptoms of a real pregnancy, including nest-making, giving birth, lactation and mothering of some surrogate offspring, whether animal or inanimate. Chocolate-box photographs of bitches mothering chickens, kittens and such are often the product of false pregnancies.

Apart from the fact that false pregnancies may prevent a bitch from competing in the ring or in other activities, there is often a marked tendency towards aggression which may upset an otherwise tranquil doggy household. Upsetting the bitch's customary regime, putting her on a spartan diet – indeed, doing all the things that a pregnant bitch should be protected from – may persuade her to abandon the false pregnancy. If all else fails hormonal injections may have the desired effect.

Refusal to Mate

Bitches may refuse to be mated for a

Potential brood-bitches who have the opportunity to mix freely with other bitches and dogs are more likely to display normal responses to a stud-dog's advances. (Photo: Jackson)

number of reasons. Their breeding or upbringing may make them unwilling to be mated, they may not be in season, or they may have physical obstructions which prevent mating from taking place.

Ensuring that potential brood-bitches are able to associate frequently with other dogs and bitches will help them to develop normal responses to the advances of dogs. Occasionally, a bitch may express a strong preference for a particular dog and refuse others. In such a situation the opportunity to become well-acquainted with the breeder's choice of mate may alleviate the problem.

If physical obstructions are met with, whether these are vaginal polyps or structural abnormalities, the mating must be abandoned and veterinary assistance sought.

However, the main reason for refusals to be mated may stem from the breeder's attempts to mate bitches either too early or too late in their season.

Fertility

Fertility levels quite naturally vary from breed to breed and from kennel to kennel. However, it is in a breeder's interests to ensure that optimum litter size is maintained, and there are several factors that will contribute to the achievement of this: the use of young, healthy and large bitches, high standards of care, mating at the optimum time, and the careful control of inbreeding.

Work by Fray, Wrathall and Knight at the University of Reading suggests that immunization against inhibin (a non-steroid hormone produced by the seminiferous tubules and ovarian follicles) can increase ovulation rates over a period of at least three years, resulting in a 35.6 per cent increase in litter size. The authors suggest that: 'active immunization against inhibin could form the basis of a practical, low-input system for promoting a recurrent increase in litter size in the less fecund species of sheep, and perhaps in other species.'

The principal cause of female infertility – apart from those that result from genetic abnormalities which are impossible to treat, and failure of the breeder to synchronize mating with ovulation (thereby producing the symptoms of infertility in a fertile bitch) – tend to stem from infections of the uterus and reproductive tract.

If a bitch fails to conceive after she has been mated at the appropriate time, to a dog whose fertility is above suspicion, a number of possibilities need to be considered.

Hypothyroidism

Hypothyroidism tends to produce irregular oestrous cycles. Diagnosis depends on thyroid blood tests and treatment on increasing the oestrogen levels.

Hypoestronism

Lack of ovarian development, small vulva and mammary glands, and the absence of oestrus resulting from hypoestronism, may be treated by increasing oestrogen levels.

Ovarian Imbalance

Ovarian abnormalities, sometimes produced by tumours or cysts, may produce infertility associated with symmetrical alopecia (causing hair loss over the loins), gynaecomastia (enlarged mammary glands), vulva enlargement and irregular oestrous cycles. The condition sometimes responds to treatment with oestrogen.

Adult Acromegaly

This is a deformity which produces abnormal enlargement of the extremities of the skeleton. It is caused either by excessive pituitary secretion of growth hormone or by the administration of prostaglandins, and may result in infertility. Spaying is indicated.

Ovarian Tumours

Ovarian tumours are composed either of granulosa or theca cells. They are associated with excessive oestrogen and, occasionally, androgen production. Surgical removal is indicated.

Ovarian Cysts

There are two types of ovarian cyst, luteal and follicular. Either of these may prevent ovulation, produce abnormal oestrous cycles or lead to abnormal sexual behaviour, including nymphomania. Surgical removal is indicated.

Pyometra

The vagina normally supports a population of bacteria that usually appears to have no adverse effects either on the bitch or on her puppies. During oestrus or after whelping, when the cervix is open, these bacteria may migrate into the uterus, which has limited resistance to infection. When the cervix closes bacteria may multiply in the uterus to produce a life-threatening condition known as pyometra or pyometritis. The bacteria will cause a build-up of pus in the uterus, which will eventually result in the belly becoming so distended that it approaches the size attained during pregnancy.

The first symptoms, however, may be loss of appetite, increased thirst, a heightened temperature and vomiting. If the cervix allows the escape of pus (open pyometra), diagnosis and treatment is easier. Often, however, the cervix remains firmly closed (closed pyometra), and the bitch becomes progressively more ill. Eventually she may become unsteady on her feet and may collapse. Urgent treatment is then necessary if her life is to be saved.

Even at an early stage veterinary surgeons tend to favour surgery involving removal of the infected uterus. In some situations, especially with young bitches or valuable breeding bitches, treatment with prostaglandins has been used with success. Although this method involves breeding from the bitch at her next season it does offer some hope that the bitch can again be bred from, which is obviously not the case following surgery.

In many respects metritis, which tends to occur post-whelping, and pyometra, which is more usually associated with bitches that have not been bred from at all or for some time, have similar symptoms and respond to similar treatment. The main difference, as far as breeders are concerned, is the most usual time of onset. Both require prompt veterinary attention.

Brucella Canis

A major cause of canine infertility in both males and females is canine brucellosis. Although the disease was only recognized in dogs in 1966 (by veterinarians at Cornell University), it has probably long been a major source of infertility, late abortions and the birth of weak puppies.

The disease is transmitted sexually and, because the bacteria live inside cells, effective treatment is difficult. Bacterial infection can remain in the blood of infected animals for up to three years. As yet there are no effective preventative vaccines. Animals that carry infection but show no obvious symptoms (other than infertility), are likely to be a major source of transmission.

The disease is prevalent in South America, Mexico and the southern states of the United States. It has been reported in Europe but is not widespread.

Influenza-like symptoms, debility, painfully swollen lymph glands in the groin and under the jaw, swollen testes in the male resulting in the production of inviable sperm but no reduction in libido, abortions or the birth of weak puppies in the female should all be treated with suspicion.

The most effective treatment following positive diagnosis based on a rapid serum agglutination test, may be castration of males and spaying of bitches to remove the infected material and subsequent isolation from breeding stock.

Cytology Tests

Cytology testing determines the peak production of nuclear cells and the ferning of cervicovaginal mucus. An investigation carried out by G.C. England showed that bitches mated at the optimum time – as indicated by vaginal cytology tests – resulted in increased

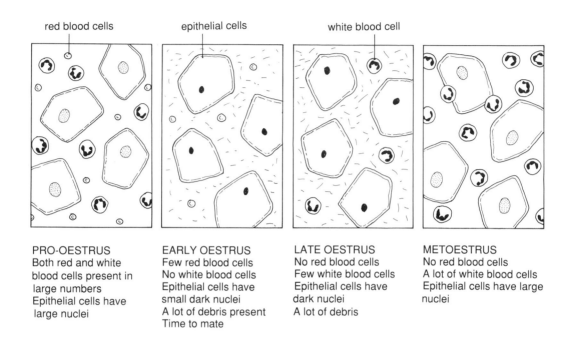

| red blood cells | epithelial cells | white blood cell | |

PRO-OESTRUS
Both red and white blood cells present in large numbers
Epithelial cells have large nuclei

EARLY OESTRUS
Few red blood cells
No white blood cells
Epithelial cells have small dark nuclei
A lot of debris present
Time to mate

LATE OESTRUS
No red blood cells
Few white blood cells
Epithelial cells have dark nuclei
A lot of debris

METOESTRUS
No red blood cells
A lot of white blood cells
Epithelial cells have large nuclei

Vaginal cytology. The cells present in the vagina will indicate the various stages of the oestrous cycle, thus making it possible to identify the best time for mating.

fertility among a test group of fifty bitches when compared with a similar group of bitches that were mated on the tenth and twelfth days after the onset of oestrus.

Forty-six (92 per cent) of the tested bitches conceived and produced 344 puppies at an average of 7.48 per litter, with a mortality rate at birth of 0.35. Thirty-nine (78 per cent) of the bitches mated at ten or twelve days conceived; they produced 279 puppies at an average of 7.08 per litter, with a mortality rate at birth of 0.41 per litter.

Although the sample is a small one, it does suggest that cytology offers the means to increase conception rates, increase litter sizes and reduce mortality rates at birth.

Contraception

The best form of contraception is strictly to keep in-season bitches away from dogs but even in the best regulated kennels accidents can happen. An oestrogen injection carried out within two or three days after an unwanted mating has taken place will cause the bitch to abort.

If there is no question that a bitch may be bred from and if, for some reason or other, the owner wishes to ensure that she will not be bred from, then unquestionably spaying, in spite of doubts discussed elsewhere, must be considered.

In the USA it is possible to buy a sort of canine chastity belt which is not only intended to prevent her from being mated

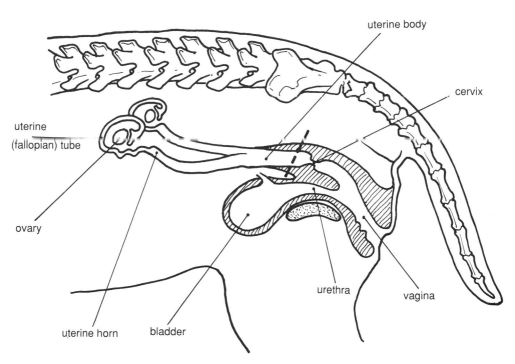

The spay operation. The uterus and both ovaries are removed.

but also to absorb her vaginal discharge. The belt will frustrate the efforts of suitors, though an unsupervised bitch may very quickly divest herself of this inconvenient garment.

It is also possible to make use of hormonal injections or tablets to prevent a bitch from coming into season. Many of the side effects which plagued the early products are no longer seen but injections seem to be unusually painful and may result in a persistant bald patch or discoloured area of coat at the site of the injection. For this reason injections are best given on the inside of the thigh. There is also some evidence to suggest that regular use of either contraceptive injections or tablets can lead to an increased incidence of pyometra, though the risk may be no higher than that faced by any bitch that is not bred from.

Spaying

Surgical neutering must also be regarded as a form of contraception, albeit a very drastic form. Proponents of surgical neutering tend to be dismissive of the possibility of subsequent problems. A survey carried out in 1986 showed that 'the view that neutered individuals are more likely to become obese is reinforced.'

In some cases it would appear that the quality of the bitch's coat may be adversely affected.

CHAPTER 6

The Stud-Dog

In the world of animal breeding it is usually the female's owner who decides which male they would like to be the father of her offspring, though, of course, the owner of the male has the right to accept or reject the proposal.

It is very unlikely that the owner of a dog will be asked to make the dog available at stud unless the dog is good or, better still, an exceptionally good specimen of his breed and has achieved the sort of success in his particular activity which will draw attention to his qualities. In some countries it is necessary to have a dog licensed for breeding, the granting of the licence being dependent on the dog's physical and temperamental qualities and his inherited characteristics. No dog will be licensed if it fails to meet the required standard, and even in countries where licensing is not obligatory no dog should be used at stud until he has been assessed for those inherited conditions known to be present in the breed. Even then wisely cautious breeders will often wait until some of the dog's puppies can be seen and evaluated.

Before a dog embarks on a stud career, his owner should be aware of the possible consequences. Stud work is likely to make him more self-assertive and, perhaps, less likely to tolerate other dogs on his territory. It may – especially when house bitches are coming into season and after visits from unfamiliar bitches – make him

less clean about the house. He is likely to reinforce ownership of his territory by cocking his leg apparently indiscriminately and so is, perhaps, often better housed in a kennel and run.

Breeders have a strongly developed tendency to claim credit for any good pups produced by their bitches but are often generously prepared to lay the entire blame for any sub-standard puppies entirely at the door of the stud-dog's kennel. Making the services of a dog available at public stud encourages public scrutiny and assessment of his performance. Dog owners who are not prepared to accept all the consequences of owning a stud-dog should avoid this aspect of breeding.

Selecting a Stud-Dog

Any dog destined for stud work should be bred, selected and reared with immense care. Raymond Oppenheimer, the quality of whose kennel of Bull Terriers provided him with a sound basis to pronounce on the matter, used to say that good stud-dogs were never bad dogs. In other words, any dog who is expected to have the ability to sire good puppies must himself be a good specimen of the breed.

If the breed is one in which inherited defects are known to exist, the dog must be subjected to the appropriate tests and

A good stud-dog of whatever breed should exude quality and masculinity. (Photo: Dalton)

his status made known to anyone who may enquire as to his use. Failure to test, and failure to disclose the results of tests, could have very serious consequences.

The dog himself must have a reliable, steady and confident temperament, if he is not later to be deterred by aggressive displays, whether real or feigned, by reluctant bitches or by the fumbling and often unwelcome attentions of their well-meaning owners; but then few breeders would want to use a dog whose temperament was in any way suspect.

Education

A dog that has been reared from puppy-hood in isolation, or that has been deterred from sexual play with other dogs, may not be easy to introduce to stud work. It is important that young dogs are allowed to practise, develop and perfect the ingrained behaviour which will be required when they are called upon to mate a bitch.

Dogs intended for stud work should be allowed to develop the ability to make relationships with others and to assert their place in those relationships without resorting to aggression. The early competitive career of a potential stud-dog not only allows him to mix with strange dogs but also develops his confidence while enabling potential users to see and appreciate his qualities.

When a prospective stud-dog has reached the age of ten or twelve months, perhaps earlier in small breeds and later in larger ones, he should be given an opportunity to mate a quiet and knowing brood-bitch. He should be allowed to play with the bitch and to respond to her provocative advances, his efforts being quietly encouraged and praised without distracting him from the purpose of the exercise. Considerable patience, perhaps extending over several days, may need to be exercised before his inexperienced efforts achieve success.

Once a tie has been achieved (*see* page 99), more patience may be called for because young dogs tend to tie for an unconscionably long time, but the owner at least has the satisfaction of knowing that his prospective stud-dog's education is progressing satisfactorily and, once the bitch has been confirmed in whelp, may confidently anticipate further satisfactory matings, though these should be carefully controlled so that the dog is not over-used or his fragile juvenile confidence undermined by difficult or uncooperative bitches.

This first mating, however, is a problematic affair. If the owner of the dog cannot provide a suitable bitch at the right time, it must be hoped that the opportunity to mate a bitch from outside the kennel will present itself. If the young dog is of outstanding quality and has been seen in favourable circumstances by other breeders it is likely that the opportunity will arrive. Traditionally the stud fee is waived for this début performance, known as a proving mating, and, at the very least, should await the arrival of the litter.

Only when a stud-dog has produced at least one litter of normal, healthy puppies should he be made available at public stud.

Responsibilities

Changes in the dog's attitude to life are not the only probable consequences of a stud career. The owner of a stud-dog provides a service for which a fee, sometimes a substantial one, will usually be charged. The service should be selective. A responsible stud-dog owner should be prepared to refuse any bitches that are below an acceptable standard and any whose owner's attitude to breeding is unacceptable. He must then be prepared to accept the consequences of refusal to mate the bitch. It follows then that the stud-dog owner should have a wide and detailed knowledge of the breed and of the individuals in it.

Some stud-dog owners have been known to attempt to justify mating their good dogs to sub-standard bitches on the grounds that refusal might mean that the bitch will be mated by a sub-standard dog and the breed would thereby be harmed. The argument is a facile one. Stud-dog owners are not responsible for what others may or may not do. Their responsibility is to their own and their stud-dog's reputation, which will be enhanced by outstandingly good puppies but will be harmed by mediocrity. Sub-standard bitches are most likely to produce mediocre puppies.

It is part of the stud-dog owner's responsibility to ensure that the dog is healthy, fertile, able and willing to mate receptive bitches brought to him and that, within reasonable limits, he is available when the bitches for whom prior arrangement has been made are in season.

If stud-dog owners knowingly or negligently fail to ensure that the service provided satisfies each of these requirements, not only might they incur the displeasure of the owners of visiting bitches but may find that they are required to explain matters before the courts. In this increasingly litigious age the possibility should not be taken lightly and especially when dealing with owners whose attitude to breeding is a very commercial one, with breeds in which hereditary problems are known to exist, or with numerically small breeds in which rarity increases the relative importance of each litter.

Stud Arrangements

Stud-dog owners should ensure that the owners of bitches are made fully aware of the details of each and every condition relative to the mating. If the conditions can be put in writing and similarly accepted, so much the better.

Certainly the bitch's owner should be made aware of all the conditions which apply to the mating. The bitch to be mated must be identified and agreement reached with regard to that particular mating. It should be made clear that the mating is dependent upon her being in good condition and free from any infectious disease at the time of the mating. The amount of and conditions relating to the stud fee must be agreed, and especially so if these give the stud-dog owner a claim to any of the puppies from the litter. It is important to define where the mating will take place and whether there are any restrictions on when it can take place. Any special provisions which may also be applicable, such as inspection of hereditary health certificates, identification documents, the availability of a second mating during the same season, the availability of return matings if the

bitch fails to conceive, should also be made known and agreed well before the mating takes place.

Normal Service

It is customary for bitches to be taken to the dog when, in their owner's opinion, they are ready to be mated. Experienced stud-dogs tend to be creatures of habit and will become sexually aroused when they recognize the start of the mating routines that in the past have resulted in their being required to mate a bitch. The routine and the background against which it takes place are, therefore, of importance. A popular stud-dog will mate a number of bitches during the course of a year, with most matings tending to take place during the spring months. In these circumstances, it would be quite impractical to expect the dog to visit all the bitches.

Although the means are available to discover precisely when a bitch should be mated, the majority of owners continue to rely on their own more or less accurate observations. This means that not every bitch will be brought to the dog at the best time and, for this reason if for no other, some are likely to show a reluctance to accept the dog's advances, and an experienced stud-dog, especially one whose libido is not of the highest, may not be interested in them.

Stud-dog owners must accept that not all matings will proceed without problems. Some bitches, having lived isolated from other dogs since they were puppies, may have become imprinted by their owners and so have had their natural impulses subdued. The owners of bitches are also notoriously likely to bring bitches for mating when it is most convenient for the owner rather than when the time is right for the bitch. Stud-dog owners must learn tolerance, but this tolerance cannot be taken to extremes without risk that the service available to other bitch owners will be affected. If, for some reason or other, a satisfactory mating is not achieved during the bitch's first visit she may be invited to return but the invitation might not be possible without affecting arrangements made for another bitch.

In some cases a second mating may be offered after a satisfactory one has been achieved. The arrangement is not by any means invariable and stud-dog owners should be careful to ensure that prior agreement has been reached regarding all the conditions which will be applicable.

Stud Fee

The fee customarily paid by the owner of the bitch is for the services of the stud-dog. It is payable immediately after a mating in which – ideally but not invariably – a tie has taken place (*see* page 99). The fee is not dependent on the subsequent birth of puppies, and although many stud-dog owners offer a free service if the bitch fails to conceive the bitch's owner should not regard this as a right. Furthermore, the offer will usually be dependent on the dog's continued availability and will be restricted to a repeat mating with the same bitch.

To charge a stud fee for the services of a dog that is known to be infertile or whose fertility is in doubt is tantamount to fraud. Even if, because of doubts about a dog's fertility, the fee is waived, a disappointed breeder may seek legal redress unless the circumstances have been carefully defined and put in writing.

The stud fee may be set at any level but is usually somewhere between one half and the full cost of a puppy. Occasionally, owners of stud-dogs may ask for a puppy or even more in exchange for the service, rather than accept a fee. The arrangement may be beneficial to stud-dog owners, but is one to which only an unwise breeder would agree.

In Scandinavia, an arrangement exists, similar in some respects to that customary among horse breeders, in which the stud fee is split into two parts. A fee, payable at the time of mating, is charged for the service; and when puppies are born a further fee, related to the number of puppies, becomes due. The arrangement has much to commend it in that it discourages those who may offer dogs of doubtful fertility at stud while rewarding dogs of outstanding fertility. On the other hand knowledge that the full fee is not payable unless the bitch produces puppies may encourage some breeders to take less care in ensuring that bitches are not taken to the dog at the wrong time.

Identification

There is little point in the owner of a stud-dog being selective about bitches accepted for mating unless these can be identified with some degree of certainty. In some, especially whole-coloured and trimmed breeds, this may not be easy. The bitch last seen, groomed to perfection, competing in the junior class at a show may look very different when, as a mature animal not trimmed for the ring, she is brought to be mated.

A growing number of countries require that all dogs and bitches used for breeding are permanently identified, usually by means of a tattoo, a tattoo being the only means of providing indelible proof of identity which can be read without recourse to complex instrumentation. This seems a sensible and even vital precaution against fraud, by either stud-dog or bitch owner, either of whom may otherwise be tempted to replace the chosen animal with a substitute. It is entirely possible that, without permanent identification, two unscrupulous owners may cheat one another in a way that will lead to the registration of puppies with totally fictitious pedigrees.

Positive identification becomes of even more importance when the dog is involved in providing any of the additional services being created by technological advances, such as the export of semen for artificial insemination (*see* page 93).

Male Reproductive System

Although it is not essential that breeders have a detailed knowledge of the canine male and female genital tracts a basic familiarity does have practical value: the mechanics of a mating are more easily understood and so a solution to any problems which might arise is more likely to be found. Knowledge of the female genital tract is of even greater importance should difficulties be encountered during the birth of puppies. At that time a delay may result in the death of puppies and in avoidable suffering for the bitch, while well-meant attempts to alleviate the problem by someone with no more than a hazy idea of the anatomy and the process which is being interfered with, may easily make an already difficult situation very much worse.

The male reproductive system produces the cells, and the fluids in which they are protected and transported, which are required to fertilize the female. The system is composed of several linked visceral tubes which begin with the testes and end in a single opening at the anterior end of the penis.

The testes, usually two in number, are normally carried in an external pouch, called the scrotum, which is situated between the rear legs. The purpose of this external arrangement is to enable the testes to remain cooler than the dog's internal body temperature, cool conditions being essential to the production of viable sperm. Thus testes retained within the body and subjected to a higher temperature do not produce viable sperm. The scrotum itself is sensitive to temperature and will adjust its relationship with the body in order to maintain the optimum internal temperature, contracting in cold weather to bring the testes within the range of the effect of bodily heat and enlarging in warm weather to provide cooler conditions. In extremely hot weather fertility may be reduced.

Typically, the testes are carried side by side but in some breeds, particularly those with a relatively narrow pelvis and heavily muscled rear limbs, restricted room may cause them to be carried in tandem. But in most breeds this should be regarded cautiously as a possible indicator of a disposition to cryptorchidism.

Sperm produced within the testes is stored in a duct, the epididymis, until mating takes place. Although semen is continually produced, the sperm stored by dogs that have not mated a bitch for some time may not be in full vigour. Two matings, at least twenty-four hours apart, will clear the old semen and allow time for it to be replaced by fresh.

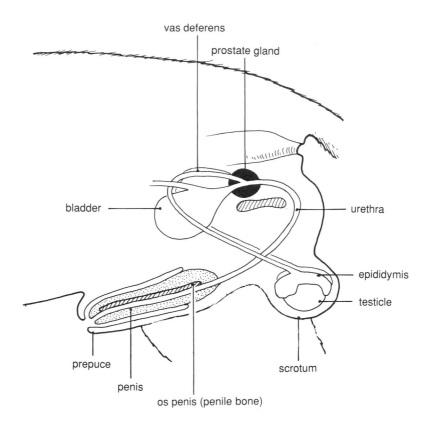

Reproductive system of the dog.

The male penetrates the female by means of a partially erect penis, partial erection being produced by the effect of a bone, the os penis. Erection is stimulated as entry to the vagina pushes back the prepuce (the penile sheath), to expose the penis itself. Erection, caused by engorgement with blood, is completed only after penetration has actually taken place. The enlargement of the *bulbus glandis*, a spherical swelling at the end of the penis, then enables the bitch to grip the penis in order to facilitate the tie. (*See* page 99.)

Male Reproductive Cycle

There is a saying that 'bitches come in season twice a year but dogs are in season every damn day', which offers no more than the simple truth. From puberty to extreme old age dogs, especially those that have been used at stud, are ever ready to mate any receptive bitch. It is this constant state of awareness that causes dogs to wander, like W.S. Gilbert's Palace sentry, 'in search of beer and beauty (And it generally happens that he hasn't far to go).'

Fertility

A healthy male dog will become fertile when he is no more than six months old and will, barring accidents and illness, remain so until advancing age makes him progressively less fertile. Even dogs of an advanced age, ten or twelve years old, may still be fertile though by this age their continued fertility may be in some doubt. The American Kennel Club requires that all dogs over the age of twelve have a certificate of fertility based on examination of a sample of semen.

Illness and occasionally the treatment of that illness, stress, dietary deficiency, lack of exercise, and too frequent use, may all have a deleterious effect on fertility. No stud-dog owner should offer the services of a dog whose fertility is in doubt without revealing those doubts to the owners of visiting bitches. All too often a stud-dog may remain available even after he has failed to impregnate a succession of bitches.

Traditionally, the fertility of stud-dogs is assessed by their ability to impregnate bitches, but this rough-and-ready method has several drawbacks, not the least of which is that it assumes that the dog carries all the responsibility for pregnancy. In fact the bitch must carry at least some of the responsibility.

Unless a dog is able to impregnate well over 80 per cent of the fertile bitches mated by him, his level of fertility must be regarded as suspect and he should be withdrawn from public stud until the problem has been identified and cured. If kennel clubs were to make registration of puppies dependent upon notification that a mating from which it is hoped to register puppies has taken place a great deal of potentially valuable information might be gained about levels of fertility while, at the same time, providing additional valuable protection against the possibility of fraud.

Infertility may be defined as the inability to impregnate fertile females. In some cases, extremes of age, bilateral cryptorchidism or with surgically neutered dogs, infertility may be absolute. More often infertility is a relative condition in which the male totally fails to impregnate several bitches, or impregnates females that subsequently abort, or give birth to stillborn young, or produce puppies that are born only with difficulty. Not all of these factors may be entirely within the male's responsibility, but undoubtedly the male can have an effect on each and every one.

In such cases the male should be subjected to a rigorous physical examination, including examination of external genitalia and of blood and sperm samples. The behaviour of the dog should be observed when bitches are in season.

The failure to mate or to mate satisfactorily may result from low sexual drive consequent upon immaturity, old age, poor physical condition, sexual inhibition produced by the presence of a more dominant male, or from females mimicking oestrus. If normal sexual drive is present, failure to mate may be the result of injury, physical defects, or of some problem of the genital tract. The absence (whether absolute or relative) of sperm, abnormal sperm, low sexual drive and physical problems which prevent or make coitus more difficult, may all be, to some extent, inherited. The conditions in which the mating takes place may also inhibit mating and should be taken into account.

Absolute or relative infertility may have any one of several causes.

Balanoposthitis or Balanitis

Most mature males emit a slight creamy discharge from the prepuce. If the discharge become excessive or purulent, it is likely that the prepuce is infected; such an infection is known as balanoposthitis. Infection may be caught from infected females or transmitted to females. Irritants within the sheath and prolonged intercourse may also result in infection.

The hair round the sheath should be removed, the sheath pushed back to expose the head of the penis and the site of the infection washed with surgical soap and treated with an appropriate antibiotic ointment. Many breeders carry out this procedure as a precautionary measure after the dog has mated a bitch.

Phimosis

Phimosis is any infection of the penis that results in swelling that may make it impossible for erection to occur. Occasionally the condition appears as a congenital abnormality.

Removal of infection or, in the case of congenital abnormality, surgery, will cure the problem.

Paraphimosis

Paraphimosis, or prolapse of the penis, describes the failure of the penis to retract following erection. It may be caused by nothing more sinister than obstruction caused by excessive hair, in which case keeping the hair trimmed will solve and avoid recurrence of the problem.

Occasionally retraction of the penis causes the skin of the sheath to roll back within itself and to form a potentially damaging constriction. Dogs should be checked after every mating to ensure that the penis has returned to its normal state.

Prostatic Disorders

The prostate is a gland, and dogs, especially but not exclusively ageing dogs, are prone to a variety of prostatic disorders. These include hyperplasia, infection, abscesses, neoplasia, cystic metapasia and paraprostatic cysts. Swelling, blood-infused urine, a discharge of pus, discomfort, frequent and apparently painful urination may all be signs of a prostatic disorder. Veterinary attention is required. Treatment with antibiotics, oestrogen, and surgery (perhaps involving castration) is indicated, but some conditions, particularly neoplasia, may be untreatable.

Cryptorchidism and Monorchidism

In order to take advantage of the cooler conditions outside the body for the production of fertile sperm, the testes are normally carried in an external bag, the scrotum. Failure of both testes to descend into the scrotum (cryptorchidism) or of one (monorchidism) produces sterility or reduces fertility. Such dogs should not be used at stud.

Orchitis

Orchitis, infection of the testicles resulting in swelling, may have any one of several causes, including injury, frostbite, cystitis, prostatitis, balanoposthitis, distemper and brucellosis. Painfully swollen testicles, a stiff-legged gait, efforts to ease the pain by sitting on cool surfaces and reluctance to submit to examination are

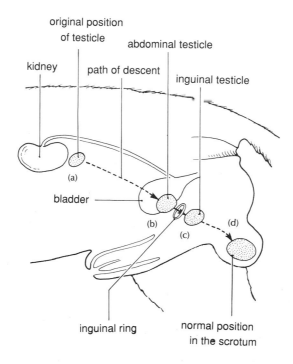

The normal descent of a testicle from behind the kidney (a) to its final position in the scrotum (d); the main sites of retention are indicated by (b) and (c).

all indications of orchitis. Treatment with antibiotics may prevent the need for castration.

Castration

In order to encourage wholesale castration of dogs as a means to reduce the population of stray and latch-key dogs, it is often suggested that castration offers all sorts of benefits. Castration certainly prevents dogs from breeding but it should not be regarded as an alternative to proper standards of care which also prevent the birth of unwanted puppies.

In 1976, the California Veterinary Medicine Teaching Hospital carried out a survey to examine changes in behaviour following castration. They found that roaming declined rapidly in 44 per cent of the dogs that had been castrated, declined gradually in 50 per cent and resulted in no change in 6 per cent. The effect of castration on mounting behaviour was less positive with 33 per cent showing a rapid decline, 33 per cent a gradual

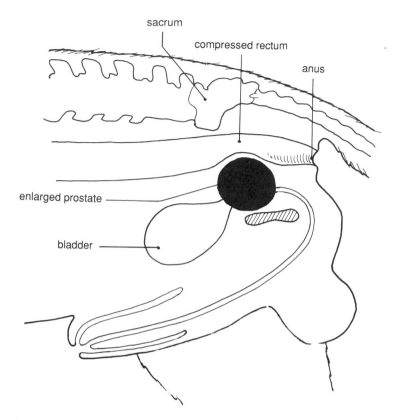

An enlarged prostate is most common in the older dog, but it is also a symptom of prostatitis. The prostate gland slowly increases in size, causing constipation and obstruction to urination. The condition can be diagnosed either on rectal examination or on X-ray, and can be treated hormonally.

decline and 33 per cent no decline at all. The effect on aggressive behaviour towards other males was even more problematic, with 38 per cent showing a rapid decline, 25 per cent a gradual decline and 38 per cent remaining as aggressive as they had been before surgery. As a means to reduce territorial aggression castration appeared to be totally useless: none of the castrated dogs showed any reduction in territorial aggressive behaviour.

Vasectomy

An alternative to castration, which avoids the possibility of subsequent unwanted changes and problems resulting from hormone imbalance, is bilateral vasectomy in which the tubes that carry sperm from the testicles to the urethra (the vas deferens) are severed or removed. Dogs continue to show all male characteristics but are sterile.

Semen Evaluation

A less wasteful, less demanding and certainly less dangerous method of assessing fertility than that offered by unfruitful matings, is to examine a specimen of the dog's ejaculate. Such examinations should be routinely carried out if the dog is not in regular use, if there are suspicions that his fertility may be reduced by illness or age, or if he fails to impregnate a receptive bitch.

The Guide Dogs for the Blind Association routinely test semen samples from their stud-dogs every six months to one year, as well as when fertile bitches fail to conceive. If semen examination and evaluation is accompanied by examination of the scrotum and testes to discern any changes in size or consistency, which may be indicative of abnormality, yet more traditional uncertainties associated with breeding might be solved.

Semen is usually collected into warmed test tubes to provide samples of each of the three components of the ejaculate. The first, stored in the prostate gland, consists of a small quantity of clear viscous liquid. The second, slightly larger, component contains the spermatozoa and is creamy in colour and consistency. The third and largest component, again emanating from the prostate gland, is clear.

If the second component is clear and watery, there may be few spermatozoa present. A yellow tinge may indicate contamination by urine or pus, while a pink coloration may be suggestive of the presence of small amounts of blood, a not unusual occurrence in middle-aged and older dogs.

A drop of the sample is then placed on a slightly warmed slide and examined microscopically. The semen will be seen as active, minute, tadpole-like creatures, with large oval heads and long, thin tails. Normal spermatozoa have straight tails whose rapid movements propel them forward in straight lines. A deformed tail will propel the spermatozoa in circles or even backwards.

The number of spermatozoa in a complete fertile ejaculate may vary between 36 and 630 million, the number tending to increase with the size of the dog and to decrease slightly with age. The counting of spermatozoa is carried out in diluted and stained samples of known volume. If fewer than 62 per cent are normal and fewer than 65 per cent show characteristic mobility the dog is likely to be infertile.

Exporting Semen

A small but assuredly growing aspect of owning a top-quality stud-dog is the export of semen. Different countries throughout the world have their own regulations, imposed both by their kennel clubs and their governments and these are, from time to time, subject to change. It is essential, therefore, that anyone wishing to export canine semen should discover what rules and regulations are currently in operation. Basic conditions are likely to include a stipulation that semen is transported in permanently identified, sealed ampoules. Documentation will include a certificate signed by a veterinary surgeon, which describes and identifies the donor dog, gives the name and address of his owner, the address of the premises on which the semen was collected, the date of the collection, and information about the health and vaccination record of the dog, especially with regard to rabies and other infectious or contagious diseases.

It is no longer unusual for puppies to be born in one country following the use of semen exported by the owners of stud-dogs in another country, and there is no doubt that this can be of enormous benefit to numerically small breeds, who may by this method extend the gene pool available to them.

The initial approach seems usually to come from the overseas owner of a bitch but there is absolutely no reason why stud-dog owners should not take the initiative by advertising the services of their dogs in other countries.

Strike Rate

There may be more felicitous phrases, but 'strike rate' serves to describe the difference between the number of available opportunities and the number of successes.

'Strike rate' might be applied to the number of bitches that become pregnant compared with the number mated, and so provide a guide to a dog's fertility.

The concept is also useful in that it offers the means to compare the likely quality of puppies produced by different dogs. For example, a dog that produces a large number of puppies may appear to have what seems to be a reasonably high level of success in the ring but closer examination might well reveal that success is dependent not on a high overall standard, but on the production of the occasional good puppy among a mass of mediocre ones. On the other hand, a dog whose use is carefully restricted may produce a far higher proportion of quality puppies from a smaller overall number.

Strike rate, then, is a measure of the level of success when the number of opportunities for success are taken into account.

CHAPTER 7

Mating

When to Mate

The fact that bitches are normally in season and available for breeding only twice a year means that breeders have a limited choice as to when puppies may be produced. Choice is further limited because bitches tend to come into season in spring and again in autumn. Spring puppies may be preferred for a number of reasons. Their growth will coincide with the onset of warmer weather when providing artificial heat for young things will not be so necessary. Kinder weather also means that very early in their lives puppies can be given the opportunity to exercise and play out of doors, where young muscles and young brains will get the sort of stimulus they need if the puppies are to grow into physically and mentally healthy adults.

Other considerations may also affect the time chosen to produce puppies. In most countries autumn-born puppies have a far better chance of a successful early show ring career than do spring-born puppies. Other considerations may apply to puppies intended for racing, coursing or other field sports.

The Kennel Club in Great Britain will not register puppies from bitches that are less than twelve months old or over eight years old. The restrictions are intended to prevent the abuse of breeding bitches and as such are welcome, though there is no physiological reason why well-grown and healthy bitches under twelve months and over eight years should not be bred from. Neither is there any certainty that bitches are not abused by being bred from at every season between their first and eighth birthdays, though the revised format of the Kennel Club's Breed Record Supplement, a quarterly publication which is essential reading for every serious breeder, now reveals the culprits and might, therefore, curb some of the callous excesses.

A bitch may be mated at the first season after her first birthday, though in practice show bitches may not be mated until they have enjoyed success in the ring. They may be mated at any time up to three or even four years old, beyond which time a bitch may be getting too old, her bones and temperament too set, to face the prospect of rearing her first litter.

When it has been decided that the bitch is ready to be mated she should be taken to the dog, whose owner has been given prior warning and has signalled acceptance of the visit. Only in rare and unusually privileged cases is the dog taken to the bitch. If distance is a problem, the bitch may be sent to the dog or arrangements may be made to use artificial insemination.

Sperm from a healthy stud-dog can remain viable in the uterus for up to ten days, though fertility begins to decline after three days. A bitch may ovulate as early as the third day of her oestrous cycle or as late as the twenty-fifth day.

Once ovulation has taken place the egg requires another forty-eight to seventy-two hours to mature and will then remain viable for about another twenty-four hours.

Natural matings using dogs with normal levels of fertility are traditionally carried out between ten and fourteen days after the first signs of oestrus have been seen or when the bitch's behaviour signals her readiness to be mated.

Some bitches, however, will 'stand' throughout their entire seasons and, particularly if they are to be mated to a dog whose fertility is not high, may be mated every third day, though obviously such a regime will require the co-operation of the stud-dog's owner and this, for very good reason, may not always be forthcoming.

The use of blood tests to enable progesterone levels to be measured now enables breeders to discover precisely when a bitch should be mated.

Hormone Assay Tests

In some breeds the optimum time for mating may last for no more than a few hours. Traditionally, breeders have had to rely on visual signs which could be unreliable, not always easy to recognize, and which might vary from bitch to bitch and from season to season.

It is now possible, by testing progesterone levels, to discover with some precision when a bitch has ovulated and thus the best time for her to be mated. Apart from its value with regard to difficult bitches, the technique is of particular importance when bitches must travel for some distance to the stud-dog and when artificial insemination (AI), particularly of chilled or frozen semen, is being used.

Progesterone levels rise slowly throughout the early days of oestrus. They rise very quickly on the day when ovulation takes place. Once a bitch has ovulated it takes about seventy-two hours for the ovum to mature and it is then that mating should take place.

There are two main methods of taking tests. One uses blood samples, the other cytology samples. In either case, the initial sample establishes a base progesterone level; any subsequent test showing a rise in that level will indicate that ovulation is taking place. Blood tests can be carried out by any vet and results known quickly but, at present, testing kits are expensive and have a short shelf life. Cytology tests require expertise and equipment which not all vets have to hand and so there may be some delay in getting results from a specialist laboratory.

A third method, simpler than the others but which appears not yet to have won total confidence from vets or breeders, relies on swabs which determine sugar levels in the vaginal discharge.

It is worth pointing out here that the theory that it is possible to determine a bitch's readiness for mating by performing an internal examination of the vagina is a fallacy, since it is impossible manually to judge the maturity of the ovum. There is really no need for laypersons to perform such examinations at any time during mating, and it may succeed only in introducing infections to the uterus.

Premises

Matings tend to be achieved more easily if the couple have had an opportunity to get to know one another, to run and play and indulge in stimulating foreplay. A secure area, if possible indoors and certainly away from public view, and appropriate for the size of the breed in question, should therefore be available. If this area is reserved for stud work or is used by the dog only when bitches are to be mated, dogs will quickly learn to associate the venue with the act of mating and will react accordingly.

The Mating

In Britain the process of mating may sometimes be referred to as 'lining'. In America, to the confusion of British breeders, the process is usually referred to as 'breeding' or 'being bred'.

It needs to be stressed that nothing is invariable during a mating. A perfectly satisfactory mating may be over in a matter of minutes, or it may take hours or even days to achieve. Some couples will get along famously, others may be almost totally uninterested or even hostile to one another. Divergence from the norm takes many forms and finding a mutually agreed solution to these problems is largely the responsibility of the stud-dog's owner.

Some bitches will even develop such a strong preference for a particular dog that all other suitors will be vigorously rejected. There is nothing anthropomorphic about the suggestion; pairs of wolves normally enter into and maintain a prolonged relationship in spite of the presence of other potential mates. The

preference is just one more example of the way in which remnants of wolf heritage remain in domestic dogs.

When the bitch arrives at the appointed place she should be allowed to cleanse herself and become familiar with her surroundings. The stud-dog owner may wish to check her health, identity, and that she is in season before introducing her prospective mate. The manner of introduction will be dependent on the routine normally followed by the stud-dog's owner, but it is customary to keep the bitch on a lead, and both in collars, until her reaction to the situation has been assessed. Breeders of profusely coated breeds may trim the area around the vulva before allowing the mating to take place, thus facilitating the stud-dog's penetration.

If the pair seem amicably disposed they can be allowed the freedom to run and play together, preferably within a securely fenced area. Even otherwise sedate creatures may at this time indulge in quite uncharacteristically skittish and flirtatious behaviour and do not always behave in their usual obedient manner.

The dog will sniff and lick the bitch's rear, probably in order to assist arousal. This behaviour, however, appears to be strongest during the early days of a bitch's season and tends, in experienced and eager stud-dogs, to become no more than perfunctory when the bitch is ready to be mated. Persistent sniffing and licking should, therefore, be regarded as an indication that the bitch is probably not quite ready to be mated or that the dog's libido is not as strong as it might be. Even so, efforts to achieve a mating might continue with some hope of success.

If a mating is not achieved after a further period it is best to give both dog and bitch a rest and to test whether a brief absence might make the heart grow fonder. The dog should be put back in his accustomed place and the bitch preferably returned to familiar surroundings, though this may not always be possible.

At this stage the possibility has to be considered that the bitch is either not ready or has passed the time for mating. The stud-dog owner may suggest that the bitch returns on the following day or that the mating is abandoned. There is little point, and there might be some harm, in trying to persuade an uninterested dog to mate a bitch that will probably not conceive. Customarily, no stud fee will have been incurred at this stage but if the mating has taken place and yet is unlikely to produce pups, the stud fee is payable.

If the bitch is ready to be mated, after a long period of foreplay, she will probably stand with her head lowered, her back slightly arched, her tail curled to one side and her vulva thrust outwards and upwards in what is known as the coital crouch. The dog will approach her rear end, and will probably sniff and lick her vulva and rear legs. He may indulge in a few pelvic thrusts by way of rehearsal and will then mount the bitch, clasping her loins with his forelegs.

At this stage the bitch may dislodge the dog by turning round and the two may indulge in more foreplay. This process may be repeated but after that it is wise to restrain the bitch, especially if the dog is inexperienced or has a fragile libido.

Mounting will again take place and unless the bitch again resists the process, mating can be allowed to proceed without further interference. The dog will thrust his penis, which by now should be partially erect, towards the bitch's vulva. The thrusts may appear to be indis-criminate but practised stud-dogs are remarkably accurate and may achieve penetration after no more than a few efforts.

If there is a disparity in size between dog and bitch, or lack of co-operation from the bitch, or inaccuracy on the dog's part, any of which may prevent penetration, various options are available. The height of one or the other can be changed, for which purpose telephone directories appear to be the recommended – almost obligatory – apparatus. A slight adjustment can be made by means of slight pressure below the bitch's tail. The accuracy of the dog's aim may also be improved by manipulating his penis. This last method is not without risk that the interference may disturb the dog, particularly one who is not accustomed to being handled in this way, and lead either to premature ejaculation or to a loss of interest. Furthermore, handling the penis with a hand that is not scrupulously clean, in conditions that are a long way from being clinically clean, creates the risk, however slight, of introducing infection to the dog and thence to the bitch.

A reflex action, the Whitney reflex, first described by Dr Leon Whitney, is sometimes used to facilitate a mating. If a dog has mounted the bitch but is not making a determined effort to gain entry, the handler may guide his penis to the vulva by holding the sheath, thus reducing the chances of infection. Once the penis is in position, pinching its base will often provoke the Whitney reflex – a vigorous reflex thrust which will achieve penetration, after which the mating can be allowed to take its usual course.

If penetration does not take place quite quickly, questions must again be raised.

Is the dog merely going through the routine expected of him in the situation with which he has become familiar? He may be simply being 'polite' and the bitch may not be ready for mating. If this appears to be the case then postponing or abandoning the mating must again be considered. If, however, the dog is eager but is having physical difficulty in achieving penetration the possibility arises, especially in the case of a maiden bitch, that he is meeting some obstruction. If this seems the most probable explanation for the problem the only solution is to have the bitch examined by a vet; perhaps, depending on the veterinary verdict, she may return on the following day.

Once penetration has taken place the bitch and, if necessary, the dog should be held in order to prevent further movement until penetration and penile erection are complete, at which stage the bitch's protests will cease. Erection may cause the bitch some discomfort and even actual pain. She is likely to be very vocal and may make quite determined efforts to end the proceedings. Her efforts could cause damage to herself and might easily end the stud-dog's career. Gentle but firm restraint is, therefore, essential.

At this stage the dog will be lying on the bitch's back, with his forelegs clasped around her loins. If the dog is heavier than the bitch she may appreciate some help in supporting his weight. A few moments or a few minutes might elapse before the dog begins to make efforts to turn into the classic tie position. He will lift one leg over the bitch's back to enable the two to take up a position in which they are stood rear to rear.

The Tie

The tie position is one that puzzles

The classic tie position. (Photo: Jackson)

canophiles. Desmond Morris has suggested that the tie takes place in order to facilitate a mating that is necessarily prolonged because of the fact that the dog's ejaculate is dispensed in three separate bursts. This begs the question as to why the tie position evolved in dogs rather than, as in most other mammals, a more rapid means of impregnation.

The tie might last for a few minutes or for as much as an hour. Ten to fifteen minutes appears to be the normal range but many stud-dog owners believe that this is often exceeded if the conditions in which the mating has taken place subject them to extreme discomfort. Rain, cold weather, the puerile curiosity of neighbours and passers by all seem to result in a prolonged tie. However, a bitch may conceive without a tie apparently taking place.

It is important that breeders appreciate that the tie is a mutual thing and not solely dependent on the dog or the bitch. The bulb at the end of a dog's penis, the *bulbus glandis*, swells, and is then grasped by the constrictor muscles within the bitch's vagina.

During the tie both dog and bitch may show every indication of boredom. It is not unusual for one or other to go to sleep and actually fall over. Vigilance should be maintained but it may not be necessary to continue to hold the pair. Nature can be allowed to take its course. Eventually the two will part, the dog licking his now flaccid penis and the bitch her vulva. The dog should then be returned to his customary place and given whatever refreshment is deemed appropriate, at the very least a drink of water though a cocktail of milk and sherry is not unknown, while an isotonic drink seems a reasonable compromise.

After the Mating

Some breeders at this stage subject the bitch to all manner of manipulations in the belief that it will improve the chances of conception. The bitch may be upended to allow semen 'to flow into her', her stomach may be massaged, and determined efforts may be made to prevent her from urinating. Such unnatural procedures are likely to do more harm than good and at best may be regarded as pointless. All should be well if the bitch receives precisely the same consideration as her mate.

All that remains is to decide whether another mating is necessary or desirable, to pay the stud fee and to complete the paperwork.

Handling the Maiden Bitch

The importance of ensuring that dogs intended for breeding should from puppyhood onwards have regular opportunity for uninhibited social contact with their own kind cannot be stressed too strongly. More breeding problems may be created by an unnatural life isolated from contact with other dogs than by any other cause.

However, even a bitch who has enjoyed the benefit of a varied social life may be easily upset when the time comes for her to be mated for the first time. It is important, therefore, that her normal routine should, as far as is compatible with security, be adhered to.

An experienced stud-dog, who will be handled by an experienced, knowledgeable and sympathetic owner, should be selected. The owner should be made aware of the fact that the bitch is a maiden. If the dog happens to be one whose behaviour towards bitches is positive without being unduly robust then so much the better.

When the time comes for her to be mated, the journey should be arranged to ensure that she is not upset. On arrival she should be allowed a few minutes to adjust to her surroundings before being introduced to the dog.

In the past some breeders insisted that maiden bitches needed to be 'broken in' by the introduction of a forefinger into the vagina. The practice may not yet be extinct, but it should be because it is both pointless and dangerous. Canids do not have a hymen that needs to be ruptured prior to mating. Any abnormal constrictions that may exist are far better dealt with by a veterinary surgeon than by a grubby forefinger ignorantly employed. Furthermore, any non-sterile object inserted into the vagina at this, or any other, time may well introduce infection which could lead to the loss of puppies or even to total sterility.

In most calmly conducted first matings instinct will eventually take over and the bitch will indicate her readiness. If this does not happen, she should be gently restrained to allow the dog to mount her. If the bitch's owner is inexperienced or disturbed by what he may regard as rape, it may be better if someone else takes charge of the bitch, to hold her head while the dog's owner restrains her hindquarters and assists the dog.

When penetration takes place she may well protest both vocally and physically and will almost certainly do so as erection is completed. Firm but sympathetic restraint should be maintained until her protests cease after which the mating can be allowed to take its customary course.

Novice Stud-Dogs

A novice dog's introduction to sexual activity should follow an upbringing in which there has been ample opportunity for social interaction with other dogs. His first partner should be a quiet, calm and sexually experienced bitch; if she is also a provocative hussy with which he has previous acquaintance then so much the better. If the two can be left, under unobtrusive supervision, to make their own arrangements then this is preferred.

Once the two are mated – and this may be achieved only after several attempts, perhaps spread over two or three days – the two should be restrained in order to accustom the dog to outside interference at this time. If the mating can be repeated on the following day the bitch might be held and the dog assisted, again in order to accustom him to interference which may be required when he is expected to mate less receptive bitches.

Especially on these first occasions, it is important to encourage the dog as much as possible in order to build his confidence, which is important if he is to develop into a reliable and useful stud.

What should be stressed is that a mating between two physically and temperamentally normal dogs with normal sexual urges should present few problems. Matings between dogs that are not physically and temperamentally normal, or that lack libido, are best avoided.

Multiple Matings

Kennel Club rules insist that if a bitch is mated by more than one dog of the same breed as herself, and during the same season, the names of all the dogs must appear on the application for puppy registration. This requirement may be set aside if scientific evidence of the identity of a single sire can be provided. Similar conditions are applied by other kennel clubs, although the availability of the means to determine parentage now make it possible, in most cases, to resolve such mysteries.

Artificial Insemination

There is nothing new or particularly difficult about the use of artificial insemination (AI). The technique has been used since at least 1780, when Spallanzani carried out a series of experiments on dogs. Although the use of AI allowed the quality of other species to be much improved, its use on dogs was officially curtailed and confined to illicit efforts by individual breeders until the 1950s when further research took place. Widespread use of AI in other forms of livestock, coupled with the inability of kennel clubs to enforce an embargo, led to its increased illicit use in dogs. The Canadian Kennel Club said that artificial insemination can easily be carried out 'by wise breeders using a plastic cup and a milk-shake straw', and because of this they, along with several other kennel clubs, make no attempt to proscribe its use.

The Kennel Club in the UK, however, forbids the use of artificial insemination unless the Kennel Club has given its prior permission. This permission will only be granted if both dog and bitch have previously produced registered progeny naturally conceived. The Kennel Club's reluctance to allow breeders free access to the undoubted benefits which AI has to offer appears to be based on a fear that the technique could be used to breed from dogs which, by reason of savage temperament or physical deformity, cannot achieve a natural mating. The fear is not unreasonable but the response to it, particularly as regards the use of chilled or frozen stored semen is concerned, may well be detrimental to the efforts of British breeders, especially to those of breeds that are not numerous in Britain, to breed top-quality dogs.

Collecting Semen

Artificial insemination is easily carried out. Semen is most easily collected in the presence of an in-season bitch used to tease the dog so that his ejaculate can be collected. Alternatively the dog may be stimulated manually. Once manipulation has stimulated erection and ejaculation has begun, continued slight pressure should be applied behind the *bulbus glandis*, to imitate that exerted during normal copulation by the bitch's constrictor muscles.

As the dog responds to stimulation, he will make the pelvic thrusts usual in a normal mating; these will be accompanied by a clear ejaculate which need not be collected. As thrusting ceases the ejaculate will become creamy and it is this that contains the semen. This should be collected into a suitable, clean receptacle that has been warmed to blood heat.

Impregnating the Bitch

The collected semen must be inserted into the bitch before cooling and dehydration begins to reduce its fertility. A suitable tube is gently inserted into the bitch's vulva to the depth to which a dog's penis would penetrate; the semen is then drawn into a syringe and passed into the tube. If the bitch is supported on her front legs for about ten minutes the semen will flow down the tube through the cervix and into the uterus. The tube can then be removed and a clean finger inserted into the vagina to stimulate contractions that will help to draw the semen into the uterus The chances of conception taking place are improved if the bitch is then walked for ten or fifteen minutes and, because contractions may be neither so vigorous nor so prolonged as they are in a natural mating, she should, if possible, be prevented from urinating.

Artificial insemination of a bitch requires expert knowledge and experience; in no circumstances should it be practised by anyone other than a veterinary surgeon or similarly qualified person. Conception rates achieved by DIY AI are usually well below those achieved by normal matings, but this may be because many are carried out by inexperienced handlers.

Chilled and Frozen Semen

Breeders may speculate as to whether they would now be benefitting if they had access to semen produced by some of their breed's great past sires, or whether future generations would benefit if they had access to semen produced by some of today's best dogs. Certainly the careful use of stored semen has been the means by which dramatic improvement has been achieved in the quality of some other domestic animals. It has also enabled some hereditary conditions, particularly those of late onset, to be brought under effective control. Even so, its use by dog breeders remains limited.

The carefully controlled use of chilled and frozen semen could be of benefit to breeds whose population in any one country may be too small to provide the sort of genetic pool which is needed if the breed is to retain its health and vigour. The technique could also be used on breeds that suffer from hereditary diseases, which reveal themselves only late in a dog's life when it may already have been bred from. It would be possible to collect and store semen for use only when it was known that donors were free from the disease.

The Guide Dogs for the Blind Association has made effective use of stored semen to reduce the incidence of hereditary diseases that reduce the working life of a guide dog, to increase the production of dogs suitable for training, and to gain access to sires, some as far away as New Zealand, which are known to produce puppies of outstanding quality. In other forms of livestock, too, the use of stored semen associated with rigorous progeny testing has proved an effective tool in the control of hereditary disease and in improving quality.

Most kennel clubs recognize that artificial insemination wisely used can offer benefits that will help breeders to produce better dogs. Semen from the very best dogs can be collected, stored and transported for use in almost every country in the world, thus making our very best dogs internationally available without depriving their home country of their availability. Procedures vary from country to country and should be carefully checked before entering into any commitment.

Importing Semen

For some years the Kennel Club in Britain exercised a total embargo on the use of artificial insemination using chilled or frozen semen and would not register puppies produced by these means. Recently, however, they have relented to the extent that a few individual applications have, after protracted negotiation, been approved.

Kennel Club permission is not, however, required before semen is imported or used to produce puppies that are not to be submitted for registration. The Ministry of Agriculture, Fisheries and Food is the controlling organization and exerts strict control over countries from which canine semen may be imported. In the past, these regulations have meant that semen could not be imported from countries where rabies was endemic, which effectively put most European countries as well as the United States, South America and Asia, out of bounds for British dog breeders. Relaxation of this total embargo now allows semen to be imported, under strict control, even from countries that are not rabies free. It is possible, and perhaps even likely, that existing regulations affecting countries in the European community may eventually be relaxed but, in spite of ill-advised political pressures, this is unlikely to happen before rabies has been eradicated from Europe.

The first step in the process of importing semen is to identify a suitable and available dog whose use will satisfy both Ministry and Kennel Club requirements. To do so may not be easy. Distance will undoubtedly reduce the opportunities to examine potential dogs. Once what appears to be a suitable dog has been identified and his availability confirmed it will be necessary to ensure that both he and his offspring are free from hereditary disease and defects. Once this information has been collected this, along with evidence which supports the need to use imported semen, must be submitted to the Kennel Club in order to ensure that when puppies are eventually born they can be registered. The KC's Breed Standards and Stud Book Sub-Committee will eventually make a recommendation to the General Committee and they will, in turn, make a decision.

Quite obviously, the breeder is likely to be in a far better position than any individual committee member to judge the necessity to use imported semen yet, as far as registration is concerned, it is the committee members who have the deciding say. Genetic evidence which demonstrates the need to import semen in order to avoid some hereditary defect prevalent in the breed may be difficult to collect. The need to breed puppies free from some defect prevalent in the breed means that the Kennel Club will want to see evidence that the bitch is herself free of this defect. If the intention is simply to avoid a dangerously high level of background inbreeding, as yet untapped evidence of which exists in the KC's own Registration Department, it would be necessary for a breeder to have the co-operation of a breed club to which the Kennel Club would make available the information from which the evidence could be extracted. The KC will want to see pedigrees of the animals concerned, to examine the nature of agreements made between the stud-dog's owner and the owner of the bitch, and to be assured that Ministry of Agriculture agreement will be forthcoming.

If the evidence fails to convince the Kennel Club of the need to import semen, its decision may be unfavourable. If the breeder does not accept the decision, he may choose to supply more evidence or select another dog. If the decision is favourable the next steps in the process can be made.

Application must be made to the Ministry of Agriculture, Fisheries and Food for permission to import canine semen. If an informal approach has already been made and the groundwork cleared, this may be accomplished in a matter of weeks, but when starting from scratch the process could take about four months.

The application will be granted only if the donor has been kept in a rabies-free area and has not been in contact with rabies for at least six months prior to collection of the semen. The dog must also be kept in a rabies-free area and away from contact with rabies for a period of six months after the semen has been collected.

Once these formalities have been observed the process of collecting the semen can begin. The dog himself must be positively identified, either by means of a micro-chip implant or, preferably by a tattoo carried out by an authorized agency. Collection itself is a simple procedure but preparing the sample for safe storage and transport is highly specialized and can only be carried out by specialists in this field of work. Customarily two collections are made. The product is examined for viability, diluted and stored in about two dozen 'straws' – sealed glass ampoules – each of which will be sufficient to fertilize a bitch. The ampoules are then frozen and stored in liquid nitrogen and will remain with the collection agency until the breeder asks for delivery.

The ampoules are then flown to the breeder, still in their liquid nitrogen flasks, which is classed as dangerous cargo and attracts commensurate transport charges. On arrival in Britain, all outside wrapping is destroyed and the frozen flasks are transported to a suitable and approved storage facility, usually a veterinary school.

When the bitch comes into season she must be taken to where the ampoules are stored. Tests will be carried out to discover when she ovulates and then the insemination will be carried out. All being well, the litter will be born nine weeks later.

Quite obviously the import of semen is not easy to arrange. The costs involved are high, but for breeds that do not have a sufficiently large British breeding population to sustain health or maintain type the benefits can be considerable. The cost, including stud fees, collection, storage, transport and insemination, is about the same as buying and importing a dog, assuming that a suitable one is available, which is not invariably the case. After one litter has been bred remaining straws may be used on other bitches, with prior approval from and due payment to the stud-dog owner, and after Kennel Club approval has been granted.

Details vary from country to country but the regulations in force in Britain will, in general terms, be similar to those that apply elsewhere.

Embryo Transfer

Techniques involving the transfer or implantation of embryos have been little used in dogs and probably, as yet, not at all by breeders. Yet as long ago as 1957, successful experiments with sheep were being carried out and in 1985 experiments with cattle showed that the techniques to make use of both fresh and stored, sexed or unsexed embryos, whether complete or split, to produce genetically identical siblings were already available.

Apart from the desire of breeders to make use of these techniques and the probable reluctance of kennel clubs to accept that use, it was difficult to synchronize ovulation in donor and recipient bitches. That difficulty has now been overcome. It may not be long before breeders can make use of embryo transfer to produce identical clones of a predetermined sex, to remove embryos from one bitch and to implant them in another.

The use of frozen semen now enables a stud-dog's career to continue after his death. The use of frozen embryos opens up the same possibility in relation to bitches.

Super-Ovulation

Sheep normally have one or two offspring once a year but the use of super-ovulation techniques now makes it possible to increase their fecundity to the point at which one sheep can be expected to ovulate and be mated several times a year and on each occasion to produce four or more embryos. The number makes it impossible for these to be carried to full term and so the embryos are routinely removed for transfer to surrogate mothers, thus leaving the more valuable donor free to produce another crop of embryos without having to undergo the strain of pregnancy, birth or rearing the young. The value of the technique is that elite animals can produce more offspring while less valuable, and possibly more

suitable ones, can be used as the recipients for valuable embryos.

The embryo transfer and super-ovulation techniques have yet to be used by breeders, and their implications appear not yet to have been considered by kennel clubs. It seems likely that kennel clubs will not welcome the use of the technique but as a means to produce top-quality dogs for use as guides and similar purposes the technique may well prove valuable. The techniques are already well established and breeders should be aware of their existence.

Parentage Testing

It is essential to pedigree dog breeding that the true parentage of breeding stock should be known. Occasionally, as a result of accident or, less frequently, deliberate fraud, parentage is in doubt. Nowadays it is a relatively simple, if still fairly expensive, matter to carry out tests to verify parentage.

The tests involve the comparison between tissue taken from the offspring and from its supposed parents. The four techniques in most common use involve examination of red cell antigens, white cell antigens, polymorphic proteins or DNA fingerprints. Each technique relies on the fact that markers, unique to each parent, will be transmitted to and will be found only in their offspring.

Identification

There are a number of methods by which individual dogs can be permanently identified. They could have a micro-chip insert, or have details of tissue samples

Permanent identification of puppies would remove the need for breeders to rely so heavily on trust. (Photo: Carey)

recorded. Both methods have the disadvantage that reading the information requires specialist equipment and/or skills. Dogs can also be freeze-branded which, though painless, leaves a disfiguring scar. Dogs may also be tattooed, usually either on the inside of the ear or the inside of the thigh. Tattooing avoids the disadvantages of other methods. It is a system that is well tried, is not painful or expensive, and provides an identify mark which can easily be read in any circumstances.

Until every dog used for breeding is permanently identified, in a way which can be easily read by individual breeders, judges and veterinary surgeons, breeding must rely heavily on trust. When a bitch is taken to be mated to a particular stud-dog the owner of the stud-dog must accept on trust the identity which its owner offers. He must also accept, on trust, that the brood-bitch has not already been mated and will not again be mated after she leaves his kennel. Similarly, the bitch's owner must accept on trust the identity of the stud-dog used. When puppies are eventually born and registered that is no way, short of tissue analysis, of verifying that they are the product of the mating described on the registration documents.

CHAPTER 8

Care of the Pregnant Brood-Bitch

It should not be assumed that after a bitch has been mated she will prevent other dogs from mating her, or that they will have no interest in her. Indeed the experience may well increase her efforts to find another suitor. Until her owner is absolutely certain that she is no longer in season, which might be anything from a week to a fortnight after she has been mated, she should be kept strictly away from all dogs.

The Stages of Pregnancy

Pregnancy lasts, on average, for sixty-three days, though the norm can vary from breed to breed. Puppies born five or six days before full term may survive, but their chances of doing so are much reduced. Those whose birth is delayed two or three days beyond full term are also at some increased risk, if only because they may have grown too big to be born naturally.

During the first four days after mating has taken place, the fertilized cell will divide into two cells; at five days it will have become four cells; at six days eight cells; and by the eighth or ninth day it will have developed into a multi-celled morula which will then pass down the uterine tube and into the uterus. By the fifteenth day of pregnancy, a hollow spherical blastocyst will have formed, and by the eighteenth day it will begin to develop a placenta.

At this stage, the conceptus begins to attach to the walls of the uterine horns, and occasionally within the uterus itself. Attachment is made through the developing placenta which produces villi (analogous to roots), which grow into depressions (crypts) in the uterine wall. Attachment serves two purposes: it gives the developing foetus more security than it had in the free-floating stage and it provides – through the umbilical cord which joins the placenta to the foetus – the means by which it can be supplied with nourishment. Much of the placenta consists of partially coagulated blood which, during the course of a developing pregnancy, normally degenerates into a dull green colour, the appearance of which during parturition may alarm those who expect any flow of blood to be bright red.

By about twenty-one days, the placentae will have attached to the uterine wall, thus ending the vulnerable, free-floating stage of the blastocyst's development. Prior to this they are very vulnerable and might be aborted if the bitch is subjected to trauma or stress. For this reason she should return to her

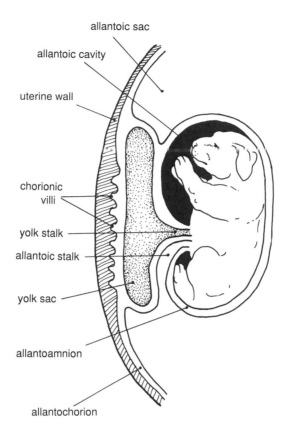

allantoic sac

allantoic cavity

uterine wall

chorionic villi

yolk stalk

allantoic stalk

yolk sac

allantoamnion

allantochorion

Structure of the foetal unit.

customary life as soon as possible after mating and be protected from any undue stress. Visits to shows or other events where infection may be picked up and where she will be under some stress are best avoided. It may be significant that some of the most remorselessly campaigned show bitches have very poor fertility records. By continuing to show them during the early stages of pregnancy their owners may well have sacrificed – for a few more weeks of competition – the chance of breeding another as good or better specimen of the breed.

At three weeks, the puppy's central nervous system will have developed and during the next week the brain and spine begin to develop. During the fourth week sex determination takes place and the puppy's eyes begin to develop.

From the sixth week, growth becomes rapid causing, especially with a large litter, the bitch's outline to undergo noticeable change. At fifty-seven days after fertilization, puppies are capable of independent existence though skilled attention would be needed if they were to survive outside the womb at this stage.

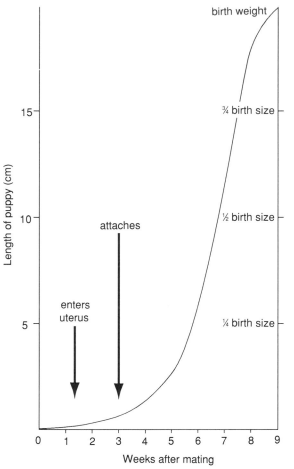

The rate of growth during pregnancy accelerates rapidly from the sixth week.

Absorption

Even during the early days after implantation, the embryos remain vulnerable to stress and may be aborted or reabsorbed if conditions become hostile. Ultrasound examination during the course of pregnancy has revealed that absorption is a far more frequent occurrence than breeders might have imagined. Vets spaying bitches that have never produced puppies frequently discover scars on the uterus wall, which shows that puppies have been implanted but not carried to full term. So it is apparent that stress during pregnancy could lead to the whole or partial loss of litters without breeders' being aware of the fact.

Pregnancy Diagnosis

As pregnancy develops, the signs become increasingly apparent: a swollen and slightly flushed vulva, enlarged teats, a slight but growing corpulence and slight behavioural changes are all indicative of pregnancy. These usual and behavioural indications of a developing pregnancy will also be present if the bitch is undergoing a false or phantom pregnancy, so they cannot be treated as wholly reliable guides.

At this stage curiosity might overcome prudence and the breeder may wish to have the pregnancy confirmed. Unless there is some better reason for doing so than merely satisfying curiosity it is usually best to let nature take her course and avoid subjecting the bitch to tests.

None of the currently available methods can do other than confirm that the bitch is in whelp at the time of the examination. None can predict the likelihood of reabsorption during the early stages of pregnancy or of spontaneous abortion at any stage. Both become more likely if the bitch is subjected to stress, possibly even the sort of stress produced by the examination itself. No method can be totally reliable as a negative indication. Solitary puppies might easily avoid all attempts to detect their presence, then emerge before a surprised and unprepared breeder. Prudent breeders should continue to treat any mated bitch as though she were in whelp until the passage of time confirms beyond all doubt that she is not.

Palpation

From about the third until the fourth week of pregnancy the developing embryos – themselves far too tiny to be felt – are surrounded by a bag of fluid which enables their existence to be verified by means of skilled and gentle palpation through the bitch's flanks providing, of course, that the bitch is prepared to co-operate by remaining relaxed throughout the procedure and is herself not obese.

By about the fifth or sixth week, the nodules will disappear under surrounding fluid and tissue. Palpation becomes much more difficult to carry out but by this time other pregnancy indicators should be apparent.

Inability to find indications of pregnancy should not be taken as conclusive proof that the bitch is not in whelp. If puppies are few in number, high in the uterus, tucked up under the rib cage, if the bitch is over-weight or if she remains tense during palpation, it may not be possible to make a positive diagnosis.

Even if palpation indicates the presence of developing puppies it is not sufficiently accurate to verify their number or that they will survive to full term.

Palpation involves some degree of risk of damaging the developing embryos. It should only be carried out by a skilled person and never without good reason.

Ultrasound

Ultrasonic pregnancy testing, using either doppler or amplitude depth equipment, utilizes sound waves which detect the pulses of unborn puppies or are reflected from the bags of fluid in which they are contained. The accuracy of the diagnosis improves as pregnancy develops. In man, the large size of a single foetus makes it possible to detect foetal abnormalities by the use of ultrasound; in dogs this use has thus far been limited to the diagnosis of *hydrops foetalis*, a condition in which the foetus becomes grossly enlarged with fluid.

Ultrasound can also detect pyometra before clinical signs appear; this enables treatment other than surgery to be considered and so increases the possibility that a bitch's fertility can be preserved.

Blood Tests

It is also possible to make use of blood samples to confirm pregnancy at three to four weeks, but again there should be a very good reason for conducting the test. As with other means, a blood test will not guarantee that the pregnancy progresses to full term.

X-Rays

Once puppies have developed to the stage at which their skeletons are formed it is possible to detect their presence by means of X-rays. Because of the risk of damage to the unborn puppies the use of X-rays on pregnant bitches should, if possible, be avoided.

Foetal Heartbeats

When the pregnancy is well advanced it becomes possible, using an aural or electronic stethoscope, to hear foetal heartbeats.

Pregnancy Termination

If an unplanned or otherwise unwanted mating takes place a single injection of the hormone oestrogen, which has the effect of bringing the bitch back into season and so aborting the, as yet, free-floating embryos, will end the pregnancy without risk or harm to the bitch. However, this method is effective only up until twenty or so days after conception.

The bitch should then be treated as though she were again undergoing a normal, fertile season and should be kept more closely confined than during her previous season. It is unlikely that she would again conceive were she to be mated but, if she had not ovulated during her previous season could do so during what is, in effect, an induced season. In which case she would become pregnant if she were to be mated again.

Sex Determination

In the past breeders have tried all sorts of weird and wonderful methods to influence the sex of unborn puppies. The use of acid or alkaline medicines and douches, mating at certain times of the year, or early or late during oestrus, have all been tried. As long ago as 1928, C.J. Davies, in his *Theory and Practice of Breeding to Type* put the whole thing in a nutshell.

It comes within the experience of every breeder to get periods when one sex preponderates; if he continues breeding on similar lines he may reasonably be assured that, according to the law of probability, approximate equality will ultimately be regained if observation is carried on over a sufficient number of cases. Disappointing as it may be to find

that sex can be controlled neither by food nor by mechanical means, yet it is at the same time satisfactory to know for certain that it is a waste of time and energy to endeavour by those methods to ensure the production of young of any particular sex.

Davies's remarks remained true until very recently when experimental attempts to produce progeny of the required sex showed a fair chance of success. When experimental methods become practically applicable, almost certainly in association with the use of AI, they will have considerable economic value to livestock farmers. In existing circumstances their value to all but a few specialist dog breeders may be less obvious but there may be circumstances in which a need to determine the sex of puppies would be an advantage.

Sperm is sorted by means of a flow cytometer, which distinguishes small differences in the DNA content of X- and Y-bearing sperm. The technique has been used on cattle, sheep and pigs since 1986, and on rabbits since 1989. No gross anatomical abnormalities were seen during the six years up to 1993. From 1993 another sorting method, using a fluorescence-activated cell sorter fitted with an ultraviolet laser, became available. Both sorting methods, however, remain too slow to produce the quantities of viable sperm required for artificial insemination. As yet their use is confined to *in vitro* fertilization to produce embryos of predetermined sex.

Diet Before Whelping

Although the development of mammary

and uterine tissue during the first half of pregnancy may make some bitches appear more than usually rotund, foetal growth during this period does not make demands which call for significantly increased nutritional intake. If the bitch was in good health when she was mated, neither under nor grossly over weight, and providing her diet is adequate, no adjustment to her intake will be required until about the sixth week of pregnancy. At this stage a progressive increase of about 10 per cent a week, resulting in an intake at birth of about one-and-a-half times her normal intake, will be sufficient to keep her and her unborn puppies in good health.

A less than adequate diet may result in her being in poor condition to face the immense demands of rearing her litter once they are born, but may have little effect on unborn puppies. Restricting a bitch's diet in the hope of restricting the pre-natal growth of her puppies is unlikely to be successful. On the other hand, a diet that is excessive in either bulk or nutrition may produce abnormal growth in the puppies or may make the bitch so fat that birth is made very much more difficult. At the very least too much food will lead to unnecessary discomfort for a heavily gravid but greedy bitch.

A heavily gravid bitch may appreciate her daily intake of food split into two or more smaller meals, which will be less likely to overload her constricted stomach.

Worming

The two main larval roundworms to affect dogs are *Toxocara canis* and *Toxascaris leonina*. In adult dogs *Toxocara canis* larvae may migrate to tissues and there remain inactive as cysts, beyond the reach of some anthelmids. Hormonal changes during pregnancy reactivate the larvae and from about the fortieth day of pregnancy they are capable of transplacental migration to infect unborn puppies. Puppies may also become infected from maternal milk. They, in turn, will reinfect the dam as she licks them and cleans up their faeces. It is entirely possible that worm infestation has a significant effect on prenatal and early postnatal survival rates, and for this reason alone is a matter of some importance. The slight but nevertheless real risk of human infection and damage demands the conscientious use of effective worming regimes.

At present, fenbendazole is the only product licensed in Britain for use on dogs which claims to reduce pre-natal transfer. In the USA, ivermectin is the preferred substance but though this is available in Britain it is not licensed for use on dogs. Work on milbemycin oxime in the USA suggests that this may also be effective against a variety of intestinal worms as well as against both demodectic and sarcoptic mange. The new substances are far more effective than the older piperazine, but themselves may soon be replaced by a cocktail of epsiprantel, nematocide and pyrantel, which promises to be effective against all or most of the worms that commonly infect dogs – something which no current wormers offer.

Trevor Turner (*see* Bibliography) has proposed a regime consisting of daily dosing with fenbendazole from the fortieth day of pregnancy until eighteen days after whelping, but concedes that such a regime would be expensive to carry out. Nevertheless, the cost would easily be recouped if the regime led to higher puppy survival rates, and would also be justified on both canine and public health grounds.

A survey carried out during 1993 by Canine Concern Scotland conclusively showed that, with regular worming, *Toxocara* infestation can be effectively eliminated from dogs. The dogs in the sample studied (mostly adults), had been wormed on average three times a year. Only one – a dog that had not been wormed for eight months – produced evidence of *Toxocara*, and even then produced an egg count that was only one sixth of the average produced by other surveys. The conclusion was spelled out by George Leslie, who organized the survey: 'Responsibly owned dogs create no serious health risk to their owners or to any other human beings.'

Whelping Quarters

The first and most important criteria for the place in which a bitch will give birth are that it should be familiar to her and meet with her approval. If the place is prepared well in advance of the event she can, after making whatever adjustments she regards as necessary, become accustomed to it and regard it as her own.

A whelping box needs to be big enough to allow the bitch to stretch out and soft enough to give her and her pups comfort. (Photo: Edminson)

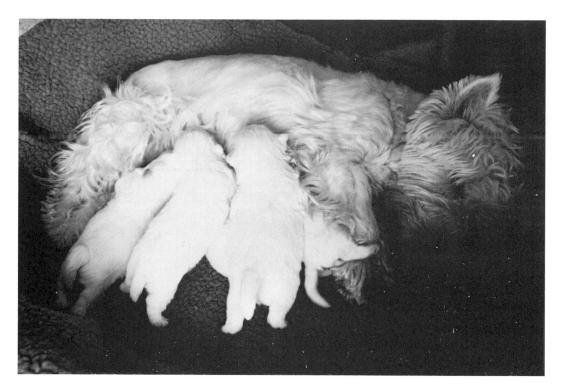

With small breeds it may be more convenient for whelping to take place in the breeder's home, rather than in an outside kennel. (Photo: Kernick)

The design of whelping quarters is almost infinitely variable, providing that certain essential requirements are met. They must be clean – clinically clean – and be capable of being maintained in that state throughout their occupation by a young and not particularly fastidious growing family. They must be warm and be capable of being kept warm, especially at and for the days immediately after the birth. The whelping quarters must be secure, both to prevent excursions by their increasingly active occupants and to prevent incursions by inquisitive members of the household.

The box must be large enough to allow the bitch to lie on her side with her head and legs fully extended. If it is fully enclosed, which improves security and retains heat, the height must be sufficient to allow the bitch to stand upright. Cramped boxes make it difficult for a bitch to adjust her position without fear that she may injure her puppies and her discomfort may quickly lead to a lack of interest in caring for their needs.

A rail round the inside perimeter of the box may help to prevent puppies from being flattened by a heavy or clumsy bitch, but the majority of bitches quickly become adept at curling themselves round their litter and forming a warm and secure enclosure between their body and legs.

Bedding might consist of newspaper, which the bitch will probably thoroughly enjoy shredding and turning into a primeval nest, prior to giving birth. Towels are easily washed but many breeders now place great faith in the synthetic fur-like washable fabrics originally developed for the comfort of long-stay hospital patients.

Size, perhaps more than anything else, may dictate whether bitches are whelped within the home or in a kennel. If space is available, it is often more convenient for the birth to take place in the breeder's home. It is easier to keep the bitch under constant surveillance and as her pups grow they will become accustomed to the sights and sounds of a busy household and the breeder will get the maximum enjoyment out of the exercise.

Temperature

During pregnancy puppies enjoy an environment which is maintained at a constant temperature of 101.5°F (38.6°C). Perhaps, in order to prepare them for their entry into the outside world, the bitch's temperature will fall before the birth takes place and their own temperature at birth is several degrees lower than this. The puppy will emerge into a world of which it has no knowledge and no experience, will be wet, tired and sore and, for the first time, must find its own food. The process of drying and getting its first vital feed will drain already depleted stores of energy and the puppy's body temperature can fall quickly.

Even in an environment that is as warm as 79°F (26°C) an isolated, newly born puppy can quickly become hypothermic. As it becomes colder it will complain pitifully and will search frantically for warmth; eventually it will cease to complain and will become torpid, its motor activities having become atrophied. At this stage the puppy can be revived by gentle warmth but beyond this stage revival becomes progressively more difficult. For the first few days of their lives puppies require a temperature of about 75°F (23.8°C), so the whelping quarters must be able to maintain this. A solicitous bitch, housed in a well-insulated whelping box, will usually provide most of the heat that is necessary but in extreme cold, or if the bitch is not as solicitous as she should be, supplementary heat might be needed.

Tolerance of low temperatures increases rapidly as the puppy grows, and by the time it is ten days old it can tolerate a temperature as low as 60°F (15.5°C).

A well-insulated, enclosed box may need no supplementary heat but, during the first few days after birth, additional insulation in the form of blankets or a foil survival blanket will help to maintain the necessary temperature.

Supplementary heat is most easily, cheaply and safely provided by means of infra-red heaters, the height of which must be carefully adjusted to ensure that the family are warmed without being cooked or dehydrated. Heat pads, which provide a gentle warmth for puppies to lie on, are also available and, providing that the bitch does not amuse herself by chewing into live wires, they are quite excellent.

CHAPTER 9

Whelping

It is usually said that the gestation period of domestic dogs is sixty-three days – nine weeks – but as experience will continually remind breeders, nothing is invariable. In the absence of other factors puppies born on or after the fifty-sixth day are usually sufficiently well developed to be able to survive; and birth may be delayed until the seventy-second day without threat to the puppies.

In addition, what may be regarded as normal varies from breed to breed. All sizes of Poodle appear to have a slightly shorter than average gestation period as do a number of toy breeds. The larger breeds, Great Danes and Dobermanns, for example, appear to have a slightly extended gestation period.

This is the time when the nerves and confidence of even the most experienced breeders are stretched almost to their limit and for the new breeder it can be a traumatic experience. All the necessary preparations will have been made both to inform themselves of what the process entails and of the signs that may signal the stage it has reached or that the process is not progressing normally. However, even experienced breeders find it difficult not to become apprehensive and nervous as a bitch approaches the time when she is due to give birth. Unless a breeder is fortunate enough to have an experienced friend who is prepared to oversee the event he will be very much

alone. Many veterinary surgeons will never have attended a normal birth and few will be able to devote sufficient time to do other than attempt to repair matters if things appear to be going wrong and this, for perfectly good reasons, they will probably only undertake in their surgeries.

Some breeds, particularly brachycephalic ones, usually small ones or those with narrow or steeply angled pelvic girdles, are prone to whelping difficulties. In these breeds problems are to be expected and a breeder should be prepared for them. In the majority of breeds, however, whelping remains a normal, if traumatic event which, given a modicum of knowledge, a degree of skill and a cool head even a new breeder need not find too daunting.

Certainly every whelping is different and few are entirely devoid of minor dramas. Breeders, of any livestock, realize that the more they breed the more problems they are likely to encounter. They seek to avoid them either by good planning or good fortune but they know that all sorts of problems are waiting in ambush.

The process of parturition is, in biological terms, composed of three phases. In practical terms it is often difficult and even impossible for even an experienced breeder to say when the first stage has started, when it gives way to the second

A whippet bitch just a few hours before whelping. The puppies are now being carried low, ready for birth. (Photo: Rawlings)

stage, and to differentiate between the second and third stages. Normal and uneventful whelpings may take no more than a few hours but can last for two or three days. Even so, events proceed according to a strict sequence and it is helpful if breeders are aware of the precise process.

First Stage

Perhaps the first firm indication that a bitch has moved into the first stage of labour is provided by a drop in her temperature, from the normal 100–100.5°F (37.7–38°C) to about 98°F (36.6°C). Use of a sterile, lubricated rectal thermometer will indicate when the temperature has fallen, after which birth

may be expected in the next twenty-four to forty-eight hours.

The first stage of parturition involves an involuntary and complex action of the pituitary gland, the ovaries, the supra-renals, and the placentae and puppies in the uterus. The signs may not in themselves be perceptible other than by clinical changes in the bitch's temperature, and in her behaviour. The bitch will probably become restless and possibly show signs of quite acute discomfort. She may wander about seeking – but seldom finding – ease, and she may be disturbed and apparently quite miserable, even apprehensive, although a phlegmatic bitch or one to whom the process is not new, may be quietly resigned to the discomfort and show few signs of the impending birth.

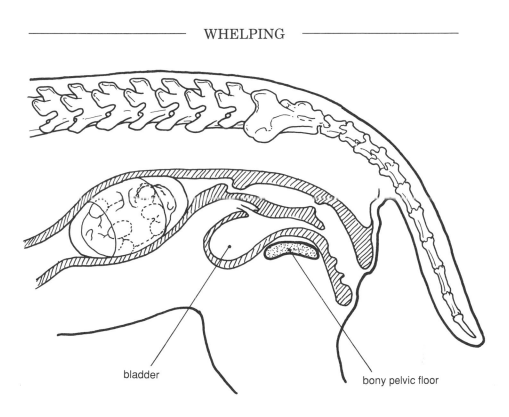

bladder

bony pelvic floor

The first puppy, in foetal posture and still enclosed in its sac, awaits the second stage of birth.

As the first stage progresses, the uterine muscle develops an irregular series of contractions which are discernible neither to the eye nor to palpation. The purpose of these contractions is to relax and dilate the uterus, vagina and vulva and not to expel the puppies. Until the process of relaxation and dilation is fully complete, the birth of puppies cannot proceed naturally. The birth passages will become softened, enlarged and lubricated to facilitate the easier passage of puppies. This first stage may be completed in the space of a few hours or may be prolonged without any need for anxiety. It does not place the bitch under intolerable strain and the puppies at this time remain in the uterus and so in safety.

Second Stage

The second stage of parturition is accompanied by more obvious symptoms. Contractions become regular and apparent, increasing in vigour as the pups' birth becomes imminent. The bitch will pant and sit or lie down in positions that help her to push more efficiently and she will lick her hind-quarters frequently.

The contractions themselves emanate from the muscular activity of the uterus, by which means the pups are forced out of the uterus encased in their foetal membranes – still attached by the umbilical cord to the placenta through which they have drawn their nutrient during the preceding nine weeks – and accompanied by a fluid which assists their journey into

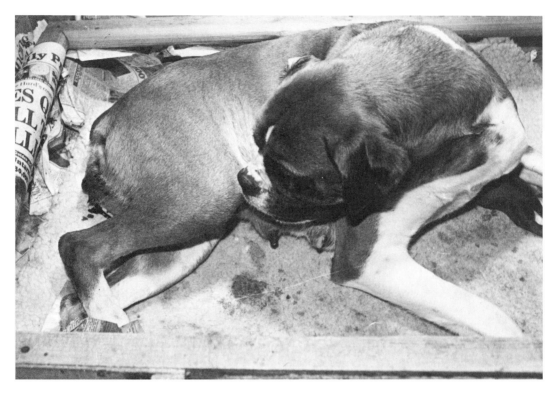

A bitch will usually turn to look at her rear end when the next puppy is about to be born. (Photo: Ward-Davies)

the outside world. The placenta becomes dislodged from its site on the uterine wall and the pup is forced from the uterus through the now dilated cervical canal and into the vagina which passes up, towards and through the pelvic girdle. It is at this point, when pups meet the unyielding bones of the pelvis, that difficulties may be encountered.

The breeds whose construction dictates a rather upright pelvis – making the angle between the floor of the pelvis and the vagina more acute – may suffer from an additional, and perhaps unnecessary, hazard in the way of natural birth. In breeds in which an upright pelvis is also expected to be narrow, thus narrowing the aperture through which the pups must pass, surgically assisted whelpings may be regarded as the norm, and especially so among the brachycephalic breeds.

Once the pelvis has been successfully negotiated, the pups encounter no further hazards to their progress. Normally the pups make the journey head first, a position which, because of the shape of the puppy and the hydraulic action of the accompanying fluids, utilizes the forces exerted by the contractions most efficiently. However, a number of pups make the journey feet first to emerge as a breech birth. Breech births, because of the reduced hydraulic effect and because

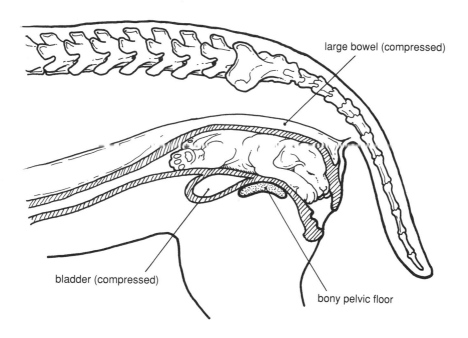

large bowel (compressed)

bladder (compressed)

bony pelvic floor

A normal presentation which makes most effective use of muscular and hydraulic forces to facilitate a trouble-free birth.

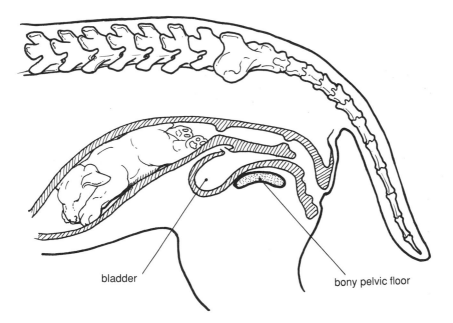

bladder

bony pelvic floor

A posterior presentation that is unlikely to present problems.

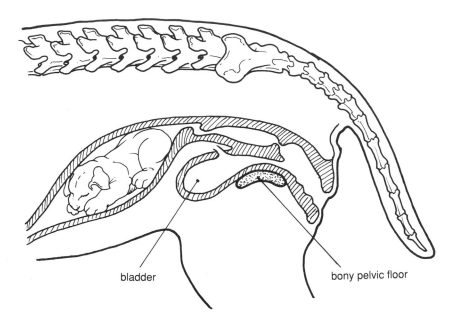

bladder

bony pelvic floor

A breech presentation in which the hind limbs are not extended can be difficult.

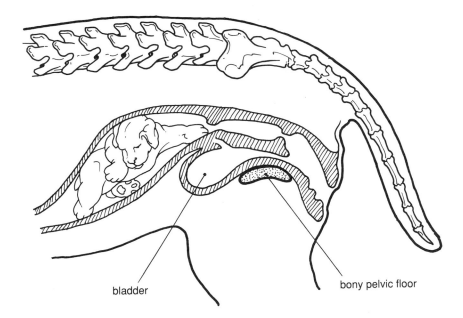

bladder

bony pelvic floor

A basically normal presentation in which one withdrawn forelimb and, consequently, a turned head, may present difficulties.

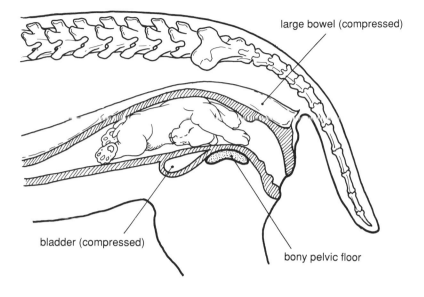

Flexion of the head may offer obstruction to normal birth.

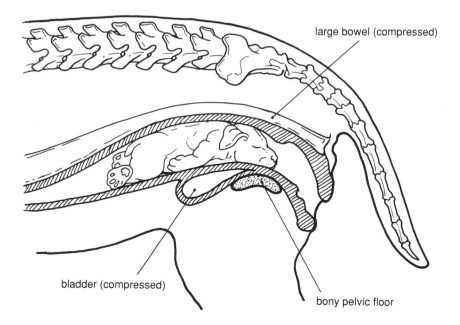

Head forward but forelimbs deflected will cause the shoulder to bulge, thus creating an obstruction.

they present more opportunity for limbs to become wedged against the pelvis are accompanied by more whelping difficulties than the more normal position, but a sufficiently large number of puppies emerge into the world feet first, without difficulty, for the position to be regarded without undue alarm in most breeds.

Puppies may be born no more than a few minutes apart, though as the bitch tires the interval between births tends to get longer. However, an interval of up to two hours is not at all unusual and, providing that the bitch is resting quietly and not distressed in any way, need cause no alarm.

Third Stage

The second and third stages of birth tend to overlap. The third stage is occupied by the process by which continued uterine contractions (allantochorion) dislodge and expel the placenta. In practice, placentae are likely to begin to be expelled before all the puppies have been born.

The Newborn Puppy

When a puppy has been born it needs to be separated from the placenta. Most bitches will do this by nibbling through the umbilical cord before eating the placenta, which contains a substance that stimulates the flow of milk; the bitch will then proceed to lick and clean the puppy. The process is often a vigorous one, accompanied by loud complaints from the puppy itself. The puppy is both cleansed and stimulated by the exercise and will quickly make its way to a nipple and begin to suckle.

Some breeders discourage the bitch from eating the placenta in the belief that it may induce vomiting. This fear is largely groundless, and probably stems – to a great extent – from the breeder's personal distaste for this natural process. Other breeders, especially when the litter is large, compromise by removing some of the placentae, and permitting the bitch to consume the rest.

Some bitches may be reluctant or unable (perhaps because of abnormal dentition) to sever the umbilical cord; others may be only too eager to do so and, in their enthusiasm, may injure the puppy. The breeder needs to supervise the process and to take a hand if the bitch seems to be behaving abnormally.

If the contents of the umbilicus are gently squeezed towards the puppy it can then be severed to leave about ¼in (1.2cm) of cord which, during the next few days will shrivel and disappear. A clean cut tends to take longer to heal than the sort of jagged edge left after the bitch has chewed through the cord, and so the breeder should try to reproduce this jagged edge when cutting the cord. It goes without saying that scissors used to sever the cord must be absolutely sterile.

If the dam's attentions do not very quickly produce a reaction from the puppy, the breeder must take over. The first task is to check that the puppy is not deformed or injured in some way, which precludes its viability. If nothing seems amiss, the puppy's mouth should be cleansed of any mucus, remnants of the amniotic sac should be removed and the puppy given a vigorous rub with a towel. If the puppy does not respond, it should then be taken in one hand, grasped around the body with a finger on each side of the head to provide support, and

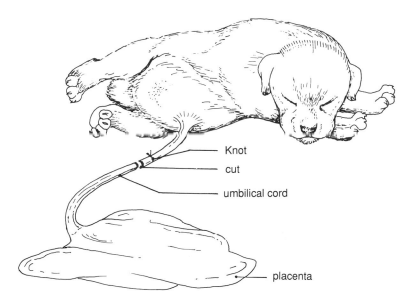

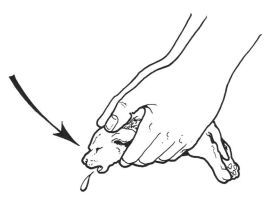

Sometimes it is necessary for the breeder to cut the umbilical cord. The contents of the umbilicus should be gently squeezed towards the puppy and the cord severed with blunt, sterilized scissors. Some breeders prefer to apply a ligature to the cord before cutting.

To clear fluids from the newborn's mouth and lungs, take the puppy firmly but gently with both hands. Then, with the head supported and pointing downwards, swing it in an arc.

swung vigorously in a long arc, the aim being to allow centrifugal force to remove any mucus or fluids from the lungs. After two or three swings, massage can continue. If there is still no reaction, opening the puppy's mouth and blowing gently into it from an inch or so away may help. Lack of response suggests that the cause is hopeless, but no harm is done if efforts are continued.

Recognizing an Emergency

If a bitch has been straining purposefully for much more than a couple of hours without making apparent headway it must be assumed that she is in some difficulty and that her puppies are at risk. To leave the situation untreated may well result in a bitch who, even if her further efforts overcome the difficulty, is so exhausted that she cannot give birth to the rest of her litter which, after such a prolonged delay, face a much reduced chance of survival.

The appearance of a dark-green or blood-infused fluid before the birth of her first puppy suggests that the placenta has separated from the wall of the uterus. The puppy is then deprived of oxygen and must be delivered quickly if it is to survive. The appearance of a similar discharge before the birth of subsequent puppies is perfectly normal.

A yellow fluid suggests that the amniotic sac has ruptured. The puppy should be born within thirty minutes if its chances of survival are not to be impaired.

It is not uncommon for bitches to rest between one birth and the next but puppies are normally born at anything from fifteen minutes to two-hour intervals, the interval tending to become longer as the bitch tires. An interval of three hours should be regarded as an indication of trouble.

If the bitch has ceased to strain, various possibilities must be considered. The first and most obvious is that she has delivered all her pups, in which case she is likely to curl herself protectively round her family to enjoy a well-earned rest. The second possibility is that she is simply taking a rest. The third is that inertia, induced by exhaustion or pain, has set in. Unless it is decided that whelping is complete or she begins to strain again within a reasonable period veterinary assistance must be sought.

Dystocia

The most common cause of puppies appearing to be moribund at birth is dystocia (a prolonged or difficult labour), the most common causes of which are small or abnormally shaped apertures in the pelvic girdle (maternal dystocia) and puppies that are too large or badly positioned to negotiate this obstacle easily (foetal dystocia).

Other causes that are unnecessarily common are obese or poorly conditioned bitches upon whom the demands of giving birth place a stress for which they are unprepared.

Inertia

There are two forms of inertia, primary and secondary. Primary inertia is characterized by a bitch that has completed the preliminary stages of whelping but is then reluctant or unable to begin contractions that will result in the birth of puppies. Primary inertia may be hereditary, and certainly seems to be familial, but it may also result from a bitch being ill at ease in the situation in which she is expected to whelp. It may also occur in bitches that are not in good physical condition or that are carrying an abnormally large litter. When and *only* when the cervix is fully dilated, a pituitrin injection may stimulate contractions and enable the birth to proceed normally, otherwise surgical intervention is called for.

Secondary inertia may occur after a bitch has had contractions and may even have produced puppies. Contractions then cease, perhaps owing to exhaustion, perhaps to some immovable obstruction. If contractions do not resume after a short rest, an injection of oxytocin should provide the necessary stimulation, otherwise a surgically assisted birth is indicated.

The incidence of inertia, in both its forms, can be reduced by eliminating from the breeding programme any bitches that have suffered from the condition, by avoiding exaggerated breed features likely to create parturition difficulties, and by ensuring that bitches are in good physical condition before and at the time of whelping.

Uterine Rupture and Torsion

Both conditions occur very rarely in dogs. Torsion is sufficiently rare to be outside the experience of all but a very few breeders and vets. Rupture is equally rare and may result from inappropriate human intervention – perhaps stimulating contractions before the cervix is fully dilated – and unless surgically repaired can lead to peritonitis. Torsion results in dystocia and calls for immediate surgical intervention.

Assisted Birth

Ideally the breeder should combine constant supervision of the birth with as little interference as possible. Well-meaning but unnecessary efforts to help are more likely to complicate the process than to ease it. However, if the amniotic fluids are expelled before the birth of a puppy, prompt attention is needed if the puppy's life is to be saved.

A hand placed under the abdomen will be able to locate the puppy and gentle pressure can prevent it from slipping back up the vagina. A clean, lubricated finger inserted into the vulva should then be able to ascertain whether the puppy is presented head first or tail first in the

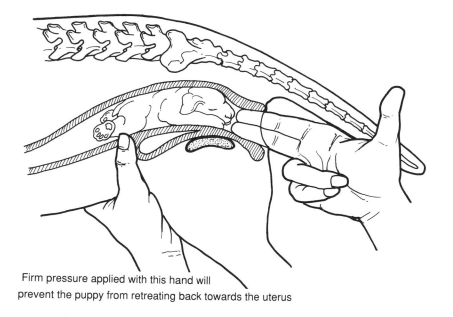

Firm pressure applied with this hand will prevent the puppy from retreating back towards the uterus

Manipulation to ease obstruction is possible only with the larger breeds.

breech position. If the head is found, gentle exploration should discover whether the problem is caused by its being bent to one side, in which case a finger gently inserted into the puppy's mouth can straighten the head and free the obstruction.

In the case of a breech birth, the obstruction is usually caused by one or other of the hind legs but in this case it is often better, once the obstruction has been freed, to take hold of the legs between two fingers and, *only* in unison with the bitch's contractions, gently ease the puppy towards the vulva. It must be stressed that the puppy must *not* be pulled towards the vulva in between contractions.

Similarly, if the obstruction caused by a normally presented puppy seems to be the product of sheer size, a finger placed on either side of the head may enable the puppy to be gently pulled to safety.

If a puppy appears at the vulva only to disappear again, one hand should be placed under the bitch's abdomen to prevent regression, while the other, holding a clean towel to provide grip, should gently ease the puppy through the vulva.

Surgically Assisted Birth

Mechanical blockage, most usually caused by the inadequate size of the pelvic cavity, or the bitch's exhaustion after a fruitless endeavour to give birth naturally, or inertia (occasioned by

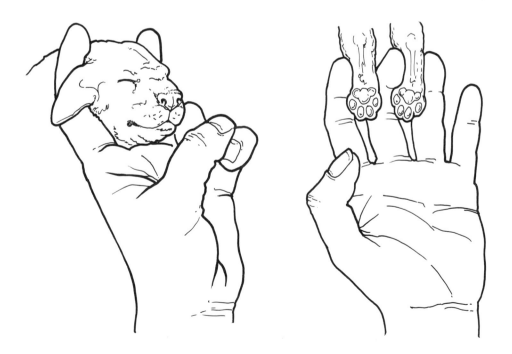

Traction by the head or by the hind limbs, having ascertained the cause of the obstruction. Again, this is possible only with the larger breeds.

exhaustion, pain, hormone deficiency or the absence of lubricants in the vaginal canal), are the most common problems that suggest that surgical intervention is necessary.

Regrettably, in some breeds, usually toys or brachycephalic breeds, the need for surgical intervention is commonplace, and it must be questioned whether the breeding of animals that are unable to give birth naturally should even be contemplated.

Caesarean section is done under general anaesthesia and, when carried out without delay, the risk to the dam is not great and puppy survival rates are good. In the hands of a skilled veterinary surgeon, the bitch will be beginning to rouse as the final stitches are being made,

puppies will suckle quickly and the litter can be raised as though it had been born normally.

If the reason for the Caesarean is unlikely to recur at subsequent pregnancies there may be no reason why the bitch should not be bred from again with every expectation that she will whelp normally. If, however, the reason is likely to recur, caring breeders will seldom submit a bitch to a second surgically assisted birth.

Litter Size

In general small breeds tend to have fewer puppies than larger ones but the general rule is frequently questioned

Large, unexaggerated breeds tend to be prolific and easy whelpers. (Photo: Jackson)

when a toy bitch unexpectedly produces a large litter and a large bitch gives birth to a single puppy. The variation is so large, and is increased by the variable number of still births, as to cast a doubt on the value of detailed figures for individual breeds. In general, however, even an unusually large litter of a small or toy breed is more likely to contain six than seven live puppies, while the average litter is more likely to contain three than four. In breeds similar in size to Basenjis, Boston Terriers, Lakeland Terriers and Miniature Poodles, unusually large litters may contain as many as eight live puppies and ten or more is not unknown, although the average litter will contain four or five live puppies. Breeds of a size similar to Chow Chows, Dalmatians, Kerry Blue Terriers, Samoyeds and Springer Spaniels might all produce ten or more puppies in an unusually large litter, while the average litter is more likely to contain seven than six puppies. The average litter in even larger breeds including the very largest, such as Newfoundlands, Rottweilers, the larger Retrievers and Setters, Siberian Huskies and St Bernards, is more likely to contain seven than eight puppies but unusually large litters may contain as many as thirteen and fifteen, and litters of even more are produced sufficiently often as to occasion no great surprise.

Still Births

Not all puppies are born alive. Some die before the process of birth begins and some during the process. Something between 2 and 2.5 per cent of all puppies are still born, accounting for about 15 per cent of total puppy mortality. The per- centage is slightly higher than the average in both unusually small and unusually large litters. For extremely large litters the number of still births may be as high as 7.5 per cent. It appears that the incidence of still birth is greater among dog puppies than among bitch puppies. Since just over 103 male puppies are born for every 100 females the lower survival rate of males goes some way towards redressing the balance between the sexes.

Culling

Whatever the size of the bitch she is unlikely to have more than eight service- able teats and many, especially in the smaller breeds may have no more than six that are fully operative. Thus a litter with more than six or eight puppies produces a level of competition for the available sustenance in which small or weak puppies in the litter will be at a disadvantage. Left to their own devices some may not survive and so the breeder has to make a choice between reducing the size of the litter to a number with which the bitch can cope, and supple- menting from birth the food the bitch is able to supply for her puppies.

In any case, all the puppies must be checked at birth to ensure that none is deformed or injured during its birth. These puppies should be destroyed at birth. In some breeds, most notably harlequin Great Danes and Dalmatians, as well as in several breeds in which all- white individuals are not acceptable and are also prone to deafness, breeders may choose not to rear grossly mismarked puppies. Destroying newly born puppies is a horrible task but it is a task that the

In several breeds, colour marking is extremely important, so breeders must decide whether or not to rear mismarked puppies. (Photo: Jackson)

conscientious breeder will not shirk. Rearing weak, injured or deformed puppies may seem humane but is likely to result in the production of still more weak or deformed puppies if these are ever bred from, as some surely will be. Culling is neither easy nor pleasant but may sometimes be necessary if the breed and the breeder's reputation are to be kept in good health.

Puppy Mortality

Puppy survival rates vary considerably from breed to breed, from bitch to bitch, and from breeder to breeder. Published information shows that somewhere between 12 per cent and 33 per cent of all puppies will die before weaning age.

These pathetic deaths are in themselves distressing enough and the sheer waste of efforts made by bitch and breeder, the lost opportunities and disappointed anticipation they represent, make it imperative that breeders, by means of good management, strive to reduce this tragic waste.

Over two-thirds of all puppy deaths occur prior to birth, during birth, or during the first week after birth, with slightly more than half of them occurring prior to birth and slightly less than half during the first week of life. This then appears to be the period towards which breeders should direct their greatest attention.

Still birth, dystocia, and death during birth account for 26 per cent of all puppy deaths. Better selection of bitches that are likely to be able to give birth without difficulty, coupled with better management during pregnancy, would have the greatest impact on losses prior to and during birth.

Better selection of bitches and better management by breeders would also appreciably reduce the losses sustained during the early weeks, and in particular the first week of life, when exposure to sub-standard conditions (16 per cent) and accidents (6 per cent) – both of which are entirely within the breeder's control – account for over one quarter of all puppy deaths. To this might also be added some part of the 10 per cent that succumb to disease – better management could surely reduce loss through this cause. Further puppy deaths are also caused by what can

in part at least be regarded as failure on the part of the bitch. Crushing, cannibalism, excessive licking and trauma together account for 29 per cent of all puppy deaths. Anecdotal evidence suggests that excessive losses from these causes are breed related. Selection of bitches for maternal qualities might dramatically reduce these unnecessary losses.

Post-Partum Care

Once the breeder is sure that the whelping is over and complete, bedding should be changed, and puppies checked once more for injury, malformation, sex

A proud bitch curls protectively round her young family. (Photo: Rawlings)

and weight. The bitch should be offered an electrolyte drink and be encouraged to cleanse herself, though she may be very reluctant to leave the nest. Her first motions after giving birth may be dark and almost treacle-like, owing to the ingested placental material. She may also have a green or brownish vaginal discharge for up to three weeks, but this is no cause for alarm.

After about twenty-four hours, her milk supply should be checked. A pearly fluid discharge is normal; a thick, yellow secretion may well suggest an infection. She should also be checked for the presence of retained puppies or placental material. If all seems well she should be left in peace with her new family and the breeder can look forward to some weeks of demanding but enjoyable activity.

Feeding the Bitch

Pregnancy and rearing a litter place enormous stresses on bitches, and especially so if the bitch is elderly or the litter large. Breeders must ensure that bitches are in tip-top physical condition before they are mated and do their utmost to ensure that pregnancy and nursing does not debilitate them. Prior to birth, food should be changed to something more nutritious than is needed for normal maintenance and the quantity slightly increased. After the birth not only should the more nutritious diet be continued but, as the puppies demands increase, the quantity of food should slowly be increased. Exact quantities and the frequency of meals will vary from breed to breed, but as a general guide by the time the pups are three weeks old the bitch should be having more than three times her normal daily intake.

The proprietary foods available for pregnant and nursing bitches provide the correct nutrition, are convenient to use for the breeder, and avoid the necessity of creating home-made dishes that may not be ideal. The packaging of proprietary foods nowadays invariably offers information about the food's nutritional values and it is a simple matter to tailor a pregnant or nursing bitch's diet to her actual needs.

CHAPTER 10

Postnatal Care and Development

By the time the puppies are born they will have been individual, if parasitic, beings for almost nine weeks and will have thrived according to how each was placed in the uterus and according to how their dam was treated before and during her pregnancy. Some puppies will die prior to or during the birth; others will die soon afterwards. Low birth weight, large litter size and low antibody levels have a great effect on survival rates. The three factors are linked: small individuals tend to occur in large litters and large litters make it more difficult for small puppies to suckle while colostrum, which boosts antibody levels to provide resistance to infection, is present in the bitch's milk. The disadvantage that small puppies labour under at birth increases as more vigorous siblings grow more quickly. Early growth rates are, therefore, important as indicators of health and vigour and so also of the potential to grow into quality adults. Weak puppies account for about 5 per cent of postnatal deaths.

The majority of postnatal deaths are

The aim of every breeder is to produce litters that are consistent in type and even in size. (Photo: Jackson)

caused by factors, of which low temperature is probably the most important, which are entirely within the control of the breeder. The bitch too is often responsible for the death of her puppies. Trauma or crushing accounts for a high proportion of all postnatal deaths.

Once a litter of healthy puppies has been born the breeder must face the demanding, but usually enjoyable, task of rearing them to the point at which they are independent and can go to their new homes. During the early days of life survival is, to a large extent, governed by birth weight, by the number of puppies in the litter, by resistance to infection, by the bitch's health and attitude towards her offspring, and by environmental conditions.

During the early days after birth a careful watch should be kept on every puppy to ensure that it is thriving, that the bitch is cleaning them up well and that umbilical cords are healing properly. The bitch's teats should also be carefully examined to ensure that all are functioning well. She should be carefully checked to ensure that any slight vaginal discharge which remains does not indicate a problem. If the discharge is slight, dark reddish or greenish brown and not smelly, all can be assumed to be well. If it is smelly it is time to summon a vet. Some vets no longer make house calls but no vet worthy of the name would expect a bitch with a litter a few days old to be subjected to the trauma and possibility of infection attendant on a visit to his surgery.

At the outset the breeder must make a decision as to whether very small and weak puppies, especially those in large litters, should be culled or whether efforts should be made to save them from otherwise inevitable decline and death.

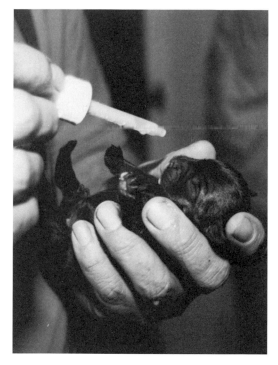

Some breeders routinely give newborn puppies a course of antibiotics. (Photo: Jackson)

Many breeders routinely use oral doses of a mild, broad-spectrum antibiotic in order to ensure that all puppies carry some degree of protection against infection. Some have found that routine use of antibiotics has dramatically increased survival rates.

Weight

Many breeders weigh all their puppies at birth and, in the course of time, collect a quantity of valuable information, but this information is seldom available to novice breeders. Weighing puppies at birth and regularly afterwards provides an effective

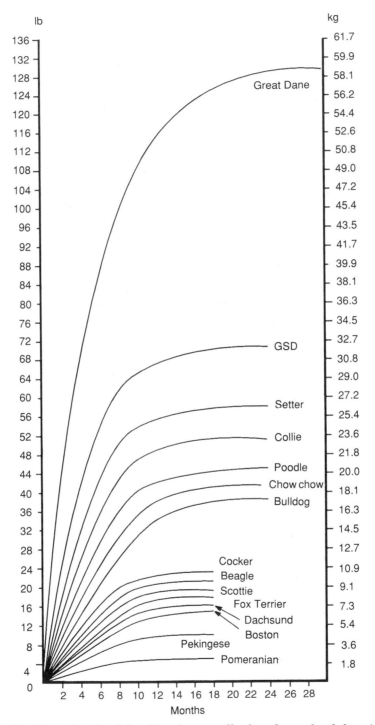

Growth curves for fifteen breeds of dog. Note how smaller breeds reach adult weight much earlier than the larger breeds. (Courtesy of R.W. Kirk, Cornell University, Ithaca, New York.)

indication of their development, enabling supplementary food to be given or withheld as appropriate.

Low birth weight is often associated with large litters and with bitches in poor health or condition.

A healthy, well-fed puppy will double its birth weight in the first nine days of life and by the time it is three weeks old will have quadrupled its birth weight. A normal human infant will double its birth weight in five months and may not quadruple its birth weight until it is well over two years old. Food intended for human babies is designed to fuel a relatively slow growth rate and so is unsuitable for rapidly growing puppies.

Growing infant mammals tend to prioritize their diets first to develop brain, then bone, then muscle and finally fat. An adequate diet is thus essential to intelligence, body size and conformation. Breeders who deliberately withhold food from growing infants in an effort to restrict growth may well achieve their aim but are likely also to produce unintelligent dogs with poor conformation.

Postnatal problems may conveniently be divided into those that affect the bitch and those that affect the puppies, though it must be realized that any that affect the bitch may also affect the puppies.

Postnatal Problems in the Bitch

Acute or Post-Whelping Metritis

Infection of the uterus and the birth canal is most likely to occur as a result of retained foetal material, a placenta or even a dead puppy. Infection may also be introduced by the use of dirty instruments or probing fingers.

A miserable bitch showing little or no interest in her puppies with an elevated temperature and a thick, greenish-brown and foul-smelling discharge should be suspected of having an infection. It is an extremely serious condition which can be fatal. Antibiotics can be effective but are by no means a guaranteed cure; occasionally an ovarohysterectomy is necessary. Veterinary advice should be sought immediately and preparations made to rear the litter by hand, although prompt attention to clear the uterus of infection and its cause may well result in the bitch's being able to continue to care for her litter.

Mastitis

A deformed nipple, small litter or a superfluity of milk may result in mastitis, in which one or more teats become swollen, hot, hard and painful. The breeder should check the teats daily to check for the onset of this condition.

Manual expulsion may relieve the condition if it is mild, and as the puppies grow and the milk supply adjusts to the demand the problem may spontaneously disappear.

Inflammation and swelling of one or more nipples resulting from infection may be caused by lacerations caused by the claws of eager puppies. The bitch may be reluctant to feed her puppies and may herself be listless and have a high temperature. The infection may be passed to any puppies that suckle from the affected nipple.

Scrupulous attention to hygiene and keeping claws well-trimmed, supported by the routine use of antibiotics, should avoid the problem. Treatment with antibiotics will cure it but may involve weaning the litter prematurely.

Eclampsia

Also called Puerperal Tetany and Milk Fever, this problem, which is most likely to affect bitches nursing large litters and toy bitches, is caused by the drain of calcium from the bitch.

She may appear restless, over-excited and may move in a jerky, unco-ordinated manner. Her face and lips may be drawn and, as the condition progresses, she may salivate profusely and be unable to stand. This is an emergency and unless treated the condition is fatal.

Intravenous calcium injections must be given as quickly as possible after symptoms have been noticed. A balanced calcium, phosphorus and Vitamin D supplement should then be added to the bitch's diet; but this is not sufficient to treat the condition initially; veterinary assistance must be sought immediately.

The condition is most frequently the result of a diet deficient in calcium, phosphorus and Vitamin D, but seems also to be familial in some breeds.

Placental Subinvolution

Placental subinvolution – the failure of the uterus to return to its normal size – may produce a slight blood-infused discharge which, though inconvenient, is not injurious to health and will usually right itself at the bitch's next season.

Placenta Retention

Prior to parturition the placenta detaches from the uterine wall and still attached to the puppy, proceeds with it down the birth canal, to be voided and subsequently eaten by the bitch as she severes the umbilical cord. Occasionally a placenta will become detached from the puppy prior to birth, it may even be that twin puppies share a placenta, so that the number of puppies born may not always correspond with the number of placenta seen by the breeder. This situation gives rise to fears that a placenta may not have been expelled during birth.

During the course of the next few days the discharge of green-tinged blood will gradually become pink before ceasing altogether. A discharge that becomes darker or foul-smelling may indicate the retention of placental or foetal material, or of developing metritis. Veterinary help should be sought without delay.

Resentment of Interference

Occasionally highly strung bitches, or those whose natural instincts have been eroded, may simply refuse to care for their puppies, may be antagonistic towards them, or may threaten their well-being with an over-solicitous display of maternal concern – constant licking, nibbling at the umbilicus, moving them from one part of the nest to another, and even attempting to hide the puppies outside the nest. In such cases the only solution to the problem may be to rear the puppies as orphans. The problem is less likely to occur if the selection of brood-bitches is, to some extent, based on maternal performance.

While it is perfectly natural for bitches to be protective of their puppies, well-adjusted bitches seem also to appreciate the attention of owners and other

A proud mother with her young litter. (Photo: Carey)

members of the household, although such attention should always respect the bitch's wishes. Some bitches, however, may be so disturbed – even by necessary efforts to keep the whelping quarters clean – that they indulge in behaviour which puts the puppies or the breeder at risk. Resentment may take the form of frantic attempts to hide the puppies or aggression towards the source of interference.

Unless the puppies can be transferred to a more tolerant bitch or can be hand-reared or weaned, the immediate problem for the breeder is to find some means of carrying out regular cleaning of the whelping quarters and inspection of the puppies. Mildly tranquillizing the bitch may also help. If the bitch can be enticed away for feeding or on some other pretext then so much the better.

Once the problem has been solved the

When youngsters are not your own, patience and tolerance may be stretched to the limit. (Photo: Edminson)

breeder will need to consider whether or not the bitch should ever again be bred from and, indeed, whether any surviving puppies should themselves be bred from.

Postnatal Problems in the Puppy

Fading Puppy Syndrome

Some puppies, apparently healthy at birth, may simply fail to thrive and may die within a few days of birth. Sometimes a single puppy in a litter will be affected, sometimes several, and occasionally an entire litter. Several possible causes have been identified for deaths resulting from this 'Fading Puppy Syndrome'. These include *Beta haemolytic streptococci, Escherichia coli, Brucella canis, Toxoplasma gondii*, canine adenovirus, canine herpes virus infections and the effects of various anaerobic organisms. Congenital defects, unsuitable environmental conditions, poor nutrition and the consequences of a difficult birth are also likely to be implicated.

Routine use of appropriate antibiotics prior to mating the bitch and in newborn puppies, coupled with strict attention to hygiene, careful control of environmental conditions and constant supervision, all help to reduce the incidence of Fading Puppy Syndrome even if they are unlikely to totally eliminate it. If a puppy is suspected of suffering with this condition the vet should be consulted.

Toxic Milk Syndrome

Another problem which appears to have a number of not yet fully understood causes is that which goes under the general label of Toxic Milk Syndrome. Symptoms, in the form of salivation, diarrhoea, bloated stomach, discomfort and distress, tend to appear from three to fifteen days after birth. Puppies must be removed from the dam and reared by hand.

Swimmers

The characteristic sprawling of swimmers (puppies suffering from Flat Puppy Syndrome) becomes progressively more apparent as puppies approach two weeks of age and make no effort to stand. Their legs remain spread to each side of the body and the chest becomes progressively flattened. The problem seems to occur most frequently with unusually heavy breeds and obese puppies. The problem may be aggravated by slippery floors which deny puppies the grip that might enable them to stand. Some puppies may recover spontaneously or after being

Lateral support of a 'swimmer's' forelimbs may help it to learn to stand.

encouraged and assisted to walk, perhaps aided by a hobble which prevents the limbs from splaying outwards. However, the likelihood of future heart and respiratory problems casts doubts on the wisdom of rearing swimmers.

Herpes

The symptoms of herpes virus infection – reluctance to feed, discarded puppies, crying, abdominal distension and spasms associated with a greenish-yellow diarrhoea – appear before puppies are three weeks of age, when their body temperature rises above the 98°F (36.6°C) necessary to the virus's incubation. Fatality is high and puppies that do recover often have residual kidney damage which may lead to death within a few months.

Umbilical Infections

Cutting the umbilicus with dirty instruments, contact with dirty surfaces in the nest, the reluctance of the bitch to cleanse her puppies, and efforts to raise orphans in less than sterile conditions, may all give rise to infections of the umbilicus. The umbilicus needs to be cleansed, treated with antibiotics and the conditions that caused the infection removed.

Haemorrhage

Puppy blood does not readily clot until the puppy is three or four days old and may then be prevented from doing so by inherited defects. Regular inspection of newborn puppies, especially around the umbilicus and anus – areas in which internal haemorrhage may be indicated – will identify the problem at an early stage

when treatment with Vitamin K may effect a cure.

Conjunctivitis

Occasionally a discharge emanating from unopened eyes may be noticed. The condition is caused by infection under the eyelids and treatment is difficult until the eyes open, when bathing the eyes will usually cure the problem.

Pyoderma

Dirty and particularly abrasive conditions may cause puppies to develop a rash of pus-filled spots. Clean bedding that does not harbour the bacteria that cause the condition is the best preventative; cure is effected by changing bedding and treating puppies with a suitable anti-bacterial agent.

Hypoglycaemia

Low blood sugar produces listlessness and depression, muscular weakness, tremors, convulsions, coma and death. Stress, caused by irregular meals, low temperatures, too much exercise or excitement, especially associated with a change of home, may all precipitate the condition. Repeated attacks may result in permanent brain damage.

Access to an electrolyte drink and sensible care and diet will avoid the problem. Treatment with glucose given orally or intravenously is usually successful unless the condition is produced by an inherited enzyme deficiency.

Juvenile Hypoglycaemia

This is the commonest metabolic disorder

to be found in young, weaned puppies. It is characterized by fits, disorientation, weakness, unco-ordination, collapse, hypothermia, depression and behavioural changes, and it appears to be aggravated by stress induced by worming, vaccination and infection.

Because puppies, especially those of toy breeds, have small livers and skeletal muscle mass, they are deficient in stores of glucose substrates and glycogen. In puppies that have been subjected to a prolonged fast these stores might become exhausted and the symptoms of hypoglycaemia will become apparent.

Affected puppies usually make a complete recovery but frequent meals – with, for puppies thought to be at risk, ready access to an ionizer enriched drink – will help to prevent the problem.

Hernias

Hernias may occur in either umbilical or inguinal forms. A hernia consists of a small external, malleable swelling, formed by the abnormal protrusion of abdominal organs and their contents.

Umbilical hernias obtrude through incompletely closed umbilical rings. The tendency is probably inherited. Umbilical hernias may disappear spontaneously or be surgically repaired.

Inguinal hernias result from protrusion through the inguinal canal to cause a small swelling in the groin. They may prevent descent of the testes and, if they involve the uterus, can cause problems for adult bitches. Inguinal hernias should be surgically corrected.

Jaw Malformations

Over- or undershot jaws may, except in the most severe cases, not be noticeable until after the eruption of primary teeth or even after permanent teeth are in place at about four months of age. In some, mainly brachycephalic breeds, an undershot jaw is acceptable; in the majority both overshot and undershot jaws are regarded as a fault. The faults are hereditary and should be avoided in any breeding stock.

Cleft Palate

If the two halves of the hard palate do not join together soon after birth, the puppy may experience difficulty in suckling and so will fail to thrive, although a small cavity may have no other discernible effect than a nasal discharge of milk. Brachycephalic and other short-nosed breeds are most susceptible. Puppies with cleft palates should be culled.

Hare Lip

Often associated with cleft palates hare lips result from a failure of the two halves of the upper lip to fuse. Puppies have trouble in suckling especially if the condition is associated with a cleft palate. Culling is indicated.

Open Fontanelle

Chihuahuas may retain an open fontanelle throughout life but in other breeds the gap that remains as a result of the failure of the bony plates of the skull to fuse is regarded as a serious problem. Such puppies are susceptible to brain damage and should be culled.

Kinked Tail

A screw tail or kinked tail, regarded as

normal only in the Bulldog, is a disfiguring rather than a disabling fault. Damage at or shortly after birth is often advanced as an explanation, but in most cases the kink should be regarded as a spinal deformation. There is some evidence that kinked tails are associated with spina bifida.

Puppy Strangles

Staphylococcal infection resulting in rapid swelling of the head and neck may occur in one or several puppies in a litter. It is thought that the condition occurs as a result of an immune system deficiency. Affected puppies must be isolated but effective treatment is problematic and the prognosis doubtful. Culling must be considered.

Orphan and Supplementary Feeding

As stronger puppies grow more rapidly than their siblings, small puppies may fall further behind in the struggle for survival. Unless the breeder makes an effort to supplement their nutrition, they can have little hope of survival and even less of growing into strong and healthy adults. Supplementing the diet of weak puppies follows basically the same pattern as rearing orphan or rejected puppies, though if the bitch or a foster mother is available to provide warmth, to lick them to promote excretion, to keep them clean, and to stimulate their physical and mental development, the task is immeasurably easier than rearing solely by hand.

Bitches' milk has over twice the calorific value of either cows' or goats' milk. It is also over twice as rich in fat, protein, calcium, phosphorous and dry matter. Neither cows' milk nor goats' milk provides an adequate substitute for bitches' milk, nor do proprietary human baby foods, which are intended for a slow-growing infant and not for the rapid development a puppy must make if it is to grow into a healthy adult.

There are a number of good proprietary substitutes for bitches' milk on the market which may be used either as a sup-

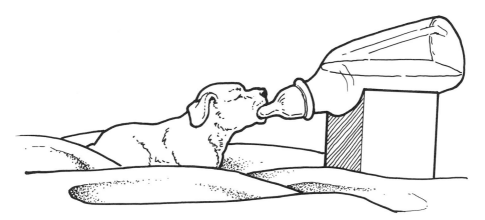

Puppy nursing from a bottle stand.

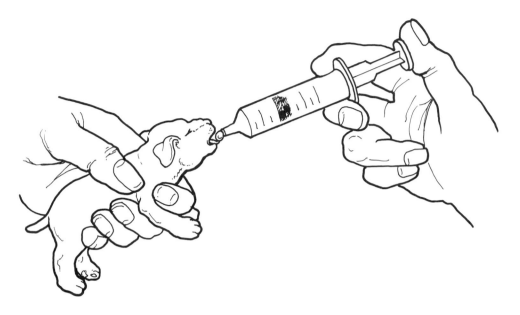

Feeding a puppy with a syringe should be carried out with great care. The puppy should be held in the position shown – never on its back – while the fluid is syringed into the mouth. It is safer to 'drip' the liquid into the mouth so that you can see that each drop is being swallowed before administering more; syringing 'unseen' may force too much food into the mouth and thence into the lungs (indicated by the appearance of liquid oozing from the nostrils), causing pneumonia.

plement to the diet or as a replacement. Care should be taken to follow the manufacturer's instructions scrupulously; well-intentioned adjustments invariably have the effect of making the food worse rather than better and may make it quite unsuitable for very small puppies. Before puppies are born, breeders should ensure that they have an emergency supply of pre-weaning food and the means to administer it. If this is not possible, boiled water will prevent dehydration while supplies are found. If more than a few hours elapse before a good proprietary bitches' milk substitute can be obtained, a pint of high-fat cows' milk homogenized

with a dessertspoonful of good-quality, fresh cooking oil and 1oz (28g) of caseinate will provide an acceptable substitute. Some breeders regularly collect very small amounts of colostrum from their suckling brood-bitches, and then freeze it, to be warmed and fed to puppies that are orphaned during whelping.

The food, given at a temperature of 100.4°F (38°C) can be administered by means of a small syringe, by a puppy feeding bottle or by an intra-gastric tube. A syringe is probably the best method of giving supplementary food because it avoids the possibility that the puppy

A dedicated brood-bitch cleaning her eighteen-day-old pups. (Photo: Kernick)

might become confused between two different sucking techniques. After a drop of food placed on the tongue has been swallowed another can be given and the puppy will quickly learn to anticipate the next drop when it has swallowed the previous one. Small feeds, given slowly at two- or three-hour intervals may be necessary at first, but as the puppy gains strength feeds may be reduced to five or six, evenly spaced throughout the day remembering, of course, that the puppies with their dam feed during both day and night, so it is a round-the-clock task.

In the case of orphan puppies, where total responsibility for feeding lies with the breeder, some people prefer to use an intra-gastric tube. Orphan puppies not only need food: they also need an artificial replacement for the humid warmth that is normally provided by a solicitous dam. An incubator is, of course, the ideal way of providing the right physical environment, but a heated pad within a box of suitable size can be used to provide adequate conditions for the puppies. If there is no foster mother available, nor even a maternal bitch who will carry out the necessary duties other than feeding, the breeder will have to perform these artificially. A warm, damp piece of cotton wool or cloth, used to massage the pups' abdomen after each meal, will encourage the pup to pass urine and faeces. This is extremely important because very young puppies will not perform this basic function spontaneously. Similarly, eyes, nostrils and anus must also be kept clean.

Some breeders may well find that the relentless physical and emotional demands made by the task of rearing an orphaned litter may be beyond them. In which case, if the puppies are to survive, someone must be found to undertake the

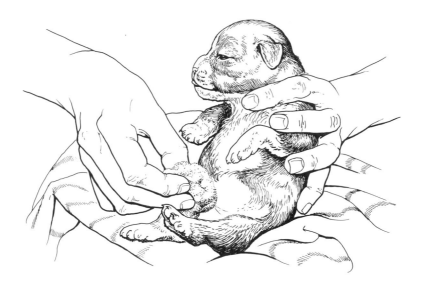

Simulating the dam's cleansing and massaging of the orphaned whelp in order to stimulate the puppy's bowel and bladder. This should be done after every feed, with dampened cotton wool or cloth.

task. Kennel clubs and veterinary surgeons should be able to provide information about the availability of specialist rearing services whose equipment and expertise will far outstrip that of all but the most practised breeders.

Novice breeders have little to guide them as to which puppies require supplementary feeding. Puppies born to breeds of similar size may themselves vary considerably in size. Even within the same breed newborn puppies may vary within a very broad range of size.

Identification

In litters in which puppies are of an even size, the same colour, and all of one sex, it is essential that some means of identifying individuals is used. Breeders have devised a number of imaginative methods ranging from clipping small areas of hair, to marking nails with nail varnish or coats with waterproof cosmetics or with some harmless, indelible substance, such as gentian violet or dye used for marking lambs.

Docking and Dew-Claw Removal

Operations to dock tails or remove dew-claws must – if they are going to be done at all – be carried out before the puppies' eyes open, usually between the third and fourth day. In some countries, including Britain, docking by lay persons is illegal although vets, in spite of vigorous discouragement from their professional bodies, remain free to carry out the

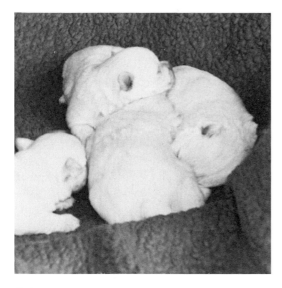

Colour apart, very young puppies are very similar whatever the breed; within one litter, it can be almost impossible to distinguish one from another. (Photo: Kernick)

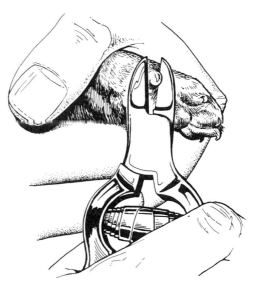

Dew-claws should be removed before the eyes open, and usually about three days after birth, either by the vet or by an experienced person using sharp sterile scissors or clippers.

operation if they believe it is in the puppies' best interests.

Lay persons may still remove dew-claws. These vestigial thumbs are normally to be found only on the front legs. In a few breeds, rear-limb dew-claws are required; in most they are regarded as undesirable and are customarily removed. They are easily removed with a pair of sharp, sterilized scissors, and the operation causes no more than momentary discomfort.

Parasites

Dogs are no different from any other animal species, including our own, in that they play host to a variety of more or less unpleasant internal parasites some of which periodically give rise to bouts of misinformed public hysteria.

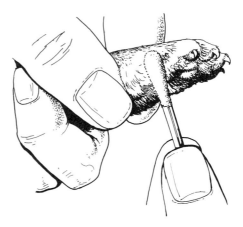

Permanganate of potash, Friar's balsam or a styptic pencil applied to the wound will seal it, stemming blood flow and preventing the entry of disease. (Drawings not to scale.)

Internal parasites range from single-celled protozoa, some harmless, some a threat to health. These variously inhabit the intestinal or bronchial tracts or the blood and lymphatic systems. They give rise to a variety of symptoms which require expert veterinary diagnosis and treatment. The majority of these problems are not present in Britain. Those which arrive in imported dogs are treated and eliminated during quarantine, an aspect of the value of quarantine which is often obscured by concentration on rabies.

Helminths, or worms, form the other main body of internal parasites. These include the nematodes or roundworms, cestadodes or tapeworms, and a variety of largely tropical trematodes or flukes. Fortunately the modern pharmacopoeia offers an increasing array of more effective treatments which will kill parasites and sometimes prevent their reappearance.

Most roundworms are transmitted from dog to dog, some can also infect humans and other species, and many – in egg and larval form – are capable of remaining viable for a considerable period. The most common species of roundworm are *Toxocara canis* and *Toxascaris leonina*. In puppies, symptoms include a cough, a pot-bellied appearance, and general loss of condition; in adult dogs, in whom *Toxacara canis* usually lies dormant, symptoms are rarely apparent.

A great deal of irresponsible and alarmist nonsense is spoken and written about the alleged dangers posed, particularly to young children, by *Toxocara* infestation. In Britain, a country with over 56 million people and over 7 million dogs, about twenty to thirty toxocariasis patients – of whom by no means all will have been infected as a consequence of contact with dogs – are treated each year

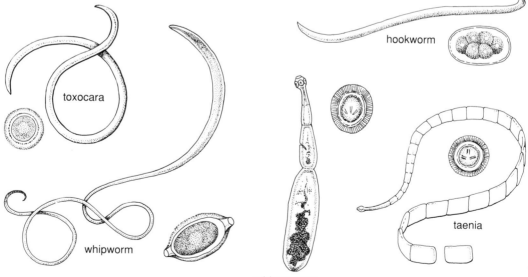

Some parasitic worms and their eggs (not to scale).

at the Hospital for Tropical Diseases in London. The majority suffer no lasting damage as a result of their infection and, contrary to sensationalist claims, there is no record of any ever having been blinded, though some have had the vision of one eye impaired.

Recent tests carried out in various parts of the country have revealed that about 3.15 per cent of the dog population tested positive for *Toxocara* infection, compared to 45.7 per cent of foxes, 11.5 per cent of domestic cats, and 53.3 per cent of feral cats (*see* paper by Bryden, A.S., Kershaw, W.E. and Storey, D.M., 'Toxocara in Dogs, Cats and Foxes, in the British Isles', 1995). All dogs and cats should be regularly wormed.

It has been shown that while piperazine used on puppies at two, four and six weeks old would reduce infestation by over 86 per cent, it had little effect on the production of eggs, the source of reinfestation. Fenbendazole, however, reduced egg production by 95 per cent. Since puppies may be infested *in utero* and from colostrum and milk, they may begin to shed eggs at three weeks of age. Treatment must, therefore, begin prior to this, preferably at two weeks of age and, with fenbendazole, should continue at two-weekly intervals until six or eight weeks of age.

An alternative regime consists of worming puppies at weekly intervals from fourteen to forty-two days and then at monthly intervals until six months, then at six-monthly intervals (or more frequently with piperazine or pyrentel embonate).

Tests have shown that treatment of adult dogs on three consecutive days with piperazine resulted in a reduction of 35.5 per cent in *Toxocara canis* infestation and a 63 per cent reduction in *Toxascaris*

leonina infestation; the same regime using fenbendazole resulted in a 94 per cent reduction in *Toxocara canis* infestation and a 92 per cent reduction in *Toxascaris leonina* infestation. Fenbendazole was also 100 per cent effective against the whipworm *Trichuris vulpis*, whereas piperazine had no discernible effect.

Tapeworms, *Dipylidium caninum* and *Echinococcus granulosus*, require a somewhat different control regime although cocktails exist that are effective against both roundworm and tapeworm. *Dipylidium* tapeworms are transmitted by fleas, *Echinococcus* tapeworms in infected offal, particularly from sheep, or from contaminated ground. *Echinococcus* is not widespread, but it is common in sheep-rearing areas of the UK. This should be of considerable concern because the larvae of this worm produce life-threatening cysts in man, one of its intermediate hosts. In other sheep-rearing countries, regular and effective worming programmes have rendered it almost non-existent. Tapeworms appear to be comparatively harmless to dogs although symptoms may include weight loss, and abdominal pain. Worm segments can often be seen in the faeces. By controlling fleas and either by thoroughly cooking all meat or, better still, avoiding feeding anything which might be infected, it is usually possible to avoid tapeworm infestation. Treatment with a praziquantel vermicide is effective.

Other types of worm include hookworms (the common *Uncinaria stenocephala*, *Ancylostoma caninum*, the tropical *Ancylostoma brasiliense* and the Asiatic *Ancylostoma ceylanicum*); whipworms *(Trichuris vulpis)*; heartworms *(Dirofilaria immitis)*; and lungworms *(Filaroides osleri)*.

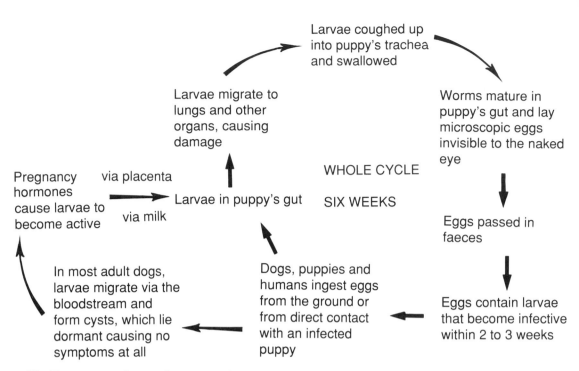

Larvae coughed up into puppy's trachea and swallowed

Larvae migrate to lungs and other organs, causing damage

Worms mature in puppy's gut and lay microscopic eggs invisible to the naked eye

WHOLE CYCLE

Pregnancy hormones cause larvae to become active

via placenta

via milk

Larvae in puppy's gut

SIX WEEKS

Eggs passed in faeces

In most adult dogs, larvae migrate via the bloodstream and form cysts, which lie dormant causing no symptoms at all

Dogs, puppies and humans ingest eggs from the ground or from direct contact with an infected puppy

Eggs contain larvae that become infective within 2 to 3 weeks

The Toxocara canis *roundworm is white, often coiled, and up to 8in (20cm) long. Its complicated lifecycle (shown here) means that almost all puppies are born already infected.* Toxascaris leonina *is similar but has a much simpler lifecycle; larvae inhabit the stomach and intestine; they do not migrate to other organs, nor can they be passed to puppies via the placenta or milk. Infection in man is not serious.*

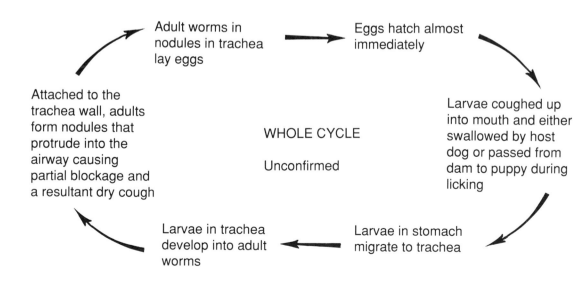

Adult worms in nodules in trachea lay eggs

Eggs hatch almost immediately

Attached to the trachea wall, adults form nodules that protrude into the airway causing partial blockage and a resultant dry cough

WHOLE CYCLE

Unconfirmed

Larvae coughed up into mouth and either swallowed by host dog or passed from dam to puppy during licking

Larvae in trachea develop into adult worms

Larvae in stomach migrate to trachea

The lungworm Filaroides osleri *is commonest in breeding kennels. It inhabits the trachea (windpipe), usually near the lungs, where it forms a nodule up to ¾ in (2cm) long.*

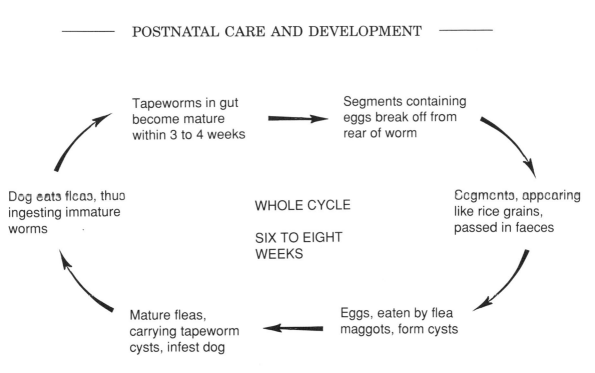

The lifecycle of Dipylidium caninum, *a tapeworm growing up to 20in (50cm) long. The worm's intermediate host is the flea; it cannot be passed directly from dog to dog.*

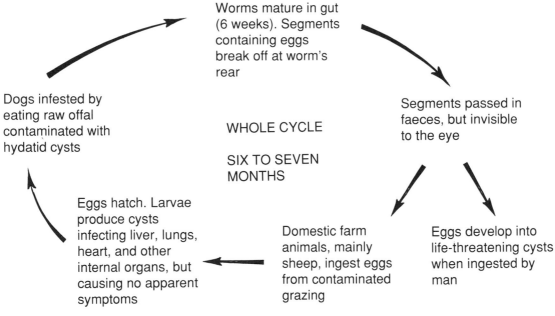

The hydatid tapeworm Echinococcus granulosus *is very small, less than ½ in (1cm) in length, and has only three or four segments. Infection in man is extremely serious.*

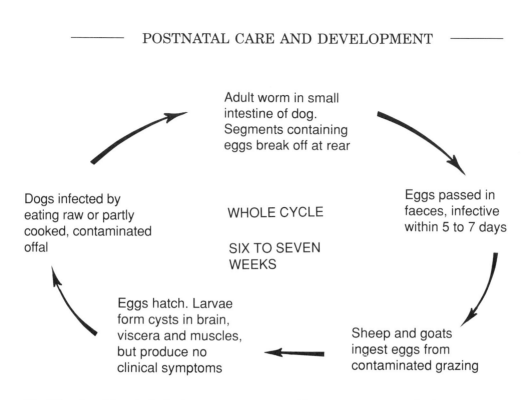

Adult worm in small intestine of dog. Segments containing eggs break off at rear

Eggs passed in faeces, infective within 5 to 7 days

WHOLE CYCLE

SIX TO SEVEN WEEKS

Dogs infected by eating raw or partly cooked, contaminated offal

Sheep and goats ingest eggs from contaminated grazing

Eggs hatch. Larvae form cysts in brain, viscera and muscles, but produce no clinical symptoms

The lifecycle of Taenia hydatigena, *a tapeworm with many segments, which can grow up to 16ft (4.8m). It is one of many* Taenia *species, all of which form cysts in the intermediate host.*

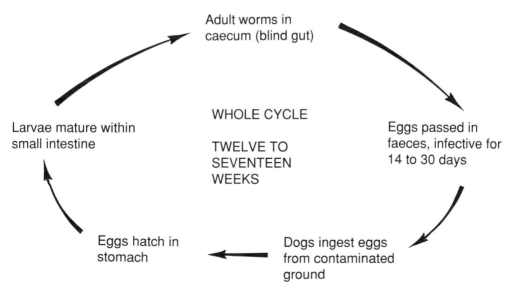

Adult worms in caecum (blind gut)

Eggs passed in faeces, infective for 14 to 30 days

WHOLE CYCLE

TWELVE TO SEVENTEEN WEEKS

Larvae mature within small intestine

Dogs ingest eggs from contaminated ground

Eggs hatch in stomach

The lifecycle of the fairly uncommon Trichoris vulpis *whipworm, which grows to about 2in (5cm).*

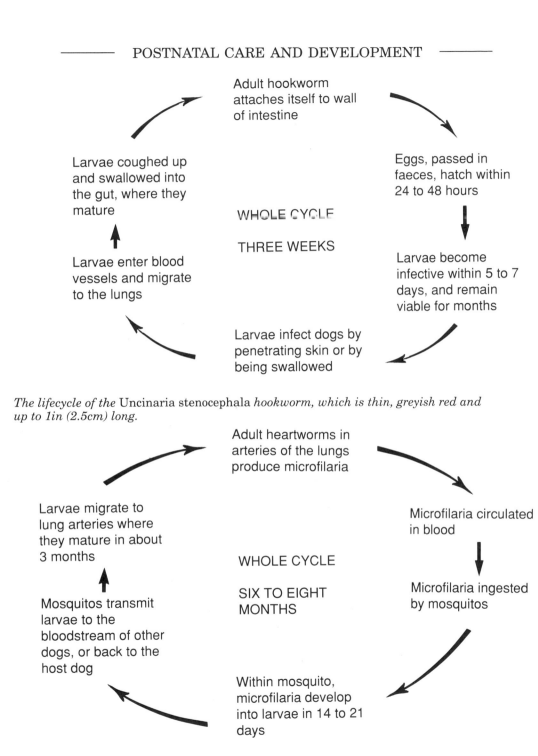

Adult hookworm attaches itself to wall of intestine

Larvae coughed up and swallowed into the gut, where they mature

Larvae enter blood vessels and migrate to the lungs

WHOLE CYCLE

THREE WEEKS

Eggs, passed in faeces, hatch within 24 to 48 hours

Larvae become infective within 5 to 7 days, and remain viable for months

Larvae infect dogs by penetrating skin or by being swallowed

The lifecycle of the Uncinaria stenocephala *hookworm, which is thin, greyish red and up to 1in (2.5cm) long.*

Adult heartworms in arteries of the lungs produce microfilaria

Larvae migrate to lung arteries where they mature in about 3 months

Mosquitos transmit larvae to the bloodstream of other dogs, or back to the host dog

WHOLE CYCLE

SIX TO EIGHT MONTHS

Microfilaria circulated in blood

Microfilaria ingested by mosquitos

Within mosquito, microfilaria develop into larvae in 14 to 21 days

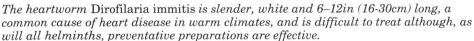

The heartworm Dirofilaria immitis *is slender, white and 6–12in (16-30cm) long, a common cause of heart disease in warm climates, and is difficult to treat although, as will all helminths, preventative preparations are effective.*

Hookworms are picked up by contact with infected dogs and infected faeces; they either penetrate the skin or are ingested orally. In large numbers they will cause weight loss, bloody diarrhoea and inflammation of the skin. Treatment with pyrantel pamoate or fenbendazole will control but not entirely eliminate infestation.

Whipworm infestation is picked up from contact with contaminated faeces. Whipworm may cause diarrhoea, which in severe cases is accompanied by dehydration and abdominal pain. Treatment with oxantel pamoate or fenbendazole every six weeks is effective.

Heartworms are found only where mosquitos (the intermediate host) are present and are a common cause of heart disease in warmer climates. A dry cough, weight loss, lassitude, oedema and anaemia are the principal symptoms. Veterinary treatment over an extended period involving injections of levamisole and dithiazine iodine may eliminate the infestation but residual heart and lung damage may occur.

Proprietary worming compounds are available in suspension form, paste, granules or tablets, the first two being the most convenient for worming young puppies.

Using a syringe to worm young puppies ensures that each pup receives the correct dose. (Photo: Rawlings)

Diet

Weaning

Wild carnivores, including wild dogs, wean their young by regurgitating partially digested food for them. The puppies solicit this food by licking the lips and mouths of adult members of the pack, a pattern of behaviour which domestic dogs retain and sometimes direct towards the human members of what they regard as their pack. Some owners may find this 'kissing' less attractive if they realized what response is expected of them!

Weaning puppies should be made as simple as possible. By the time the puppies are about three weeks old they will be exploring their nest and soon after will be giving every sign of being dissatisfied with their diet of mother's milk. If they are offered a bowl of suitable food while the bitch is absent, sharpening appetites will soon direct their attention towards it.

A circular trough designed so that the litter can feed from one bowl. (Photo: Photovogue)

When the bitch returns she may be allowed to finish the food, her example providing further stimulation to the puppies. Within a few days the puppies will be eating independently and should then have the number of meals increased to four or five as the bitch's ability to satisfy growing nutritional needs decreases.

There are several good proprietary puppy foods on the market. The dry foods should, at this early stage in the weaning process, be well soaked in warm water but as the puppies adapt to their new diet it can be fed dry, providing, of course, that the puppies have access to a constant supply of clean water – which should be available regardless of the type of diet. The puppies may be allowed to feed to repletion from a generously charged dish. Care should be taken to ensure that every puppy receives its fair share of food and that none is being bullied by stronger siblings. By the time the puppies are five weeks old they should be having four or even five meals a day and the bitch will be spending little time with them. They will effectively be weaned and can become accustomed to living without contact with their mother in order to prepare them for transfer to their new homes from about eight weeks of age.

Expert rearing contributes to good bone, straight limbs and optimum growth. (Photo: Jackson)

Dietary Additives

Breeders are sometimes persuaded to supplement proprietary diets, which are already well balanced, with added vitamins and minerals. By doing so they undo much of the careful work of those who research, formulate and manufacture these foods. Worse still they expose their puppies to the risk of ingesting too much of some vitamin or mineral which, in excess, can cause positive harm.

The range of foods now available makes the use of dietary supplements obsolete, except in the most exceptional cases when under veterinary supervision.

Vaccines

Young puppies, like young children, have to combat a number of diseases that appear to prey, if not exclusively then certainly primarily, on the young. Fortunately several of these juvenile infections that used to wreak such havoc among puppies, killing many and leaving others permanently damaged, have largely become a thing of the past thanks to the effect of vaccines.

Although the first vaccines against distemper were produced before the turn of the century, they were not markedly successful, and in 1907 the British Board of Agriculture organized the first of several official investigations into the disease. Even so it was not until after the Second World War that vaccines provided reasonably reliable protection against this and other diseases but even these might have unfortunate side effects.

Even the modern generation of vaccines are not 100 per cent reliable. They may provoke a reaction, may be masked by maternal antibodies, or be overwhelmed by massive infection, a new or more virulent strain of the disease, or, especially where dogs are subject to stress and insanitary living conditions, may fail to provoke the appropriate immune response. Such failures are, however, very rare and certainly do not provide any reason for withholding the protection that modern vaccines offer.

Puppies derive some relatively small degree of immunity to disease through the placenta. This is boosted, to about 75 per cent of their dam's level by the colostrum, hence the importance of suckling during the first few hours of milk production when colostrum is present in the milk. Hence also the importance of ensuring that the vaccination programme of brood-bitches is up to date before they are mated.

Vaccines that utilize killed viruses still provoke the desired immune response, but since the virus itself is dead, there are no problems with 'shedding' or danger of reversion to an infectious state.

Puppies receive some degree of protection from their dam but vaccination should be carried out as soon as this maternally derived immunity begins to fade, usually at about eight or ten weeks of age but sometimes even earlier. Puppies will need an initial injection followed, at not less thán fourteen days, by a second. Occasionally, especially if the first injection was made while puppies were under about ten weeks of age, a third injection may be needed. Annual booster doses are required for some of the diseases.

Initial injections usually cover canine distemper, hepatitis, the two forms of leptospirosis, parainfluenza and parvovirus, which are given in the form of a vaccine 'cocktail', abbreviated to DHLPP. In countries where rabies is endemic, vaccines to protect against this disease are usually compulsory and subject to strict controls.

Alternative Treatment

Concern about the long-term effect of reliance on modern veterinary techniques has led to increased interest in the use of homoeopathic and herbal remedies. The absence of reliable clinical studies, coupled with what appear to be outrageous claims (to prevent hip dysplasia or cure rabies), do little to inspire confidence. Nevertheless, a growing number of dog breeders rely on the use of alternative treatments and have faith in their efficacy.

Behavioural Development

Satisfying the bodily needs of puppies is only a small part of rearing a litter. It is equally important to ensure that their mental development is such that it will enable them to grow into well adjusted adults capable of taking their proper place in society.

Puppies that are deprived of human contact and a wide range of experience for the first few weeks of their lives are unlikely to make satisfactory pets: they may be difficult or even impossible to

Play is an important part of growing up. (Photo: Kernick)

train, and will lack the ability to make a close attachment either with human beings or their own kind. The term applied to the process of gaining the experience that will enable puppies to grow into well-adjusted adults is 'socialization'.

For puppies, the period between five and twelve weeks of age is critical. In human beings the same critical period of development occurs between twelve and fifty-two weeks. Deprived of social contact they will grow up to be emotionally isolated, shy, anti-social, possibly aggressive and unhappy, but given an overprotective environment they will lack independence, will be maladjusted and emotionally inadequate. Puppies that are reared during these critical weeks entirely by people, will lack the ability to

make normal relationships with other dogs, they may become aggressive or fearful, and might be useless for work, show or even breeding. Given a stimulating environment they will have the opportunity to develop normally.

The canine equivalent of the traditional supposed seven ages of man are reduced to six, each well defined by changes in behaviour, response to stimulus and ability. However, the time when different breeds move from one period to another is subject to considerable variation. Scott and Fuller have shown that Beagle and Cocker Spaniel puppies open their eyes, produce teeth and wag their tails more quickly than Fox Terrier puppies.

The Six Ages of Dogs

Neonatal Period

The neonatal period begins at birth and continues for about two weeks during which time puppies, in normal circumstances, are entirely dependent on their dam for their survival. At this stage neurological development is not advanced though head nerves and muscles associated with a strong rooting reflex necessary for feeding, and the ability to regain an upright position, are well developed. During the first four or five days a puppy will adopt a prenatal flexor position, its back arched, its limbs retracted under its body. From about five days this position is replaced by an extensor response in which the back is hollowed and the limbs are extended.

During these first few days of life puppies will normally spend up to a third of their time, day and night, feeding. Vigorous puppies may suckle up to

Any object that carries a familiar scent is a source of security to a youngster.
(Photo: Anderson)

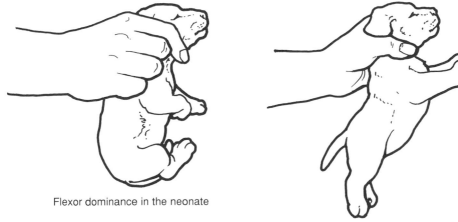

Flexor dominance in the neonate

Extensor dominance in the four- or five-day-old puppy

Early tonal reflexes.

The unfocused gaze of a fortnight-old puppy. (Photo: Jackson)

seventy times during a twenty-four hour period – once every twenty minutes.

Sleep, which occupies two thirds of the day, is characterized by constant slight movement and a contented vocal refrain of grunts, whines and mews.

At about ten days the eyes will open, but not until the next stage of development do puppies respond to light.

Transitional Period

During the third week of life puppies are learning to become independent of the bitch. Their neurological and physical development is rapid. Sense organs, the ears and eyes become functional. The puppy will begin to walk rather than crawl and will learn to lap rather than suck.

Socialization Period

Once the spinal cord has developed sufficiently to enable puppies to stand and walk they are able to explore their surroundings and to experience new activities. They will respond to one another, will begin to play, and will be quite content when the bitch leaves them to their own devices.

The development of instinctive behaviour essential to survival in the wild – stalking, pounding, holding and shaking prey, as well as sexual behaviour – is evident during this period. A hierarchy develops within the litter, which can result in physically or temperamentally weaker puppies being subjected to merciless bullying. In some gladiatorial breeds it is sometimes necessary to separate puppies at this stage.

The way in which puppies are treated during this period, from four to seven weeks, is critical to their subsequent development. Reared in isolation, with limited opportunity to explore and play, subjected to unpleasant experiences at the hands of man, they are likely to grow into nervous and fearfully aggressive creatures unable to make attachments with either man or other dogs.

Hound puppies welcome a young visitor in a generous grass run. (Photo: Edminson)

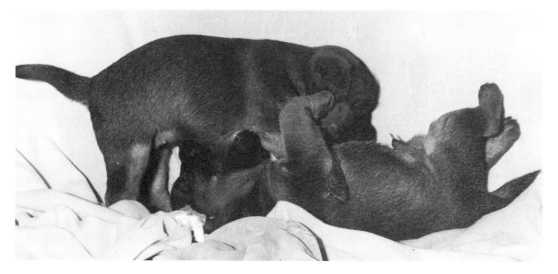

Puppies at play are great time-wasters! (Photo: Jackson)

Breeders should play with the puppies, giving them toys – a cardboard box, a piece of cloth, or anything that will safely encourage them to play – and in all sorts of imaginative ways enable the puppies to enlarge their experience and to grow in confidence as a consequence. Kennels may have a radio, usually tuned to some pop music programme, in order to accustom puppies to strange noises; runs will be converted into miniature adventure playgrounds, with boxes to hide in, tables to climb on and crawl under, ramps, tunnels and all manner of things to explore.

Good breeders are instinctively aware of the critical nature of this short period. They spend a lot of time with their puppies. They ensure that puppies meet other dogs, the household cat and any other animals that share their home. They are exposed to all the sights and sounds of a busy household or kennel and they learn to associate people with a pleasant experience. The lessons learned during this period will never be forgotten and will decide just how well adjusted the puppies are as adults.

Towards the end of this period puppies will become totally independent of their dam and may be allowed to go to their new homes. In many respects puppies appear to adjust more readily to a new environment when they are between seven and twelve weeks old, but at seven or eight weeks they may not be physically robust enough to withstand the conditions they might have to endure in a household unaccustomed to dogs.

According to Dr Hellmuth Wachtel:

In addition to feeding and socializing with humans, regular physical exercise, congeneric socialization and a versatile,

changing environment challenging the pups' latent developing attitudes are essential, but often neglected. So pups need a spacious and secure run, but this should be partly structured to add quality to an often insufficient quantity of space. The optimum is to provide both a well-planned indoor and outdoor 'adventure playground'. The indoor playground could have a miniature agility course with small implements like hurdles, a low table (for playing 'King of the Castle'), tunnels, see-saws, dogwalk, etc. Of course this is only for spontaneous exercise of the pups, not for training them; but a variable structure provides challenges for the pups' curiosity and investigating instincts. Just like an agility course it should be rearranged daily to produce new situations and tasks to keep them and their minds active, counteracting any tendency towards developing kennel syndrome.

The outdoor playground should be well structured, too, but focused on a nature-related structure, partly lawn, partly sand or soil, with means for exercise like tree trunks, non-poisonous shrubs, ditches, holes and a small hill. For mental training, a not-too-complicated maze made of boards and baited with food could be provided. Here again the environment should vary somewhat every day by putting in hurdles, boxes, tubes, etc.

According to Weidt:

When sold to their new owners, imprinting playdays, Prägungsspieltage, are a good thing. These are regular meetings with the siblings and/or other pups of about the same size and age and their new owners in order to satisfy the interrupted congeneric, as well as intensifying the human, socialization process. As human toddlers, pups develop most

Chewing is just one way in which puppies explore their surroundings. (Photo: Jackson)

Strong and inflexible attachments and an inability to adjust to new situations may make it difficult to rehome older dogs and may even mean that the loss of older companions or the loss of a familiar habitat or regime causes unusual distress. Some breeds, however, appear to retain a relaxed attitude which enables them to make new attachments and to adjust to new environments at any stage without undue difficulty.

Juvenile Period

From about ten weeks of age until sexual maturity at seven months or later, depending on the breed, the puppies may be regarded as teenagers, with all the appetites, energy and rebellion that is associated with that period.

Although neurological and physical development is complete by this stage, training for complex tasks cannot progress owing to the short span of attention of which puppies are capable.

Adulthood

If adulthood is not measured solely on a basis of sexual maturity, but also includes behavioural patterns, the ability and readiness to accept training, confidence in novel situations and so on, it may be said that adulthood lasts for the rest of the dog's life. It is entirely possible to teach an old dog new tricks and for old dogs to adjust to new situations providing that their breeding and early upbringing has given them the ability to do so.

intelligence and physical abilities when able to use them early in their lives. A day not utilized to practise mental and physical abilities is a day lost for ever, and a day lost for character and personality forming and strengthening.

After about fourteen weeks, the ability to adjust to new environments may decline rapidly and especially so in some breeds.

Old Age

One of the most difficult and distressing aspects of dog ownership to come to terms

Something else to chew! (Photo: Jackson)

with is the relatively short canine life span. In some large and heavy breeds what is generally accepted as the normal life span may be no longer than eight or nine years. Smaller breeds may live twice as long without exciting comment, but though some dogs have lived beyond their twentieth birthday any dog that reaches the age of fifteen or sixteen must be regarded as aged.

Although dogs deteriorate physically as they age, they do not seem to go through temperamental changes. They retain interest in both work and play and in spite of advancing physical infirmity may show a continued desire to be involved in both.

Sheep dogs, retired from active work, may relieve their frustrations by herding farmyard poultry. Very old dogs will romp with puppies. Show dogs whose careers have come to an end may become distressed when kennel companions are taken to shows while they, Cinderella-like, are obliged to stay at home.

Loss of physical attributes, hearing and even sight, does not appear to distress dogs and they have an enviable ability to make whatever adjustments may be necessary. They should, however, be carefully observed for signs of pain or discomfort which canine stoicism may make it difficult to detect. Sitting or standing in unusual attitudes, a slightly

Young things growing up together derive mutual benefit from the association.
(Photo: Edminson)

The supplicant kneading attitude of an unweaned puppy is retained in adulthood when it is sometimes anthropomorphically seen as 'shaking hands'.

open-mouthed, narrow-eyed expression, licking or chewing or scratching at one part of the body, restlessness or a reluctance to move, and irritability, may all indicate that the dog is in pain.

At any stage owners with an anthropomorphic attitude towards dogs are likely to create problems for themselves and to lose some of the enjoyment that stems from regarding dogs as dogs, with their own particular way of doing things, their own dignity and their own priorities. As dogs age, such an attitude becomes a real barrier to giving dogs the care they deserve.

Euthanasia

Sometimes the last kindness we can offer

our dogs is to have them humanely destroyed in order to protect them from the misery and suffering that an intractable illness will produce. All too often, a sentimental and anthropomorphic attitude denies dogs this final service. It can reasonably be assumed that dogs have no foreknowledge of death and no worries about the hereafter; they are not sustained by pleasant memories and have no fear of the future; dogs live for the moment. If the moment is filled with pain and suffering and there is little prospect of relief, dog owners have a responsibility to put their own attitude to death to one side and do their old companions one final, kind service.

No breeder can reasonably expect to avoid the need to grapple with what, for any caring dog owner, is a most distressing situation: to decide whether or not the life of a dog, adult or puppy, should be brought to an end.

Andrew Edney has defined the conditions that indicate that a dog's life should be brought to an end. Is the dog free from pain, distress, or serious discomfort which cannot be effectively controlled? Is he able to walk and balance reasonably well? Is he able to eat and drink enough for normal maintenance without much difficulty and without vomiting? Is he free from tumours that cause pain or serious discomfort and are judged inoperable? Is he able to urinate and defecate reasonably frequently without serious difficulty or incontinence? Is the owner able to cope physically and emotionally with any nursing that may be required? Dr Edney suggests that if the answer to any of these questions is no, there are probably grounds for euthanasia.

There may also be other grounds: if a dog is dangerously aggressive or unreasonably nervous and fearful; if treatment of his condition would place an intolerable economic burden on his owner; and if treatment is unlikely to restore life to a reasonable quality.

The decision can never be an easy one for any caring owner, but facing the decision and coming to terms with its consequences are part and parcel of a breeder's lot. To allow a dog to suffer because of an inability to make the decision that could bring the suffering to an end is not an act of kindness. The decision to end a dog's life for good reason is one for which an owner should be able to expect support from his veterinary surgeon.

CHAPTER 11

Kennel Management

Managing a breeding kennel, whether it exists as part of a hobby and consists of no more than a few dogs, or is a business venture with a great many dogs, makes a number of demands that cannot be avoided if the enterprise is to achieve success. These demands begin even before any puppies are born.

In many countries breeding kennels are subject to a number of controls. In Britain a breeding kennel is defined as one in which more than two bitches, whether in the same ownership or not, and from which there is an intention to breed, are kept. Only the number of bitches from which there is an intention to breed are relevant. The number of very young or old bitches, spayed bitches, those prevented from breeding by other means, bitches that are awaiting a buyer and male dogs, are irrelevant to licensing conditions. Local authorities have the right to enter premises, but not dwelling houses, where they believe dog breeding is taking place.

In the USA breeding kennels may be set up only where planning zones allow for such an activity. The number of dogs that may be kept is subject to strict control. In Germany, as well as in some other European countries, both the premises and the animals kept for breeding must be officially approved. In most countries breeding kennels are licensed and are subject to regular inspection of their premises, and of the condition of the breeding stock (if not of the quality of breeding stock), and of records.

Official discovery of a clandestine breeding kennel may incur penalties and could invoke the need for planning and building permissions which might not be forthcoming. Environmental health legislation may be invoked if staff are employed. Safety and taxation authorities may take an interest in even the smallest venture.

Before anyone embarks on a career as a breeder, he must ensure that what he is doing does not bring him into conflict with the law. So it is important to obtain the necessary information and advice from the appropriate authorities.

Advertising

Once a kennel has established a reputation for producing good-quality puppies there may be little or no real need to advertise. Most successful breeders do so not to increase sales but simply to boast about success. The saying that 'Good wine needs no bush' is entirely appropriate to the breeder's art.

Advertisements should not be worded in a way that gives rise to unreasonable expectations on the part of buyers. Nor should they make false or misleading claims.

If a puppy is advertised as a show or

working prospect but ultimately fails to reach the quality required, if it is described as physically or temperamentally sound but grows into an unsound adult, the buyer may claim redress which may take account of the cost of the puppy, the cost of any veterinary fees or loss of earnings resulting from the deficiency, as well as the cost of the legal action itself.

Breeders should be careful – in both written and verbal advertisement of their stock – not to be tempted to make unreasonable claims.

Registration

It is customary for breeders to begin the process of registration as soon as it is apparent that puppies are thriving, though some wait longer in order to give buyers an opportunity to choose the name by which their puppy will be registered.

Most established breeders employ a kennel name, an affix, the exclusive use of which is protected by the payment of a fee. Regulations concerning the use of affixes vary from country to country. Some kennel clubs insist that all breeders must register an affix; others reserve the right to do so for established breeders.

Kennel clubs will not usually allow a name, other than a registered affix, to be repeated within the same litter, and some, for example the Kennel Club in Britain, may refuse to accept single-word names or may restrict the number of letters used in the registered name. All such regulations or provisos are usually fully explained on registration forms.

It would be going too far to suggest that the original meaning of the aphorism 'Give a dog a bad name and hang him' may be attributed to the naming of puppies, but it is certainly true that an inappropriate name may well reduce a dog's value. Names that are disrespectful of celebrities, carry obscene connotation, or refer to fictional or real characters whose fame is transient, could easily deter potential buyers. So too could names that are inappropriate to the breed.

Registered names tend to say more about the breeder than they do about the dog. Some show a want of imagination, others an uncontrolled imagination; some are pompous, others ignorant. Some display a misplaced sense of humour. Other names are merely inappropriate either to the dog or to the breed. Rather than running the risk of future embarrassment it is worth while giving some thought to the names chosen for puppies. Because of the number of requests to change inappropriate names, the Kennel Club in 1993 decided to allow owners to change names other than by the addition of an affix (which was the only change previously allowed).

Records

If a kennel is being run as a business – and there may well be advantage in doing so for even a very small establishment, especially if it is part of a larger dog-related concern such as showing, racing, working, training, boarding, grooming, writing or photography – it is important to keep such records as are required of any business enterprise.

Even if the enterprise is simply a hobby, records will be important. Whether records are kept in a simple diary or in a more complex filing system, they should provide instant access to information about age, parentage, identification marks, health, past and future competitions, seasons, matings, and detailed information about puppies produced – their number, sex, weight, colour, health, cost, new owners, and so on.

Memory is a very unreliable guide, and even a brief note made at the time can provide valuable information years after details of the event have been blurred by the passage of time.

Pedigrees

The format of pedigrees is fairly standardized and easily understood. They provide details of the particular dog's parents in the left-hand column, his grandparents in the next column, and on through great-, great-great-, and great-great-great-grandparents, depending on how many generations the pedigree deals with. The minimum is three, four more usual, five something of a luxury. Breeders sometimes amuse themselves by compiling ten-generation pedigrees for their favourites but to do is is a time-consuming labour of love and not something a purchaser could ever reasonably expect.

Blank pedigree forms or forms overprinted with the breeder's kennel name and address, may be bought from several kennel stationery firms. They are also provided, free of charge, by some pharmaceutical and petfood firms.

Buying and Selling

Although *caveat emptor* – let the buyer beware – must be the principle that guides every puppy buyer, the vendor is by no means absolved from responsibility.

A purchaser may establish an implied warranty by telling the vendor of the purpose for which the dog is being bought. A warranty may be established if the intended purpose is put in writing. A vendor may even offer a warranty in an unwisely worded advertisement, in correspondence with potential buyers, or in speech.

If the dog subsequently fails to fulfil his intended purpose or falls short of the claims made for him by the vendor, the new owner may confidently seek redress in the courts.

Breeders who fail to take such precautions as are available to them to ensure that breeding stock is free from hereditary disease, or who fail to warn buyers that a puppy may be carrying hereditary defects, may also be called upon to explain matters before the courts.

In Britain, falsifying pedigrees – a commonplace practice among puppy farmers and dealers – with the intention to deceive is a criminal offence (obtaining money by false pretences). Genetic fingerprinting techniques now make it a simple matter to uncover such deceit.

Insurance

In the author's experience of a small breeding kennel run over a period of thirty years, insurance premiums would have cost far more than any claims that might have been made, as must be the case if insurance companies are to remain in business. Nevertheless, insurance certainly has a place for any dog owner.

During puppyhood, and especially during the first few weeks after a puppy moves to its new home, insurance offers worthwhile protection both to the breeder and the new owners. Insurance should provide cover for any expenses likely to be incurred as a result of illness, accident, loss and theft, advertising the loss or theft, and provision of a reward for the finder.

Cover, at very modest rates, taken out by the breeder before puppies go to their new homes usually lasts for a period of about six weeks, after which the new owner has the option to renew the policy.

In some countries third-party insurance is compulsory, but in any country it is advisable. Dog owners are liable for any damage or accident caused by their dog. If damage is caused to livestock or an accident involves injury to or the death of a person, the dog owner's liability may well be extremely heavy. Many breed clubs are able to provide members with access to third-party insurance through block policies; but whether through a block or individual policy there is no doubt that third-party insurance is essential.

Identification

Even in those countries where there is no legal or kennel club imposed requirement to do so, many breeders have all their dogs and all the puppies they produce permanently identified, either by means of a micro-chip insert or, more conveniently, by means of a tattoo.

Micro-chip inserts, though favoured by the veterinary profession and by some welfare organizations, suffer from several disadvantages, the most obvious and serious of which is that the information they contain is not accessible without a scanner.

Tattoos, usually sited in the ear or, less often, on the inside of the thigh, provide the means to identify dogs at a glance and so not only act as a deterrent to thieves and enable dogs to be quickly and easily identified should they stray, but also ensure that their identity can be positively verified when they are used at stud or taken to a stud-dog, when they require veterinary attention and when they are tested for the presence of hereditary disease.

Freeze-branding, still used in some countries to identify individual pack hounds, is an effective method of identification but one that is seldom employed for other dogs.

It is not totally unknown for the breeders of an exceptional puppy to find that the exhibitor to whom it was sold subsequently appears in the ring with a very similar puppy claimed to have been home-bred. A tattoo would help to allay any suspicion of fraud. Tattoos also act as effective deterrents against unscrupulous dealers who pose as private buyers in order to purchase puppies that would otherwise not be available to them.

Diet Sheet

Even if a puppy is being sold to someone who is knowledgeable about dogs, it will ease the transfer to a new home and new regime if its diet remains unchanged at least for a few days. A simple diet sheet detailing the type of food to which it is accustomed, how it is fed, how often and in what quantities, as well as any supplements the puppy may have been having, will be appreciated by the new owner and the puppy.

If the puppy goes to its home with a bag of its accustomed food, so much the better.

Ready to move on to new homes. (Photo: Carey)

Vaccination Certificate

The veterinary surgeon's certificate, on which are all the details of the vaccinations that the puppy has received and on which it is identified by name and identity mark, should be handed to the new owner. These will provide assurance of its treatment and will provide valuable guidance as to future treatment.

Evidence of vaccination carried out by breeders (where this is allowed), should perhaps be treated with some caution even though a breeder may carry out vaccinations for about one tenth of the price customarily charged by veterinary surgeons. If a second vaccination, as part of a course, is necessary, the new owner should be informed of when it is due.

Other Information

Detailed information about the puppy's worming regime and recommendations for future worming should be provided for the new owner.

In addition, if the dog is sold with a known status in relation to any hereditary disease or other health condition, whether carried by himself or his parents, the buyer must expect details in writing. These may consist of veterinary certificates or certificates supplied through a test scheme or kennel club. Verbal assurances cannot be regarded as sufficient evidence and a wise purchaser should treat any reluctance to provide documentary evidence with suspicion.

A new dog owner or one new to the

breed will probably appreciate a list of the relevant breed clubs and publications about the breed. Some commercial firms as well as some kennel clubs make informative packs available which will also prove both interesting and useful to a new owner.

Breeders should take great care to ensure that pedigrees are clearly and accurately filled in. Errors may take on the complexion of a deliberate attempt to deceive, and may be treated as such by disappointed buyers and even by the courts.

Receipt

A receipt on which the puppy is identified by name and identity number, signed by the vendor and giving the name and address of the purchaser, setting out the cost of the puppy, all the details of its purchase, including any arrangements that limit the purchaser's rights, to stud work, puppies bred, exhibition, work, export and so on, is an important document which offers protection to both vendor and purchaser.

The vendor should keep a copy of that receipt, signed by the purchaser.

Presentation

It is a simple matter to present all the documents – pedigree certificate, registration documents, diet sheet, vaccination certificate, insurance certificate, list of breed clubs and useful publications and the receipt – all neatly written and kept together in a clean envelope.

Finally

Although reference has been made to beliefs and practices of bygone times, the emphasis throughout this book has been on the importance of new knowledge and techniques. Even so, it would be quite wrong to give the impression that breeders have nothing to learn from their predecessors. The way in which C.J. Davies in 1928 ended his book *The Theory and Practice of Breeding to Type* demonstrates that some aspects of breeding are immutable:

1. The more good points the parents possess in common the greater the likelihood of their producing good progeny.
2. It is better to breed from an animal with no bad points, and no outstanding good ones, than from one with one good point and a number of bad ones.
3. It is not to be expected that the progeny of good sires and inferior dams will inherit all the good qualities of the sire and none of the bad ones of the dam. The best strains are always built up on a foundation of good dams as well as good sires.
4. Inbreeding is sometimes essential and often desirable. It will not cause deterioration if the related animals are carefully chosen for their good qualities and freedom from constitutional defects; but
5. The closer the inbreeding the more rigid must be the selection.
6. The key to success in breeding to type lies in the one point – SELECTION. Everything else is subordinate to it.

Appendix I

Schedule of Hereditary Abnormalities

The following table indicates the mode of inheritance of a number of diseases and conditions. The first column gives the disease or condition; the second column the symptoms or definition of it; the third the means by which it is genetically inherited. The following abbreviations are used in the third column:

r=recessive	**f**=familial	**sl**=sex-linked
d=dominant	**gp**=genetically predisposed	**u**=uncertain
c=complex	**p**=polygenic	**xr**=x-linked recessive
ca=chromosomal anomaly	**t**=threshold	**?**=unknown

Modes of Inheritance Defined

Mode of Inheritance	Definition
Recessive	A gene which has no apparent effect unless it is carried by both parents.
Dominant	A gene that has apparent effect when carried by only one parent.
Complex	Influenced by both genetic and environmental factors.
Chromosomal anomaly	Resulting from abnormalities in the number or composition of individual chromosomes.
Familial	Tending to occur within families.
Genetically predisposed	The characteristic itself may not be inherited but the predisposition to it may well be.
Polygenic	Controlled by the combined effect of several genes.
Threshold	Dependent on several genes which need to exert combined effect in order to achieve expression.
Sex-linked	Determined by a gene that is carried on the sex chromosome, usually the X-chromosome.
Uncertain	There is uncertainty about the precise mode of inheritance.
Linked recessive	Recessive linked to the X-chromosome.
Unknown	The precise mode of inheritance is not known.

Disease/Condition	Symptoms/Definition	Mode of Inheritance
Abiotrophy (PNA)	Premature loss of vitality in tissues, organs and nervous system.	r
Acrodermatitis enteropathica	*See* Enteropathic acrodermatitis.	
Achondroplasia	Bone-growth failure, leading to dwarfism	r
Alopecia	Total absence of hair regarded as normal in hairless breeds but occasionally found in some others.	r
Anal furunculosis	*See* Perianal fistula.	
Angiohaemophilia	*See* Von-Willebrand's Disease.	
Angiosarcoma	*See* Haemangiosarcoma.	
Anorchidism	Absence of testes.	?
Anterior terminal hemimelia	Absence of forelimb bones.	r?
Anury	Absence of caudal vertebrae, regarded as normal in some breeds.	r
Aortic subvalvular stenusis	Constriction of the aorta, leading to congestive heart failure.	t
Aphakia	Absence of eye lens.	r?
Ataxia	Lack of muscular co-ordination, often associated with unusual vocalization.	r
Ataxic demyelination	Progressive lack of muscular co-ordination.	r
Atopic dermatitis	*See* Canine atopy.	
B12 malabsorption	Poor appetite, lethargy, anaemia.	r
Bird tongue	Lethal condition in which the tongue is folded laterally so preventing the puppy from suckling or swallowing.	r
Bithoratic ectronelia	Absence of forelimbs.	r
Bjeras leukodystrophy	Ataxia, paralysis and blindness.	r
Black-hair-follicle dysplasia	Thinning and dullness of black coat in piebald animals.	r

Disease/Condition	Symptoms/Definition	Mode of Inheritance
Bloat	*See* Gastric dilation-volvulus.	
Blue Dobermann Syndrome	*See* Blue Dog Syndrome.	
Blue Dog Syndrome	Thin, poor-quality coat, hair loss and scaly skin.	f
Boxer Cardiomyopathy	Heart disease characterized by slow heartbeat, weakness, arrhythmia and heart failure.	u
Brachydactyly	Abnormally short limbs.	r?
Brachyury	Abnormally short tail.	r
Calcinosis circumscripta	*See* Calcium gout.	
Calcium gout	Development of calcium nodules in subcutaneous tissue.	f
Cancer	Malignant tumours.	p
Canine atopy	Seasonal allergic response resulting in pruritus and self-trauma.	u
Cardiomyopathy	Frequently lethal pulmonary oedema; dilation of heart chambers.	u
Cardiovascular disease	Assorted heart and vein defects.	p
Carpal subluxation	Dislocation of the carpal joint, associated with Haemophilia A.	f
Cataract	Opacity of the eye lens, which may affect either juveniles or have a later onset to affect only adults.	d or r
Centralized progressive retinal atrophy	*See* Progressive central retinal atrophy	
Cerebellar ataxia	Unco-ordinated and exaggerated movement resulting from progressive brain damage.	r
Cerebellar ataxia hydrocephalus	Enlarged cranium associated with lack of muscular co-ordination.	r
Cerebellar cortex atrophy	Prancing gait and progressive ataxia.	r
Cerebellar cortical abiotrophy	Lack of muscular co-ordination.	r
Cerebellar degeneration	Muscular inco-ordination.	r

Disease/Condition	Symptoms/Definition	Mode of Inheritance
Cerebellar hypoplasia	Cerebellum cell deficiency.	u
Ceroid lipofuscinosis	Brain atrophy resulting in blindness, mental dullness and abnormal behaviour.	f
Cervical spondylosis	Hind limb muscular inco-ordination, progressing to paralysis.	r
Cervical vertebral deformity	*See* Wobbler Syndrome.	
Chondrodystrophy	*See* Chrondrondysplasia.	
Chondrondysplasia	Abnormal cartilage growth, often associated with dwarfism.	r
Chondrodystrophia fetalis	*See* Epiphyseal dysplasia.	
Choroidal hypoplasia	Eye defect characterized by scleral ectasia, coloboma of the optic disc, and microthalmia.	r
Chronic degenerative radiculomyelopathy	Disease of the nerve roots and spinal cord.	u
Cleft palate	Fissure of the hard or soft palates, temporary or permanent.	r
Cleft palate and hare lip	Fissure of palate and lip.	f
Collie eye anomaly	*See* Choroidal hypoplasia.	
Colour mutant alopecia	*See* Blue Dog Syndrome.	
Complement 3 deficiency	Increased susceptibility to bacterial infection.	r
Connective tissue dysplasia	*See* Ehlers-Danlos Syndrome.	
Copper toxicosis	Copper storage malfunction leading to liver degeneration.	r
Corneal dystrophy	Developmental condition leading to oedema and ulceration of the eye.	r
Craniomandibular osteopathy	Abnormal enlargement of the jaw, occipital and temporal bones, causing deformity.	r
Cranioschisis	*See* Cranium bifidum.	
Cranium bifidum	Failure of the cranial bones to close.	r

Disease/Condition	Symptoms/Definition	Mode of Inheritance
Cruciate ligament rupture	Rupture of the knee ligament.	u
Cryptorchidism	Having testes which fail to descend into the scrotum.	f
Crystalline corneal dystrophy	Developmental condition producing crystalline granules, leading to corneal oedema and ulceration.	r
Cutaneous asthenia	*See* Ehlers-Danlos Syndrome.	
Cutis hyperelastica	*See* Ehlers-Danlos Syndrome.	
Cyclic haematopoiesis	Lethal fluctuation in the number of circulating neutrophils, characterized by grey coat coloration.	r
Cyclic neutropenia	*See* Cyclic haematopoiesis.	
Cystine uriliths	Calculi caused by secretion of high levels of cystine.	u
Cystinuria	*See* Cystine uriliths.	
Day blindness	*See* Hemeralopia.	
Deafness	Partial or complete inability to hear, sometimes associated with white and merle dogs.	f
Degenerative myelopathy	Progressive paralysis, initially of the hind limbs but then of the forelimbs.	r
Degenerative pannus	Cellular infiltration, vascularization and pigmentation of the cornea.	u
Demyelinating myelopathy	Progressive muscular weakness, leading to paralysis, first of the hind limbs then of the forelimbs.	r
Dental defects	Additional, absent or crowded teeth.	f
Dermatomysitis	Acute skin and muscle condition characterized by inflammation of the skin, subcutaneous tissue and necrosis of the muscle fibres.	d

Disease/Condition	Symptoms/Definition	Mode of Inheritance
Dermoid cysts	Fibrous cysts lined with hair follicles, which occur in subcutaneous sites.	r?
Dermoid sinus	Abnormal sinus running from the skin to the spine; the anterior opening of the sinus is surrounded by a tuft of hair.	r
Dew-claw	A rudimentary first digit normally found only on the forelimbs; sometimes (abnormally) found on the rear limbs, and in some breeds occurs in a double form, regarded as normal in some pastoral guarding breeds.	d?
Diabetus mellitus	Insulin inbalance resulting from pancreas malfunction.	r
Diaphragmatic hernia	Intestinal protrusion through the diaphragm.	f
Distiachiasis	Double rows of eyelashes.	f
Dobermann cardiomyopathy	Heart disease characterized by acute pulmonary oedema, cardiogenic shock and occasionally sudden death.	u
Dobermann eye anomaly	Opaque cornea, prominent third eyelid, retinal detachment.	r
Dwarf anaemia	Abnormally short limbs and large red blood cells.	r
Dwarfism	*See* Pituitary dwarfism and Primordial dwarfism.	
Dwarf ocular	Abnormally short limbs and eye lesions.	r
Dyshormonogenetic goitre	*See* Goitre.	
Dystocia	Difficulty in giving birth, often a result of the combined effect of several features – abnormally large heads, narrow or upright pelvic girdles, etc., of the breeds in question.	

Disease/Condition	Symptoms/Definition	Mode of Inheritance
Ectromelia	Incomplete development of the long bones of the limbs.	r
Ectropic ureter	Incontinence.	u
Ectropion	Eversion of the eyelids.	f
Ehlers-Danlos Syndrome	Condition characterized by fragile bones and skin.	d
Elbow dysplasia	Developmental defects of the elbow joint, especially in growing puppies, leading to forelimb lameness and arthritis.	r
Elbow subluxation	Dislocation of the elbow joint leading to forelimb lameness.	r
Enostosis	Bony growth within the cavity or internal surfaces of long bones and bone cortex.	f
Enteropathic acrodermatitis	Inflammation of the skin produced by defective zinc uptake.	r
Entropion	Inversion of the eyelids resulting in extreme irritation and abrasion of the eyeball.	u
Epidermolysis bullosa	Blistered skin, especially at points of pressure, or trauma.	f
Epilepsy	Spasmodic fits.	c
Epiphyseal dysplasia	Abnormally shortened limbs and early generalized arthropathy.	
Esophageal achalasia	*See* Megaoesophagus.	
Everted membrane nictinans	Curled third eyelid causing runny and watering eyes.	r?
Factor VII deficiency	Anaemia.	r
Familial anaemia	Nonspherocytic haemolytic anaemia.	r
Familial necropathy	Degeneration of the kidneys.	r
Fawn Irish Setter Syndrome	*See* Blue Dog Syndrome.	
Foramen magnum	Large fissure in the occipital bone between the cranial cavity and spinal canal.	u

Disease/Condition	Symptoms/Definition	Mode of Inheritance
Forbe's Disease	*See* Glycogen storage disease III.	
Fragmented coronoid process	*See* Elbow dysplasia.	
Fucosidosis	Enzyme deficiency resulting in an excess of tissue fucose producing cerebral and neural degeneration.	r
Fused incisors	Abnormal front-tooth growth.	f
Gangliosidosis GM1	Deficiency of the lipid storage system resulting in stunted growth and muscular dysfunction.	r
Gangliosidosis GM2	Muscular dysfunction, fits, poor sight, death.	r
Gastric dilation-volvulus	Gastic dilation leading to haemorrhage, ulceration and death.	f
Gaucher's Disease	*See* Glucocerebrosidosis.	
Generalized progressive retinal atrophy	*See* Progressive retinal atrophy (PRA).	
Giant axonal neuropathy	Disease characterized by ataxia, hypotonia, loss of feeling and hind-limb reflexes.	r
Gingival hyperplasia	*See* Gingival hypertrophy.	
Gingival hypertrophy	Abnormal growth of gingiva resulting, in extreme cases, in an inability to close the mouth.	f
Glaucoma I	Eye disease caused by increased pressure on the optic disc, resulting in blindness.	r
Glaucoma II	As Glaucoma I, but different mode of inheritance.	d
Globoid cell leukodystrophy	Lysomal storage disease, resulting in neurological dysfunction.	r
Glomerulo nephritis	Kidney malfunction leading to excessive thirst, vomiting and urination.	f
Glossopharyngeal defect	*See* Bird tongue.	
Glucocerebrosidosis	Tremors, unco-ordinated, stumbling movement.	f

APPENDIX I

Disease/Condition	Symptoms/Definition	Mode of Inheritance
Glucosuria	*See* Renal tubular dysfunction.	
Glycogen storage disease I	Enzyme deficiency.	r
Glycogen storage disease II	As Glycogen storage disease I.	r
Glycogen storage disease III	As Glycogen storage diseases I and II.	r
Goitre	Enlarged thyroid gland, sparse coat, nervousness and excitability, neonatal mortality.	f
Granulocytopathy	Defective neutrophils resulting in recurrent infections.	r
Grey Collie Syndrome	*See* Cyclic haematopoiesis.	
Haemangiosarcoma	Malignant tumour of endothelial cells.	u
Haematopoiesis	*See* Cyclic haematopoiesis.	
Haemolytic anaemia	Dysfunction of the immune system, leading to death.	r
Haemolytic PK anaemia	Anaemia caused by immune-response disorder, often associated with jaundice; frequently fatal.	r
Haemophilia A	Loss or impairment of normal blood-clotting ability caused by Factor VIII anomaly.	sl
Haemophilia B	Loss or impairment of normal blood-clotting ability caused by Factor IX anomaly.	sl
Hairlessness	Total absence of coat; absence of hair other than on legs and feet.	r
Harada's Disease	Inflammation of the eyes and skin.	u
Hare lip	Defect of the upper lip: failure to fuse.	r
Hemeralopia	Inability to see in bright light.	r
Hemivertebra	Underdevelopment of one side of a vertebra.	u
Hepatic encephalopathy	Degenerative brain disease resulting in excitability, tremors, compulsive movement, blindness and death.	u

Disease/Condition	Symptoms/Definition	Mode of Inheritance
Hepatitis	Lethal liver disease.	s
Hereditary collagen dysplasia	*See* Ehlers-Danlos Syndrome.	
Hereditary myelopathy	Muscular weakness; incontinence.	r
Hip dysplasia	Abnormally shallow acetabulum and small or misshapen femoral head.	p
Histiocytosis	Skin, scrotal and nasal cancers.	u
H-Y antegen	Confused sex differentiation.	r
Hyperkalaemia	Abnormally high concentration of blood potassium resulting from renal abnormality.	u
Hyperlipoproteinaenia	Metabolic disorder leading to fits.	f
Hyperthermia	Abnormally high body temperature, nervousness and excitability	f
Hypertrophic neuropathy	Myelin production defect leading to early weakness, loss of reflexes and paralysis.	r
Hypofibrinogenaemia	Blood fibrogen deficiency leading to mild or severe bleeding.	d
Hypomyelinogenesis	Inadequate synthesis of myelin leading to nervous tremors and degeneration of the central nervous system.	r
Hypoproconvertinaemia	Reducing levels of clotting Factor VII producing mild bleeding.	r
Hypoprothrombinaemia	Blood prothrombin deficiency.	r
Hypothyroidism	Thyroid gland inactivity.	u
Ichthuosis	Keratin deficiency leading to dry, rough and scaly skin.	f
Immotile Cilla Syndrome	Lack of movement of ciliary structures of the eye.	r?
Inguinal hernia	Groin hernia.	t
Intersexuality	Partial hermaphrodite.	ca
Intervertebral disc protrusion	Pain and neurological problems, sometimes leading to paralysis and caused by displacement of an intervertebral disc, slipped disc.	p

Disease/Condition	Symptoms/Definition	Mode of Inheritance
Intestinal malabsorption	Persistent diarrhoea, debility, weight loss, death.	r
Jaw panosteitis	Inflammation of the jaw bones.	f
Juvenile cellulitis	Inflammation of facial tissue.	f
Keratitis	Inflammation of the cornea.	r?
Kinked tail	Deformity of the caudal vertebrae.	f
Krabbe's Disease	*See* Globoid leukodystrophy.	
Laryngeal paralysis	Paralysis of the larynx.	d
Laryngostenosis	Restriction of the larynx; laboured breathing.	f
Legg-Calve Perthes Disease	Femoral head necrosis leading to lameness.	r
Lens luxation	Displacement of the eye lens.	r
Lentiginosis profusa	Dark-pigmented skin.	f
Lethal oedema	Grossly bloated puppies; lethal.	r
Lipid storage disease	Cellular metabolic disorder resulting in excessive tissue lipids.	r
Lymphocytic thyroiditis	Auto-immune disease in which thyroid follicles are progressively destroyed.	f
Lymphoedema	Localized chronic swelling.	d
Lymphosarcoma	Malignant tumour of the lymph glands.	c
Malabsorption	Malfunction of the small intestine.	u
Mammary gland tumours	Cancers.	c
Mandibular prognathism	Abnormal protrusion of one (usually lower) jaw, or both jaws.	r? f?
Mast cell tumour	Skin tumours.	c
Megaoesophagus	Dilation and slackness of the oesophagus; persistent vomiting leading to weight loss.	u
Meningitis	Inflammation of the brain.	u
Merle	Coat coloration associated with deafness and ocular defects.	d

Disease/Condition	Symptoms/Definition	Mode of Inheritance
Microphthalmia	Abnormally small eyes, related to merle coloration.	r
Mitral insufficiency	Heart valve dysfunction causing abnormal blood flow within the heart.	c
Mononephroptosis	Lacking one kidney.	f
Monorchidism	Having only one testes.	u
Mucopolysaccharidosis	Metabolic disorder producing mental retardation, stunted growth and ocular defects.	f
Multifocal retinal dysplasia	Ocular defect characterized by several small defective areas in the retina and tapetum; vision appears not to be disturbed.	r
Muscle-fibre deficiency	Weakness; uncertain movement.	r
Muscular dystrophy	Degenerative disease of the muscles.	x
Myasthenia gravis	Episodic muscular weakness.	r
Myopathy	Muscular weakness; inco-ordination.	r
Myotonia congenita	Muscular spasms with stiff and stilted movement.	r?
Narcolepsy Cataplexy Syndrome	Fits precipitated by excitement or exercise.	u
Necrotizing myelopathy	Spinal cord degeneration.	d
Neuroaxonal dystrophy	Progressive loss of muscular co-ordination, tremors.	r
Neurogenic muscular atrophy	Progressive weakness of the neck and limb muscles.	f
Neuronal abiotrophy	Early onset, progressive neural tetraplegia and muscle atrophy.	r
Neuronal ceroid lipofuscinosis	*See* Ceroid lipofuscinosis.	
Ocular dermoids	Corneal cysts.	r?
Oedema	*See* Lethal oedema.	
Oesophageal achalasia	*See* Megaoesophagus.	

Disease/Condition	Symptoms/Definition	Mode of Inheritance
Oesophageal dysphagia	Difficulty in swallowing caused by malfunction of the oesophagus.	d?
Osteochondritis dissecans	Malformation of the cartilage, especially between the femur and humerus.	p
Osteochondrodysplasia	Abnormal bone and cartilage growth leading to a form of dwarfism.	r
Osteogenesis imperfecta	Abnormally brittle bones.	f
Osteosarcoma	Malignant bone tumours.	f
Otocephalic Syndrome	Hydrocephalus, cranial abnormalities, agnathia and neurological abnormalities.	f
Pancreatic acinar atrophy	Condition caused by insufficient secretion of digestive enzymes.	r
Pannus	*See* Degenerative pannus.	
Panosteitis	*See* Enostitis.	
Patellar luxation	Dislocation of the kneecap resulting in characteristic hind limb hopping movement.	p
Patent ductus arteriosus	Abnormal persistence of foetal open lumen.	t
Pelger-Heut anomaly	Heart murmurs of no clinical significance.	d
Perianal fistula	Inflammation and ulceration of anal sinuses.	f
Peripheral vestibular disease	Head tilt; lack of balance.	r
Persistent hyperplastic primary vitreous	Persistence of embryonic eye tissue producing a white or opaque pupil; sometimes associated with microphthalmia.	f
Persistent pupillary membrane	Remnants of non-vascular tissue across the iris and cornea producing opacity.	f
Persistent right aortic arch	Heart murmur.	t

Disease/Condition	Symptoms/Definition	Mode of Inheritance
Perthes Disease	*See* Legg-Calves Perthes Disease.	
Pig jaw	*See* Mandibular prognathism.	
Pinnal alopecia	Hair loss on the ear flap.	u
Pituitary dwarfism	Juvenile panhypopotuitarism resulting in slow and abnormal growth, retention of puppy hair and teeth, immaturity and shortened life-span.	r
Plasma thromboplastin antecedent	Blood clotting Factor XI deficiency producing mild bleeding.	r
Polyneuropathy	Disease involving nerves in several parts of the body.	r?
Polyostotic fibrous cysts	Lameness caused by cysts between the radius and ulna.	f
Pompe's Disease	*See* Glycogen storage disease II.	
Primary ciliary dyskinesia	*See* Immotile Cilia Syndrome.	
Primordial dwarfism	Generalized disproportionate growth.	u
Prognathism	*See* Mandibular prognathism.	
Progressive axonopathy	Disease of the peripheral and central nervous systems.	r
Progressive central retinal atrophy	Progressive degeneration of the retina resulting in blindness.	f
Progressive lens luxation	Displaced lens of the eye producing irritation and leading to blindness.	r
Progressive muscular dystrophy	Progressive weakness of the muscles; awkward movement.	sl
Progressive peripheral retinal atrophy	Progressive degeneration of the retina resulting in blindness.	r
Progressive retinal atrophy (PRA)	A group of degenerative eye diseases that vary in age of onset Initially producing impairment of vision in bright light and progressing to impairment, though not always total blindness, in all conditions.	r
Pseudo-achondroplastic dysplasia	*See* Epiphyseal dysplasia.	

Disease/Condition	Symptoms/Definition	Mode of Inheritance
Pseudohaemophilia	*See* Von-Willebrand's Disease.	
Pulmonic valve stenosis	Heart murmur and fibrillation.	t
Pyoderma	Purulent skin disease.	u
Pyruvate kinase deficiency	Anaemia caused by enzyme deficiency.	r
Quadriplegia	Inability of young puppies to stand and walk, head tremors, defective vision.	r
Renal cortical hypoplasia	Kidney insufficiency leading to poor growth and weakness.	f
Renal cystic adenocarcinoma	Kidney and skin tumours.	f
Renal dysplasia	Small and misshapen kidneys, loss of appetite and weight, leading to death.	f
Renal tubular dysfunction	Kidney malfunction leading to thirst and excessive urination, loss of weight and poor coat condition.	f
Retinal dysplasia	Blindness caused by retinal detachment.	r
Rod-cone dysplasia	Impairment of night vision leading to blindness.	r
Samoyed glomerulopathy	Progressive renal failure, lethargy and weight loss.	d
Scottie cramp	Muscular stiffness and hypertension caused by serotin deficiency.	r
Scottie jaw	*See* Craniomandibular osteopathy.	
Semen defects	Missing and deformed tails, deformed heads, feeble movement.	u
Seminoma	Tumour of the testes.	u
Sensory neuropathy	Loss of digital sensitivity, self-mutilation.	r
Severe pathesis	Muscle wasting, intolerance of exercise.	r
Sex reversal	Female sex reversal.	r
Short mandible	Underdeveloped lower jaw.	r

Disease/Condition	Symptoms/Definition	Mode of Inheritance
Short spine	Abnormally short, curved spine.	r
Skeletal lethal	Multiple skeletal defects.	d
Spinal dysraphism	Incomplete closure of the neural tube leading to characteristic 'bunny hopping' movement of the rear limbs.	f
Spinal muscular atrophy	Wasting of the spinal muscles.	r
Spondylosis deformans	Chronic lumbar vertebrae disease.	f
Stockard's Paralysis	Progressive hindquarters weakness, inco-ordination and paralysis.	f
Stuart-Prower Syndrome	Clotting deficiency leading to serious bleeding in neonates.	d
Stub	Spinal abnormalities, abnormally short tail, and spina bifida.	d
Sub-aortic stenosis	*See* Aortic subvalvular stenosis.	
Swimmers	*See* Quadriplegia.	
Tail short	Abnormally short tail.	d?
Tay-Sach's Disease	*See* Gangliosidosis GM2.	
Testicular feminization	Males with female sex organs.	sl?
Tetrology of fallot	Lethal multiple defect of the heart.	t
Thoracic-lumbar disc disease	Various vertebrae problems.	c
Thoracic hemivertebra	An anomaly in which one side of the thoracic vertebrae are underdeveloped.	
Thrombasthenia	Blood clotting deficiency.	d
Thrombocythaemia	Increase in the number of blood platelets.	?
Thrombocytosis	*See* Thrombocythaemia.	
Thyroiditis	Thyroid inflammation.	f
Tumoral calcinosis	*See* Calcium gout.	
Ulnar physis closure	Deformed ulna.	r
Umbilical hernia	Tissue protrusion through the umbilical ring.	r?

Disease/Condition	Symptoms/Definition	Mode of Inheritance
Ununited anconal process	Failure of the anconal process to unite with the ulna.	p
Ununited coronoid process	*See* Elbow dysplasia.	
Uric acid excretion	Inability to convert uric acid to allantoin.	r
Urinary calculi	*See* Cystine urolith.	
Uveodermatitis	Dermatitis associated with multiple eye defects.	f
Valvular incompetence	Failure of heart valves to close completely, causing heart murmurs and inefficient operation of the heart.	
Vascular haemophilia	*See* Von-Willebrand's Disease.	
Vertebrae osteochondrosis	Lesions of the spinal column producing lameness.	f
Von-Willebrand's Disease	Haemorrhagic diathesis producing prolonged bleeding following injury and poor coagulation.	d
Waterlogged puppies	*See* Lethal oedema.	
Wheat sensitive enteropathy	Inability to digest wheat products.	u
Wobbler syndrome	*See* Cervical vertebral deformity.	

Appendix II

Whelping Calendar

Columns are given in pairs: the first column of each pair shows the mating date; the second shows the expected whelping date.

Jan	Mar	Feb	Apr	Mar	May	Apr	June	May	July	June	Aug	July	Sept	Aug	Oct	Sept	Nov	Oct	Dec	Nov	Jan	Dec	Feb
1	5	1	5	1	3	1	3	1	3	1	3	1	2	1	3	1	3	1	3	1	3	1	2
2	6	2	6	2	4	2	4	2	4	2	4	2	3	2	4	2	4	2	4	2	4	2	3
3	7	3	7	3	5	3	5	3	5	3	5	3	4	3	5	3	5	3	5	3	5	3	4
4	8	4	8	4	6	4	6	4	6	4	6	4	5	4	6	4	6	4	6	4	6	4	5
5	9	5	9	5	7	5	7	5	7	5	7	5	6	5	7	5	7	5	7	5	7	5	6
6	10	6	10	6	8	6	8	6	8	6	8	6	7	6	8	6	8	6	8	6	8	6	7
7	11	7	11	7	9	7	9	7	9	7	9	7	8	7	9	7	9	7	9	7	9	7	8
8	12	8	12	8	10	8	10	8	10	8	10	8	9	8	10	8	10	8	10	8	10	8	9
9	13	9	13	9	11	9	11	9	11	9	11	9	10	9	11	9	11	9	11	9	11	9	10
10	14	10	14	10	12	10	12	10	12	10	12	10	11	10	12	10	12	10	12	10	12	10	11
11	15	11	15	11	13	11	13	11	13	11	13	11	12	11	13	11	13	11	13	11	13	11	12
12	16	12	16	12	14	12	14	12	14	12	14	12	13	12	14	12	14	12	14	12	14	12	13
13	17	13	17	13	15	13	15	13	15	13	15	13	14	13	15	13	15	13	15	13	15	13	14
14	18	14	18	14	16	14	16	14	16	14	16	14	15	14	16	14	16	14	16	14	16	14	15
15	19	15	19	15	17	15	17	15	17	15	17	15	16	15	17	15	17	15	17	15	17	15	16
16	20	16	20	16	18	16	18	16	18	16	18	16	17	16	18	16	18	16	18	16	18	16	17
17	21	17	21	17	19	17	19	17	19	17	19	17	18	17	19	17	19	17	19	17	19	17	18
18	22	18	22	18	20	18	20	18	20	18	20	18	19	18	20	18	20	18	20	18	20	18	19
19	23	19	23	19	21	19	21	19	21	19	21	19	20	19	21	19	21	19	21	19	21	19	20
20	24	20	24	20	22	20	22	20	22	20	22	20	21	20	22	20	22	20	22	20	22	20	21
21	25	21	25	21	23	21	23	21	23	21	23	21	22	21	23	21	23	21	23	21	23	21	22
22	26	22	26	22	24	22	24	22	24	22	24	22	23	22	24	22	24	22	24	22	24	22	23
23	27	23	27	23	25	23	25	23	25	23	25	23	24	23	25	23	25	23	25	23	25	23	24
24	28	24	28	24	26	24	26	24	26	24	26	24	25	24	26	24	26	24	26	24	26	24	25
25	29	25	29	25	27	25	27	25	27	25	27	25	26	25	27	25	27	25	27	25	27	25	26
26	30	26	30	26	28	26	28	26	28	26	28	26	27	26	28	26	28	26	28	26	28	26	27
27	31	27	May 1	27	29	27	29	27	29	27	29	27	28	27	29	27	29	27	29	27	29	27	28
28	Apr 1	28	May 2	28	30	28	30	28	30	28	30	28	29	28	30	28	30	28	30	28	30	28	Mar 1
29	Apr 2			29	31	29	July 1	29	31	29	31	29	30	29	31	29	Dec 1	29	31	29	31	29	Mar 2
30	Apr 3			30	June 1	30	July 2	30	Aug 1	30	Sept 1	30	Oct 1	30	Nov 1	30	Dec 2	30	Jan 1	30	Feb 1	30	Mar 3
31	Apr 4			31	June 2			31	Aug 2			31	Oct 2	31	Nov 2			31	Jan 2			31	Mar 4

Gestation table. The first column shows the mating date; the second column shows the expected whelping date.

Appendix III

Postnatal Development

Weeks	0	1	2	3	4	5	6	7	8	9	10
Days	0	7	14	21	28	35	42	49	56	63	70

0 – 3 days
- Birth
- Body temperature 94.1°F (34.5°C) – 99°F (37.2°C)
- Heart rate 220 per minute
- Respiratory rate 15 to 35 per minute
- Suckles
- Crawls forward
- Flexor responses dominant
- Grunts and squeals

3 – 7 days
- Yelps in complaint
- Reflexes begin to develop

7 – 8 days
- Extensor responses develop

8 – 10 days
- Birth weight doubled
- Eyes fully developed
- Co-ordinated movement
- Shivering reflexes develop

10 – 13 days
- Eyes open

13 – 14 days
- Ears open

15 – 18 days
- Learns to crawl backwards and attempts to walk
- Begins to respond to light and movement

18 – 20 days
- Learning to stand

20 – 24 days
- SOCIALIZATION BEGINS
- Beginning of play
- Communication skills begin with raised forepaws
- Startled by loud noises
- Begins to bark in play
- Teeth erupt
- First interest in solid food

25 – 27 days
- Visual perception develops

27 – 29 days
- Complex play movements develop

29 – 43 days
- Capable of existence independent of dam

56 days
- Weaning complete
- Begins to avoid unfamiliar experiences

Appendix IV

The purpose of this table, which has been well received by the geneticists who have checked it, is to enable breeders to work out degrees of inbreeding within a four-generation pedigree without becoming involved in complex calculations. It works like this:

1 represents the parental generation, 2 grandparents, 3 great-grandparents and 4 great-great-grandparents. So since Grove Willie appears once as Foiler's paternal grandfather (2) and once as his maternal grandfather (2) Foiler is 12.5 per cent inbred to him. However, Grove Tartar appears twice as paternal great-grandsire (3 3), and twice as paternal great-great-grandsire (4 4), and the pattern is repeated on the maternal side. So through his sire, Foiler is inbred (3 3 4 4) and to his dam (3 3 4 4) which produces a coefficient of 28.1 per cent.

Position and Frequency of Progenitor within Pedigree

Male Side	1	2 3 4	2 3 2 4 4 3 3 4 4	2 4 3 3 4 3 4 4 4	2 3 3 3 4 4 4 4 4 4	3 4 4 4 4	3 4 4	4
Female Side								
1	–	43.8	37.5	31.3	25.0	18.8	12.5	6.2
2 3 4	43.8	38.3	32.8	27.3	21.9	16.4	10.9	5.5
2 3 2 4 4 3 3 4 4	37.5	32.8	28.1	23.4	18.8	14.1	9.4	4.7
2 4 3 3 4 3 4 4 4	31.2	27.3	23.4	19.5	15.6	11.7	7.8	3.9
2 3 3 3 4 4 4 4 4 4	25.0	21.9	18.8	15.6	12.5	9.4	6.3	3.1
3 4 4 4 4	18.8	16.4	14.1	11.7	9.4	7.0	4.7	2.3
3 4 4	12.5	10.9	9.4	7.8	6.2	4.7	3.1	1.6
4	6.3	5.5	4.7	3.9	3.1	2.3	1.6	0.8

Appendix V

Registration Totals, Litter Size and Weight

NB Recorded figures exclude stillborn and early postnatal deaths. Dr Malcolm Willis has suggested that, in German Shepherd Dogs, these may represent 1.3 puppies per litter (about 20 per cent). The figure will vary from breed to breed, and is said to vary between 12 and 33 per cent.

In the following table, column 1 gives Kennel Club (and American Kennel Club) registration totals for each breed. Column 2 gives litter sizes, based on registrations, for the Kennel Club (and the American Kennel Club). Column 3 gives the difference – in numbers – between the litter sizes recorded by the two kennel clubs. Column 4 gives the weight range specified by the Kennel Club (and the American Kennel Club) breed standards. However, not all breed standards offer guidance on weight; and with the standards that do, it is not certain that breeding bitches conform to the weights specified or, in some breeds, even with the weight of show dogs. For several years, Pedigree Petfoods Waltham Centre weighed dogs at shows; they have not yet published the results, but have given me permission to publish the data collected on bitches (column 5). Unfortunately, this falls far short of covering every breed, but it does show that actual weights may differ from those laid down in breed standards.

Breed	1 KC 1987 (AKC 1989) pups registered	2 KC 1987 (AKC 1989) litter size	3 Diff. +/–	4 KC (AKC) wt (kg)	5 Waltham Survey wt (kg)
Affenpinscher	39 (212)	3.0 (2.8)	–0.2	3–4 (–)	–
Afghan Hound	698 (3,416)	6.8 (6.0)	–0.8	– (22.7)	22.8
Airedale Terrier	1,747 (9,189)	6.5 (7.7)	+1.2	– (–)	–
Alaskan Malamute	48 (12,069)	4.4 (6.3)	+1.9	38–56 (34)	–
American Cocker Spaniel	552 (246,639)	4.0 (5.2)	+1.2	– (–)	–
American Foxhound	– (78)	– (6.8)	–	– (–)	–
American Staffordshire Terrier	– (1,596)	– (6.8)	–	– (–)	–
American Water Spaniel	– (482)	– (6.5)	–	– (11.4–18.2)	–
Anatolian Shepherd Dog	118 (–)	6.6 (–)	–	41–59 (–)	–
Australian Cattle Dog	13 (2,418)	4.3 (5.8)	+1.5	– (–)	–

Breed	1 KC 1987 (AKC 1989) pups registered	2 KC 1987 (AKC 1989) litter size	3 Diff. +/-	4 KC (AKC) wt (kg)	5 Waltham Survey wt (kg)
Australian Silky Terrier	86 (7,019)	3.3 (3.7)	+0.5	4 (–)	–
Australian Terrier	80 (1,332)	4.4 (4.5)	+0.1	6.34 (–)	–
Basenji	91 (2,731)	3.8 (4.8)	+1.0	9.5 (10)	–
Basset Hound	1,152 (47,478)	6.2 (6.3)	+0.1	– (–)	–
Beagle	1,185 (102,833)	4.8 (5.1)	+0.3	– (–)	13.0
Bearded Collie	1,844 (1,266)	5.9 (6.1)	+0.2	– (–)	20.0
Bedlington Terrier	251 (372)	3.6 (3.9)	+0.3	8.2–10.4 (–)	7.6
Belgian Shepherd Dog (Groenendael)	286 (1,033)	6.6 (5.9)	–0.7	– (–)	–
Belgian Shepherd Dog (Laekenois)	5 (–)	5.0 (–)	–	– (–)	–
Belgian Shepherd Dog (Malinois)	15 (269)	7.5 (6.4)	–0.9	– (–)	–
Belgian Shepherd Dog (Tervueren)	309 (675)	7.2 (6.1)	–1.1	– (–)	24.2
Bernese Mountain Dog	610 (1,566)	5.0 (5.8)	+0.8	– (–)	41.2
Bichon Frise	1,877 (27,961)	4.1 (4.6)	+0.5	– (–)	5.2
Black and Tan Coonhound	– (323)	– (6.1)	–	– (–)	–
Bloodhound	117 (2,507)	6.5 (6.9)	+0.4	45 (45.5)	–
Border Collie	1,267 (–)	5.2 (–)	–	– (15.9)	17.8
Border Terrier	2,216 (718)	4.0 (4.0)	=	5.1–6.4 (5.2–6.4)	6.9
Borzoi	207 (1,947)	5.6 (6.1)	+0.5	– (27.3–38.6)	31.2
Boston Terrier	119 (33,735)	2.7 (4.1)	+1.4	6.8–11.4 (6.8–11.4)	–
Bouvier des Flandres	253 (3,527)	6.0 (6.5)	+0.5	27–35 (–)	–

Breed	1 KC 1987 (AKC 1989) pups registered	2 KC 1987 (AKC 1989) litter size	3 Diff. +/–	4 KC (AKC) wt (kg)	5 Waltham Survey wt (kg)
Boxer	8.082 (42,289)	5.1 (5.6)	+0.5	25–27 (–)	–
Briard	315 (354)	7.2 (8.2)	+1.0	– (–)	–
Brittany	81 (28,288)	5.2 (6.6)	+1.4	13 (13.6–8.2)	–
Bull Terrier	3,268 (2,342)	4.8 (4.7)	–0.1	– (–)	23.0
Bull Terrier, Miniature	125 (–)	3.6 (–)	–	– (–)	–
Bulldog	1,196 (17,073)	3.9 (4.3)	+0.4	– (–)	47.6
Bullmastiff	1,159 (2,060)	5.3 (5.7)	+0.5	41–50 (45.4–54.5)	–
Cairn Terrier	5,181 (19,706)	3.8 (4.2)	+0.4	6–7.5 (5.9)	7.2
Canaan Dog	7 (–)	7.0 (–)	–	18–25 (–)	–
Cavalier King Charles Spaniel	17,983 (–)	3.8 (–)	–	5.4–8 (–)	7.9
Chesapeake Bay Retriever	65 (8,272)	7.2 (7.5)	+0.3	– (25–31.8)	–
Chihuahua	2,742 (59,188)	2.7 (3.5)	+0.8	–2.7 (–2.7)	–
Chihuahua (Long-coat)	1,858 (–)	2.7 (–)	–	–2.7 (–2.7)	2.0
Chihuahua (Smooth-coat)	884 (–)	2.6 (–)	–	–2.7 (–2.7)	2.0
Chinese Crested	314 (–)	2.9 (–)	–	–5.5 (–)	–
Chow Chow	989 (116,814)	3.7 (4.8)	+1.1	– (–)	–
Clumber Spaniel	127 (128)	5.1 (4.3)	–0.8	29.5 (25–31.8)	–
Cocker Spaniel	13,664 (246,639)	4.7 (4.2)	–0.5	12.5–14.5 (11.8–14.5)	–
Collie	7,161 (38,717)	5.0 (6.2)	+1.2	– (22.7–27.3)	–

Breed	1 KC 1987 (AKC 1989) pups registered	2 KC 1987 (AKC 1989) litter size	3 Diff. +/–	4 KC (AKC) wt (kg)	5 Waltham Survey wt (kg)
Rough Collie	7,043 (–)	5.0 (–)	–	– (22.7–27.3)	–
Smooth Collie	118 (–)	4.9 (–)	–	18–25 (22.7–27.3)	– –
Curly-Coated Retriver	139 (202)	6.6 (7.5)	+0.9	– (–)	–
Dachshund	5,878 (95,469)	3.5 (4.0)	+0.5	– (–)	–
Dachshund (Long-haired)	577 (–)	4.8 (–)	–	9–12 (–)	–
Dachshund (Miniature long-haired)	2,397 (–)	3.3 (–)	–	4.5 (–)	–
Dachshund (Short-haired)	439 (–)	4.2 (–)	–	9–12 (–)	–
Dachshund (Miniature short-haired)	1,293 (–)	3.2 (–)	–	4.5 (–)	–
Dachshund (Wire-haired)	291 (–)	4.7 (–)	–	9–12 (–)	–
Dachshund (Miniature wire-haired)	881 (–)	3.6 (–)	–	4.5 (–)	–
Dalmatian	1,290 (39,670)	6.3 (7.6)	+1.3	– (–)	–
Dandie Dinmont Terrier	215 (164)	3.0 (3.7)	+0.7	8–11 (8.2–10.1)	–
Deerhound	282 (257)	5.9 (5.8)	–0.1	36.5 (34.1–43.2)	–
Dobermann	12,495 (51,864)	6.4 (6.9)	+0.5	– (–)	–
Elkhound	136 (8,290)	6.1 (5.6)	–0.5	20 (–)	–
English Setter	1,186 (1,374)	5.5 (5.7)	+0.2	– (–)	–
English Springer Spaniel	11,629 (41,830)	5.8 (6.8)	+1.0	– (22.3–25)	–
English Toy Terrier	73 (–)	2.7 (–)	–	2.7–3.6 (–5.4)	–
Eskimo Dog	3 (–)	3.0 (–)	–	27–41 (–)	–

Breed	1 KC 1987 (AKC 1989) pups registered	2 KC 1987 (AKC 1989) litter size	3 Diff. +/–	4 KC (AKC) wt (kg)	5 Waltham Survey wt (kg)
Estrela Mountain Dog	3 (–)	1.5 (–)	–	– (–)	–
Field Spaniel	98 (91)	4.5 (4.1)	–0.4	18–25 (15.9–22.7)	–
Finnish Spitz	68 (224)	3.1 (4.1)	+0.6	14–16 (–)	–
Flat-coated Retriever	1,185 (492)	7.0 (8.0)	+1.0	25–34 (–)	–
Fox Terrier (Smooth)	440 (1,660)	3.9 (4.0)	+0.1	6.8–7.7 (–)	–
Fox Terrier (Wire)	1,215 (7,706)	3.7 (4.5)	+0.8	8.25 (7.3)	–
Foxhound	– (73)	– (8.0)	–	– (–)	–
French Bulldog	178 (790)	2.9 (3.1)	+0.2	10.9 (10–12.7)	–
German Pointer (Short-haired)	1,051 (18,944)	6.7 (7.4)	+0.7	– (20.5–27.3)	24.9
German Pointer (Wire-haired)	209 (2,218)	7.5 (7.7)	+0.2	20.5–29 (–)	–
German Shepherd Dog (Alsatian)	31,846 (123,175)	6.4 (6.6)	+0.2	– (–)	28.9
German Spitz (Klein)	71 (–)	2.8 (–)	–	– (–)	–
German Spitz (Mittel)	45 (–)	3.5 (–)	–	– (–)	–
Glen of Imaal Terrier	62 (–)	4.8 (–)	–	– (15.9)	–
Golden Retriever	18,586 (120,473)	6.6 (7.9)	+1.3	– (25–29.5)	30.4
Gordon Setter	627 (2,456)	6.2 (6.8)	+0.6	25.5 (20.5–31.8)	28.7
Great Dane	3,065 (17,611)	6.0 (6.7)	+0.7	46+ (–)	58.6
Greyhound	70 (199)	4.6 (6.9)	+2.3	– (27.3–29.5)	–
Griffon Bruxellois	254 (603)	2.6 (3.1)	+0.5	2.2–4.9 (3.6–4.5)	–
Hamiltonstovare	5 (–)	5.3 (–)	–	– (–)	–
Harrier	– (55)	– (6.9)	–	– (–)	–
Hungarian Kuvasz	– (683)	– (6.3)	–	– (31.8–40.9)	–

Breed	1 KC 1987 (AKC 1989) pups registered	2 KC 1987 (AKC 1989) litter size	3 Diff. +/−	4 KC (AKC) wt (kg)	5 Waltham Survey wt (kg)
Hungarian Puli	73 (358)	4.6 (4.9)	+0.3	10–13 (−)	−
Hungarian Vizsla	335 (2,949)	7.0 (6.5)	−0.5	20–30 (−)	−
Ibizan Hound	18 (176)	5.4 (6.8)	+1.4	− (20.4)	−
Irish Red-and- White Setter	137 (−)	5.7 (−)	−	− (−)	−
Irish Setter	1,944 (5,368)	7.0 (7.9)	+0.9	− (27.3)	25.1
Irish Terrier	201 (431)	4.9 (4.5)	−0.4	− (11.4)	−
Irish Water Spaniel	144 (152)	5.9 (7.6)	+1.7	− (20.5–26.4)	−
Irish Wolfhound	971 (1,798)	5.8 (6.5)	+0.7	40.9+ (47.7+)	56.3
Italian Greyhound	64 (2,054)	2.4 (3.8)	+1.4	2.7–4.5 (−)	−
Italian Spinone	136 (−)	7.0 (−)	−	29–34 (−)	−
Japanese Akita	521 (17,357)	6.4 (6.3)	−0.1	− (−)	34.9
Japanese Chin	317 (1,813)	2.6 (3.1)	+0.5	1.8–3.2 (−)	3.0
Japanese Shiba Inu	27 (−)	3.4 (−)	−	− (−)	−
Japanese Spitz	191 (−)	2.9 (−)	−	− (−)	−
Keeshond	264 (19,403)	4.6 (5.6)	+1.0	− (−)	17.6
Kerry Blue Terrier	376 (703)	4.3 (4.9)	+0.6	15.9 (15–18.2)	−
King Charles Spaniel	296 (−)	2.9 (−)	−	3.6–6.3 (−)	−
Komondor	7 (389)	7.0 (5.7)	−1.3	36–50 (−)	−
Labrador Retriever	26,392 (175,129)	6.6 (7.6)	+1.0	− (25–31.8)	31.8
Lakeland Terrier	369 (466)	3.2 (3.5)	+0.3	6.8 (−)	−
Lancashire Heeler	180 (−)	3.5 (−)	−	− (−)	−
Large Munsterlander	114 (−)	6.0 (−)	−	25 (−)	27.3
Leonberger	31 (−)	7.8 (−)	−	− (−)	−
Lhasa Apso	2,818 (77,171)	4.2 (4.9)	+0.7	− (−)	6.14

Breed	1 KC 1987 (AKC 1989) pups registered	2 KC 1987 (AKC 1989) litter size	3 Diff. +/–	4 KC (AKC) wt (kg)	5 Waltham Survey wt (kg)
Löwchen	138 (–)	2.9 (–)	–	– (–)	–
Maltese	878 (37,072)	3.1 (3.2)	+0.1	– (–)	7.9
Manchester Terrier	117 (885)	3.4 (3.9)	+0.5	– (5.4–10)	–
Maremma Sheepdog	61 (–)	6.1 (–)	–	30–40 (–)	–
Mastiff	458 (3,919)	5.5 (5.5)	=	– (–)	66.6
Miniature Pinscher	287 (15,177)	3.1 (3.6)	+0.5	– (–)	–
Miniature Schnauzer	2,116 (91,253)	4.3 (4.7)	+0.4	– (–)	6.6
Neapolitan Mastiff	8 (–)	4.0 (–)	–	50–70 (–)	–
Newfoundland	813 (4,544)	6.9 (5.9)	–1.0	50–54.5 (45.4–54.5)	52.9
Norfolk Terrier	460 (405)	2.3 (2.5)	+0.2	– (5–5.4)	–
Norwich Terrier	158 (370)	2.4 (3.0)	+0.6	– (5.4)	–
Old English Sheepdog	3,218 (8,736)	5.7 (6.5)	+0.8	– (–)	29.9
Otterhound	72 (73)	5.3 (7.3)	+2.0	– (29.5–45.4)	–
Papillon	925 (3,278)	2.4 (3.0)	+0.6	– (–)	–
Pekingese	2,617 (48,847)	2.7 (3.8)	+1.1	5.5 (–6.4)	4.15
Petit Basset Griffon Vendeen	106 (–)	5.2 (–)	–	– (–)	–
Pharaoh Hound	28 (186)	5.2 (5.4)	+0.2	– (–)	–
Pinscher	21 (–)	3.0 (–)	–	– (–)	–
Pointer	771 (558)	5.9 (5.9)	=	– (–)	23.2
Pointing Wire-haired Griffon	– (169)	– (7.0)	–	– (–)	–
Polish Lowland Sheepdog	12 (–)	6.0 (–)	–	– (–)	–
Pomeranian	1,568 (74,843)	2.1 (3.0)	+0.9	2–2.5 (1.4–3.2)	2.10
Poodle	– (190,995)	– (3.6)	–	– (–)	–
Poodle (Miniature)	2,575 (–)	3.6 (–)	–	– (–)	–

Breed	1 KC 1987 (AKC 1989) pups registered	2 KC 1987 (AKC 1989) litter size	3 Diff. +/–	4 KC (AKC) wt (kg)	5 Waltham Survey wt (kg)
Poodle (Standard)	2,033 (–)	6.4 (–)	–	– (–)	23.6
Poodle (Toy)	5,861 (–)	3.1 (–)	–	– (–)	–
Portuguese Water Dog	9 (641)	3.0 (7.8)	+4.8	16–22 (15.9–22.7)	–
Pug	835 (27,929)	3.5 (4.3)	+0.8	6.3–8.1 (6.4–8.2)	–
Pyrenean Mountain Dog	365 (5,808)	6.8 (6.3)	–0.5	40+ (40.9–52.3)	47.9
Rhodesian Ridgeback	950 (2,984)	7.0 (7.2)	+0.2	– (29.5)	35.5
Rottweiler	16,837 (109,087)	6.8 (6.7)	–0.1	– (–)	39.1
Saint Bernard	732 (8,692)	5.9 (6.9)	+1.0	– (–)	70.9
Saluki	114 (747)	4.6 (5.5)	+1.1	– (–)	19.8
Samoyed	1,096 (19,974)	4.9 (5.5)	+0.6	– (–)	20.4
Schipperke	136 (7,159)	3.1 (3.9)	+0.8	5.4–7.3 (–8.2)	–
Schnauzer	220 (826)	6.1 (6.5)	+0.4	– (–)	–
Giant Schnauzer	230 (2,183)	7.0 (7.4)	+0.4	– (–)	–
Scottish Terrier	2,447 (20,717)	3.9 (4.7)	+0.8	8.6–10.4 (8.2–9.5)	–
Sealyham Terrier	145 (156)	3.9 (3.8)	–0.1	8.2 (10.4–10.9)	–
Shar Pei	177 (–)	4.1 (–)	–	– (18.2–25)	–
Shetland Sheepdog	5,429 (77,455)	3.4 (4.4)	+1.0	– (–)	7.8
Shih Tzu	3,806 (97,485)	4.0 (4.3)	+0.3	4.5–7.3 (4.1–7.3)	6.4
Siberian Husky	328 (45,386)	4.8 (5.2)	+0.4	16–23 (15.9–22.7)	–
Skye Terrier	169 (334)	5.0 (5.5)	+0.5	– (–)	–
Soft-coated Wheaten Terrier	127 (2,063)	5.5 (5.5)	=	16–20.5(–)	17.9

Breed	1 KC 1987 (AKC 1989) pups registered	2 KC 1987 (AKC 1989) litter size	3 Diff. +/–	4 KC (AKC) wt (kg)	5 Waltham Survey wt (kg)
Staffordshire Bull Terrier	10,222 (399)	4.6 (4.8)	+0.2	11–15.4 (10.9–15.4)	16.2
Sussex Spaniel	92 (67)	4.8 (4.5)	–0.3	22.5 (15.9–20.5)	–
Swedish Vallhund	69 (–)	5.3 (–)	–	11.4–15.9 (–)	–
Tibetan Mastiff	30 (–)	4.3 (–)	–	– (–)	–
Tibetan Spaniel	515 (378)	3.4 (3.3)	–0.1	4.1–6.8 (–)	5.5
Tibetan Terrier	757 (984)	4.3 (5.1)	+0.8	– (8.2–13.6)	9.0
Weimaraner	1,704 (6,842)	6.2 (6.6)	+0.4	– (–)	27.9
Welsh Corgi (Cardigan)	148 (872)	4.8 (5.0)	+0.2	– (11.4–15.4)	–
Welsh Corgi (Pembroke)	2,234 (8,385)	4.5 (4.8)	+0.3	– (11.4)	–
Welsh Springer Spaniel	800 (468)	5.3 (6.0)	+0.7	– (–)	18.6
Welsh Terrier	314 (1,303)	3.3 (4.1)	+0.8	9–9.5 (9.1)	–
West Highland White Terrier	15,086 (30,267)	4.2 64.2)	=	– (–)	–
Whippet	1,554 (2,619)	4.9 (6.1)	+1.2	– (–)	–
Yorkshire Terrier	31,912 (78,524)	3.8 (3.4)	–0.4	–3.1 (–3.2)	2.2

Appendix VI

Canine Calorie Intake (kCal)

From weaning to about six months, a puppy will need approximately twice the normal adult intake. During late pregnancy a bitch needs about 1.5 times her normal maintenance intake; at peak lactation she will need about 3.5 times her normal diet.

Weight of dog kg	Maintenance kCal
1	130
2	225
3	300
4	370
5	435
6	500
7	570
8	635
9	690
10	740
15	1,000
20	1,250
25	1,480
30	1,690
35	1,900
40	2,100
45	2,300

Bibliography

Books and Pamphlets

Anderson, R.S. (Ed.), *Nutrition and Behaviour in Dogs and Cats*, Pergamon Press, UK (1984)

Bowman, J.C., *An Introduction to Animal Breeding*, Camelot Press, UK (1974)

Darwin, C.R., *The Origin of Species*, John Murray, UK (1859)

The Variation of Animals and Plants Under Domestication, John Murray, UK (1868)

Davies, C.C., *The Theory and Practice of Breeding to Type*, Our Dogs Publishing, UK (1928)

Desmond A. & Moore, J., *Darwin*, Michael Joseph, UK (1991)

Done, J.T., *Vol 20, Advances in Veterinary Science and Comparative Medicine*, Academic Press, New York (1976)

Edney, A.T.B., *Dog and Cat Nutrition*, Pergamon Press, UK (1988)

Heredity and Disease in Dogs and Cats, BSAVA & BVA Animal Health Foundation, UK (1988)

England, Dr G., *The Use of Diagnostic Ultrasound in Canine Reproduction (Technical Review No. 1)*, The Guide Dogs for the Blind Association, UK (1991)

Semen Evaluation and Artificial Insemination in the Dog (Technical Review No. 3), The Guide Dogs for the Blind Association, UK (1992)

Evans, J.M., *The Henston Veterinary Vade-Mecum (Small Animals)*, Henson Ltd, UK (1983)

Holmes, R.L., *Reproduction and Environment*, Oliver & Boyd, UK (1968)

Kirk, R.W., *Current Veterinary Therapy III*, W.B. Saunders & Co., Philadelphia (1966)

Lane, D.R. (Ed.), *Jones's Animal Nursing*, Pergamon Press, UK (1980)

Lytton, The Hon. Mrs. N., *Toy Dogs and Their Ancestors*, Duckworth, UK (1911)

Messent, P. & Horsfield, S., et al, *The Human-Pet Relationship*, Institute for Inter-disciplinary Research on the Human-Pet Relationship, UK (1985)

Moody, B., *A Programme for Puppy-Rearing (Technical Review No. 7)*, The Guide Dogs for the Blind Association, UK (1993)

Morris, D., *Dog Watching*, Jonathan Cape, UK (1986)

Pitcairn, R.H., *Natural Health for Dogs and Cats*, Rodale Press, UK (1983)

Robinson, R., *Genetics for Dog Breeders*, Pergamon Press, UK (1989)

Thorne, C. (Ed.), *The Waltham Book of Dog and Cat Behaviour*, Pergamon Press, UK (1992)

Trumler, E., *Understanding Your Dog*, Faber & Faber, UK (1973)

Turner, T. (Ed.), *Veterinary Notes for Dog Owners*, Popular Dogs, UK (1990)

Wansborough, P., *Caring for Brood-Bitches at Home (Technical Review No. 6)*, The Guide Dogs for the Blind Association, UK (1992)

Willis, Dr. M., *Practical Genetics for Dog Breeders*, Witherby, UK (1992)

Articles

Beacock, J., 'Keeshond Breed Notes', in *Our Dogs*, UK (1993)

David, Dr H., 'AKC Statistics Fall Under Scrutiny', in *Dog World*, UK (1990)

Gunn, Dr I., 'The Revolution in Canine Breeding Technology for the 90s', in *The Kennel Gazette*, The Kennel Control Council, Australia (1990)

Logan, I. (Ed.), 'An Analysis of All Litters Recorded by The Kennel Club in 1987', in *The Kennel Gazette*, The Kennel Club, UK (1988)

Miller, P.S., 'Pet Therapy Advances: Seizure-Alert Dogs', in *Dog World*, UK (1992)

Papers

Boundy, T. et al, Embryo transfer in sheep under practice conditions, *The Veterinary Record*, BVA, UK (1985)

Cran, D.G., et al, Production of bovine calves following separation of X- and Y-chromosome bearing sperm and *in-vitro* fertilisation, *The Veterinary Record*, BVA, UK (1993)

Edney, A.T.B., Companion animals and human health, *The Veterinary Record*, BVA, UK (1992)

Dogs and human epilepsy, *The Veterinary Record*, BVA, UK (1993)

The management of euthanasia in small animal practice, *The Journal of the American Animal Hospital Association*, USA (1979)

Edney, A.T.B. & Smith, P.M., Study of obesity in dogs visiting veterinary practices in the United Kingdom, *The Veterinary Record*, BVA, UK (1986)

England, Dr G., Vaginal cytology in the breeding management of bitches, *Journal of Small Animal Practice*, BSAVA, UK (1992)

Fisher, M.A., et al Efficacy of fenbendazole and piperazine against developing stages of *Toxocara* and *Toxascaris* in dogs, *The Veterinary Record*, BVA, UK (1993)

Fray, M.D., Wrathall, J.H.M., and Knight, P.G., Active immunisation against inhibin promotes a recurrent increase in litter size in sheep, *The Veterinary Record*, BVA, UK (1994)

Gillespie, S.H., The epidemiology of *Toxocara canis*, *Parasitology Today*, USA (1988)

Hanssen, I., Hip dysplasia in dogs in relation to their month of birth, *The Veterinary Record*, BVA, UK (1991)

Jolly, R.D. & Healy, P.J., Screening for carriers of genetic diseases by biochemical means, *The Veterinary Record*, BVA, UK (1986)

Jolly, R.D. et al, Screening for genetic diseases: principles and practice, *The Veterinary Record*, BVA, UK (1981)

Leslie, G., The incidence of *Toxocara canis* eggs in dog faeces in a survey of regularly wormed dogs, Canine Concern Scotland Trust (1994 report)

Logue, D. & Greig, A., Infertility in the bull, ram and boar, *In Practice*, BVA, UK (1985)

Macartney, L. et al, Canine parvovirus enteritis 2: pathogenesis, *The Veterinary Record*, BVA, UK (1984)

Picard, L. et al, Production of sexed calves from frozen-thawed embryos, *The Veterinary Record*, BVA, UK (1985)

Renton, J.P. et al, A spermatozoal abnormality in dogs related to fertility, *The Veterinary Journal*, BVA, UK (1986)

Robinson, R., Relationship between litter size and weight of dam in the dog, *The Veterinary Record*, BVA, UK (1973)

Scott, D.W., Canine demodicosis, *Small Animal Practice*, Veterinary Clinics of North America, USA (1979)

Serpell, Dr. J., The beneficial effects of pet ownership on human health and behaviour, *Journal of the Society for Companion Animal Studies*, UK (1992)

Sreenan, J.M., Recent developments in embryo transfer and related technologies, *The Veterinary Record*, BVA, UK (1987)

Stallbaumer, M., Treatment of helminths in dogs and cats, *In Practice*, BVA, UK (1993)

Thrusfield, M.V., Association between urinary incontinence and spaying in bitches, *The Veterinary Record*, BVA, UK (1985)

Turner, T., Anthelmintics currently licensed for use in dogs and cats, *The Veterinary Record*, BVA, UK (1987)

Unpublished References

Johnson, J.V., Burger, I.H., & Markwell, P., Survey of bodyweights in adult dogs, Waltham Centre for Pet Nutrition, UK (1993)

Wachtel, H., Private correspondence, Austria, (1993)

Index

absorption of foetus, 110
acquisition, 64
acute metritis, 137
adult acromegaly, 78
advertising, 167
allantochorion, 124
alleles, 23
allelomorphs, 23
Ancylostoma: brasiliense,
    149
    caninum, 149
    ceylanicum, 149
anoestrus, 72
anthelmids, 113
antibiotics, 135
antibodies: in colostrum, 157
    levels, 134
artificial insemination (A1),
    102
    See also exporting semen

background inbreeding, 16
balanoposthitis, 90
bedding, 116
behavioural development,
    157
birth, assisted, 127
    surgically assisted, 128
    weight at, 146
blastocyst, 108
blood tests, 96, 111
booster, annual, 157
bottlenecks, 16, 34
breech birth, 120, 128
breed, choosing a, 64
    concept of, 42
breed standard, 19
breeding: bitches, ages of, 68
    kennel controls, 167
    reasons for, 18
    stock, testing all, 62
    terms, 66
brood-bitch, 65
    diet of, 68, 112, 133
    postnatal problems in,
        137
    See also female

brucellosis, 79, 90
bulbus glandis, 88, 100
bursa, 68
buying, 66

Caesarean section, 129
calcium, drain of, 138
    injections of, 138
canine: brucellosis, 79, 90
    distemper, 157
    genome, 62
carriers, 61
castration, 91
cell division, 23
cervix, 69
cestadodes, 148
characteristics, acquired,
    14
    inherited, 14
chastity belt, 80
chlorophyll tablets, 73
chromosomes, 23
cleft palate, 142
close breeding, 33, 51
closed stud system, 53
Code of Ethics, 20
coital crouch, 98
colostrum, 134, 157
conception rates, 103
conjunctivitis, 141
contraception, 80
contractions, uterine, 119,
    124
crossbreeding, 47, 48
cryptorchidism, 26, 29, 87,
    90
culling, 130
cystitis, 90
cytology tests, 79

demodectic, *see* mange
dew-claws, removal of, 147
dietary additives, 156
diet: sheet, 170
    See also brood-bitch;
        feeding
diploid number, 23

Dipylidium caninum, 149,
    151
Dirofilaria immitis, 149, 153
distemper, 90
docking, 146
dog: ownership, 10, 11
    population, 10, 13
dystocia, 126, 131

Echinococcus granulosus,
    149
eclampsia, 138
embryo transfer, 105
epididymis, 87
epistasis, 26
epsiprantel, 113
euthanasia, 165
exaggerated features, 42
exporting semen, 93
extensor response, 158

Fading Puppy Syndrome,
    140
fallopian tubes, 69
fashion, 29
feeding: cost of, 10
    orphans and
        supplementary, 143
    See also brood-bitch; diet;
        weaning
female: reproductive cycle,
    70
    reproductive system, 68
fenbendazole, 113, 149
fertility, 44, 77, 89, 95
Flat Puppy Syndrome, 140
foetal heartbeats, 111
follicular cysts, 78
fontanelle, open, 142
foreplay, 97
freeze-branding, 107, 170
frostbite, 90

gene: dominant/recessive, 23
    pool, 31
    register, 37
    replacement therapy, 62

genetic: abnormalities, 36
  screening, 37
  variation, 28
genetics, 22
  population, 27, 29
genotype, 38, 58
gestation period, 117
Gonadotrophin Releasing
  Hormone (GnRH), 75
growth rate, 137

haemorrhage, 141
haploid number, 23
hare lip, 142
heartworms, 154
heat, 74
heated pads, 116
helminths, 113, 148
hepatitis, 157
hereditary defects, 20, 36,
  56, 58
  carriers of, 61
  incidence of, 62
hernia, 142
herpes virus, 141
heterozygous, 24
homoeopathy, 157
homozygous, 24
hookworms, 149, 154
hormone assay tests, 96
hybrid vigour, 48
hydrops foetalis, 111
hypoestronism, 78
hypoglycaemia, 141, 142
hypothyroidism, 78

identification, 86, 106, 146,
  170
inbreeding, 15, 16, 27, 45,
  46, 49, 51, 52
incubator, 145
infertility, 78, 89
infra-red heaters, 116
inhibin, 78
insurance, 169, 170
intra-gastric tube, 144
ivermectin, 113

jaw malformations, 142

kennel: blindness, 55
  records, 168
  type, 33

kinked tail, 142

labour, difficult, 126
leptospirosis, 157
libido, 98
life span, 164
like to like, 46
line-breeding, 15, 49
lining, 97
litter size, 77, 78, 129, 134
locus, 23
low birth weight, 137
luteal cysts, 78

maiden bitches, 100
male: reproductive cycle,
  88
  reproductive system, 87
mange, demodectic, 113
  sarcoptic, 113
mastitis, 137
mating, 85, 97
  compensatory, 47
  repeat, 55
  second, 86
  See also refusal to mate
meiosis, 23
metoestrus, 74
micro-chip implant, 105, 170
milbemycin oxime, 113
milk, bitch's, 143
  substitutes for, 143
milk fever, 138
monorchidism, 26, 90
morula, 108
multiple matings, 101
mutation, 26

nematocide, 113
nematodes, 148
neonatal period, 158
neutering, 81
nutritional intake, 113
nymphomania, 78

oestrogen, 112
oestrus, 71, 74, 76
  See also seasons
old age, 163
orchitis, 90
outcrosses, 34
outcrossing, 31, 48

ovarian: cysts, 78
  imbalance, 78
  tumours, 78
ovaries, 68
overshot, 142
ovulation, 96

palpation, 111
parainfluenza, 157
paraphimosis, 90
parasites, 147
parentage testing, 106
parturition, first stage of,
  118
  second stage of, 119
  third stage of, 124
  See also labour; whelping
parvovirus, 57, 157
pelvis, 69, 117
phenotype, 29, 33, 38, 58
phimosis, 90
piperazine, 113, 149
placenta retention, 138
polygenic, 24
praziquantel, 149
pregnancy, 108
  diagnosis of, 110
  phantom, 76
  pseudo, 76
  stress during, 109
  temperature during, 116
  termination of, 112
  testing for, 111
prenatal: flexor position, 158
  growth, 113
  influences, 14
prepuce, 88
progesterone levels, 96
pro-oestrus, 72
prostaglandins, treatment
  with, 79
prostatitis, 90
proving mating, 84
puberty, 71
puerperal tetany, 138
puppies, naming of, 168
puppy: farms and mills, 21
  in utero development,
    108–110
  mortality, 45, 131
  postnatal development,
    157–63, 192

postnatal problems, 140
strangles, 143
survival rates, 131
weight, 135, 146
See also feeding
pyoderma, 141
pyometra, 78–9, 111
pyometritis, 79
pyrantel, 113
pyrentel embonate, 149

rabies, 157
random matings, 31, 46
receipts, 172
refusal to mate, 76
registration, 168
regurgitating, 154
roundworms, 113, 148, 149, 150

sarcoptic, *see* mange
saturation, 14
scented sprays, 73
screw tail, 142
scrotum, 87
seasons, interval between, 71
silent, 74
synchronized, 71, 75
See also oestrus; scented sprays
selection, 25, 26, 40, 41, 173
semen, 87, 93
chilled, 103
service, free return, 86
sex determination, 25, 112
sex-limited, 26
shows, early dog, 12
sib mating, 52

siblings, 52
socialization, 160
spaying, 80
spina bifida, 143
standing, 74
still birth, 130
strain, definition of, 49
straws, 105
strike rate, 94
stud-dog, 82, 84, 85
novice, 101
See also service
stud fee, 84, 86, 98
super-ovulation, 106
supplementary heat, 116
surgical neutering, 81
survival rates, 113
swimmers, 140

Taenia species, 152
tail-female descent, 15
tail-male descent, 15
tapeworms, 148, 149, 151, 152
tattoos, 87, 105, 107, 170
telegony, 14
temperature, 116, 118
testes, 87
threshold traits, 26
tie position, 99
tissue samples, 106
Toxascaris leonina, 113, 148, 149, 150
toxic milk syndrome, 140
Toxocara canis, 113, 148, 149, 150
toxocariasis, 148
transitional period, 160
Trichuris vulpis, 149, 152

ultrasonic pregnancy testing, 111
umbilical: cord, 124
infection, 141
Uncinaria stenocephala, 149, 153
undershot, 142
unlike to unlike, 47
urethra, 69
uterus, 69

vaccination, 156, 171
annual booster doses, 157
vagina, 69, 70
vaginal: cytology tests, 79
discharge, 73, 74, 81, 96, 126, 133, 137
variation, 32
vasectomy, 92
veterinary confidentiality, 20
vulva, 69

warranty, 169
weaning, 154
weighing puppies, 135, 146
weight, birth, 146
low birth, 134, 137
whelping: quarters, 114
temperature during, 118
See also contractions, uterine; parturition
whipworm, 149, 154
Whitney reflex, 98
worming, 113, 149

X-rays, 111